F.I.A.S.C.O.

FRANK PARTNOY is the author of *The Match King: Ivar Kreuger and the Financial Scandal of the Century* and *Infectious Greed: How Deceit and Greed Corrupted the Financial Markets*. He has worked as an investment banker at Morgan Stanley and a corporate lawyer, and has testified as an expert before both the United States Senate and House of Representatives. A graduate of Yale Law School, he is currently the George E. Barrett Professor of Law and Fi~~nance~~

"Most of us enter the investment business for the same sanity-destroying reasons a woman becomes a prostitute: It avoids the menace of hard work, is a group activity that requires little in the way of intellect, and is a practical means of making money for those with no special talent for anything else."
RICHARD NEY, *The Wall Street Jungle*

"Behind every great fortune there lies a great crime."
HONORÉ DE BALZAC

F.I.A.S.C.O.

Blood in the Water
on Wall Street

FRANK PARTNOY

P

PROFILE BOOKS

For the mouse

First published in Great Britain in 1997 by
Profile Books Ltd
58A Hatton Garden
London EC1N 8LX
www.profilebooks.com

This paperback edition published in 2009

First published in the United States in 1997 by
W. W. Norton & Company, Inc.
500 Fifth Avenue
New York
NY 10110
http://www.wwnorton.com

A CIP catalogue record for this book is available from the British Library.

Typeset in Times by MacGuru
info@macguru.org.uk

Printed and bound in Great Britain by
CPI Bookmarque, Croydon, Surrey

ISBN 978 1 84668 238 4

Contents

Acknowledgments

The author thanks: Starling Lawrence, editor in chief at W. W. Norton, and Patricia Chui, his assistant, for their comments and advice; Robert Ducas, literary agent, for his encouragement and insight; the law firm of Covington & Burling for its liberal leave policy; Michele and Denny Partnoy, for agreeing to purchase at least one copy; Laura Adams, Bruce Baird, and Chris Bartolomucci for comments on a draft; and numerous Morgan Stanley employees, named and unnamed, for providing and corroborating the material that became this book.

Preface

From 1993 to 1995, I sold derivatives on Wall Street. During that time, the seventy or so people I worked with in the derivatives group at Morgan Stanley in New York, London, and Tokyo generated total fees of about $1 billion – an average of almost $15 million a person. We were arguably the most profitable group of people in the world.

My group was the biggest moneymaker at the firm by far. Morgan Stanley is the oldest and most prestigious of the top investment banks, and the derivatives group was the engine that drove Morgan Stanley. The $1 billion we made was enough to pay the salaries of most of the firm's ten thousand worldwide employees, with plenty left for us. The managers in my group received millions and millions in bonuses; even our lowest level employees had six-figure incomes. And many of us, including me, were still in our twenties.

How did we make so much money? In part, it was because we were smart. I worked with the greatest minds in the derivatives business. We mastered the complexities of modern finance, and it is no coincidence that we were called "rocket scientists."

This was not the Morgan Stanley of yore. In the 1920s, the white-shoe investment bank developed a reputation for gentility and was renowned for fresh flowers and fine furniture, an elegant partners' dining room, and conservative business practices. The firm's credo was: "First class business in a first class way."

However, during the banking heyday of the 1980s, the firm faced intense competition from other banks and slipped from its number one spot. In response, Morgan Stanley's partners shifted their focus from prestige to profits – and thereby transformed the firm. By the time I arrived in 1994, Morgan Stanley had swapped its fine heritage for a slick sales-and-trading operation – and a lot more money.

Other banks – including First Boston, where I worked before I joined Morgan Stanley – could not match Morgan Stanley's aggressive new sales tactics. By every measure, the firm had been recast. The flowers were gone. The furniture was Formica. Busy managers ingested lunch, if at all, at a crowded donut stand jammed between two hallways along the trading floor. Aggressive business practices inspired a new credo: "First class business in a second class way." After decades of politesse, there were savages at Morgan Stanley.

The derivatives group received its marching orders from the firm's leader, John Mack. Mack had worked his way up from the depths of the trading floor, where he still was known as "Mack the Knife." On his desk, Mack kept a large metal spike, upon which, it was rumored, he would threaten to impale inept employees. For one banking deal, in place of the traditional firm memento – a clear rectangular block with a copy of the firm's "tombstone" advertisement – Mack had received a smashed phone handset encased in lucite, a legacy from his job working the trading floor phones. With Mack at the helm, the halcyon days of J. P. Morgan obviously were over.

Following Mack's lead, my ingenious bosses became feral multimillionaires: half geek, half wolf. When they weren't performing complex computer calculations, they were screaming about how they were going to "rip someone's face off" or "blow someone up." Outside of work they honed their killer instincts at private skeet-shooting clubs, on safaris and dove hunts in Africa and South America, and at the most important and appropriately named competitive event at Morgan Stanley: the Fixed Income Annual Sporting Clays Outing, F.I.A.S.C.O. for short. This annual skeet-shooting tournament set the mood for the firm's barbarous approach to its clients' increasing derivatives losses. After April 1994, when these losses began to increase, John Mack's instructions were clear: "There's blood in the water. Let's go kill someone."

We were prepared to kill someone, and we did. The battlefields of the derivatives world are littered with our victims. As you may have read in the newspapers, at Orange County and Barings Bank and Daiwa Bank and Sumitomo Corporation and perhaps others no one knows about yet, a *single* person lost more than a billion dollars. At some companies it took more than one person to lose a billion dollars. Dozens of household names, including Procter & Gamble and numerous mutual funds, lost hundreds of millions each, billions total, on derivatives. The $50 billion Mexican currency debacle included its share of derivatives victims, too. As the late Senator Everett Dirksen once said, "A billion here and a billion there, and pretty soon you're talking about real money." If you owned stocks or mutual funds during the past few years, a portion of the real money lost on derivatives very likely was yours.

Derivatives have become the largest market in the world. The size of the derivatives market, estimated at $55 trillion in 1996, is double the value of all U.S. stocks and more than ten times the entire U.S. national debt. Meanwhile, derivatives losses continue to multiply.

Of course, plenty of firms *made* money on derivatives, including Morgan Stanley, and the firm's derivatives group is thriving, even as derivatives purchasers lick their wounds. Some clients tired of having their faces ripped off or being blown up, and business declined briefly in 1995 and 1996. Many of us quit during this period, some leaving for less brutish firms. Morgan Stanley transferred a few of the group's most aggressive managers to more "suitable" areas of the firm. But several employees remained. Today the group survives, reconstituted but still profitable, poised for the next battle, prepared to fire on command.

1

A Better Opportunity

I sat by the phone and willed it to ring. It was Tuesday morning, February 1, 1994, two weeks before bonus day. I was working as a derivatives salesman at First Boston, the investment bank in New York.

I was waiting for a call from an executive recruiter – a "headhunter" – who already had called me several times during the past few days. His timing was flawless. Bonus time was approaching, derivatives were hot, and I had been a featured speaker at a recent emerging markets derivatives conference. I was marketable, willing to switch jobs, and I was especially valuable to the headhunter: If he placed me at a new firm, he would receive one-third of my starting salary. Good Wall Street headhunters made millions of dollars, and I knew this guy wasn't calling me to be nice. He wanted my head.

It wasn't easy camouflaging these calls. If you've ever seen a trading floor, you might wonder how a salesman can even speak to a headhunter without arousing suspicion from the other salesmen just a few feet away. I knew detection could be fatal. Several salesmen had been disciplined or fired for negotiating with headhunters at work. To be safe, we devised elaborate systems to conceal our job searches, including code language and late-night meetings. My new system, copied from a colleague, was simple but not foolproof: The headhunter called using a friend's name, and I picked up the phone and pretended to be talking to the friend while the headhunter described the job he had to offer. If I wanted to discuss the job, I would hang up, leave the trading floor, and call the headhunter from one of the pay phones in the lobby. Others used this system, too, and around bonus time, salesmen besieged those phones.

Thus far I had risked several trips to the lobby and listened calmly to many job offerings. Each time I said no. The jobs were at firms of First Boston's caliber – that is, they were second tier. Although First Boston had been a top firm in the early 1980s, it had slipped several notches in the past decade, and numerous employees had left for better firms. I was tired of second-class status, and I, too, wanted to move up. I coveted one job in particular, at the firm I thought had the hottest derivatives group on Wall Street. I told the headhunter if he could get me that job, I would take it. He promised to explore and to let me know what he discovered.

Finally, the phone rang. It was the headhunter, and he sounded excited.

"Frank?" he whispered.

"Yes?" I whispered back. A nearby colleague eyed me suspiciously. No one whispered on a trading floor.

"I've got it."

"You've got what?"

"It." He paused. "Your job. The job you want. Call me."

Now *I* was excited. I told my colleague I'd be back in a few minutes. He seemed to know what I was doing. I practically sprinted to the lobby pay phone.

As I waited for the headhunter to answer, I grabbed a pen and paper to take notes. The phone rang for what seemed like a full minute. I looked around the lobby and smirked at my firm's new logo: a blue-on-white sailboat placed next to the firm's new name, CS FIRST BOSTON. The CS stood for Credit Suisse, a large Swiss bank and the firm's new owner. However, the stylish new logo couldn't change the fact that First Boston's voyage had been neither cosmopolitan nor smooth sailing. The boat looked like it belonged in Boston, not Berne, and the only thing global about my firm was its losses.

I recalled one example, when First Boston had loaned $450 million – 40 percent of its equity capital – to just one firm, Ohio Mattress, in a disastrous deal Wall Street wits had christened "the burning bed." Profits at First Boston were so pathetic that the firm had to sell a stake in its derivatives business just to pay bonuses. Meanwhile, it was rumored that Allen Wheat, the firm's new chief executive officer, had received compensation of $30 million, although reports later indicated his compensation was a mere $9 million. The firm had been tagged Wheat First Securities, a reference to a small-time, relatively impoverished brokerage firm. It was no surprise that top salesmen were fleeing in droves. I, too, wanted out.

The headhunter finally said, "Hello."

I began whispering again. "What do you have?" I scanned the lobby, to be sure no one was listening.

He must have sensed my anxiety because he began toying with me cruelly. "It's a hot derivatives group at a *very* prestigious investment bank, and they're looking for an emerging markets salesman. It's you. It's perfect. You're all over this."

I cut him off. Emerging markets was my area, but there were many "prestigious" investment banks. "Who is it? Just give me the name."

He hemmed and hawed for a few minutes as I struggled to keep calm. I pressed him again. Finally he spilled the name. "*Morgan Stanley.*"

I knew that for negotiating purposes I should pretend to be only mildly interested in the job. That way my headhunter wouldn't think I was desperate or that I would switch jobs for a pittance. I knew I should preserve my bargaining power. The key to negotiating was saying I liked the job ... but not that much. I fought to contain my excitement.

I couldn't. I nearly screamed. "I want it! I want it! Get me this job! When can I talk to them? *I want it!* I want this job!" I looked around the lobby to see if anyone was watching me.

"How soon do you want to talk to them?"

I couldn't help shouting. "*Now!* Soon! This afternoon! Tomorrow, at the very latest!"

The headhunter laughed confidently, knowing he had me lassoed. "Whoa, boy. Calm down. I'll try to set it up for tomorrow. I'll call you tonight at home and let you know the details."

When I replaced the receiver, my hand was trembling with excitement. I scrambled back to the desk and hoped no one had noticed my absence – or heard my shouting. Fortunately they hadn't; my previously suspicious colleague had settled comfortably into his second chocolate Dove Bar of the morning.

That night my headhunter called me at home, telling me, "You're done." He already had arranged a full interview schedule for next Monday, February 7. He said Morgan Stanley's decision would be quick, probably within a week.

I awoke early the day of my interview and called in sick to First Boston. My bosses would interrogate me, but I didn't care. My only concern was impressing the derivatives salesmen at Morgan Stanley. The firm's derivatives group was the best in the world, and its business was booming. Although I knew the firm needed emerging markets people, I suspected they would hire only one or two of the top candidates. I prayed for Morgan Stanley to hire me.

When I arrived at Morgan Stanley for my interview, the firm's cavernous trading floor was buzzing. As with other trading floors I had seen, space was at a premium; even the gray reception area was windowless and cramped. Although Morgan Stanley encouraged clients visiting the investment bankers on the top floors of its Sixth Avenue skyscraper to gawk at the building's glass-rimmed views of Manhattan, it did not afford the same luxuries below, in the bowels of the fourth-floor trading dungeon.

If you haven't had the pleasure of physically comparing different Wall Street trading floors, you needn't bother. They are all basically alike. The floor itself is a checkerboard of stained carpet squares covering a maze of twisted wires and electronic equipment. These removable squares serve as the lid of a massive trash can, and hidden below are dozens of half-empty Chinese food containers and mice. (Mice love trading floors, and banking employees are constantly discussing creative ways to trap and kill them.) If you stop by virtually any trading floor on Wall Street, this is what you will inevitably encounter:

Hundreds of telephones are ringing. Television monitors are blasting news and flashing scattered bond quotes. One of the checkerboard squares is upended, and several maintenance men are taking a break to yell at each other in front of a pile of circuits and cables. Dozens of traders and salespeople are standing at three-foot intervals face-to-face at several long rectangular desks, which are stacked with a rainbow of colorful computers, flashing monitors, blue Reuters and green Telerate screens, beige Bloomberg data systems, and customized black broker quote boxes.

Every few seconds a nearby loudspeaker hoots a deafening stream of gibberish: "Fifty GNMA eights to go at a half." "Non-farm payrolls expected down thirty." "The long bond buyer I saw earlier is now in the two-year sector, putting on a butterfly spread." The loudspeaker is appropriately named the hoot and holler, or just the hoot for short. Every salesman and trader is tapped into the hoot and holler, using it to announce important issues, to publicize requests to the entire trading floor, or to broadcast to everyone that the head government bond trader is, once again, acting like an asshole. If you only want to speak to one or a few people instead of the entire floor, and they are more than ten feet away, you have to call them by phone. Yelling is useless in the din, and unlike commodities traders in the Chicago trading pits, Wall Street traders typically do not use hand signals, except when they are flashing someone a middle finger. Everyone does read lips, however, just enough to distinguish the infrequent

F. I. A. S. C. O.

"You're done" from the more commonly used "You mother-fucker."

Even in this maelstrom, it's easy to differentiate traders from salesmen. The traders are the men with rolled up sleeves and loosened ties, who hold several phones each and periodically smash one phone against a desk, computer, or trading assistant, and then grab another donut out of a monstrous box. In contrast, the salesmen calmly adjust their cufflinks while they hold one phone to each ear and, by alternatively squeezing hidden mute buttons inside their handsets, carry on several composed conversations at once. A good salesman can simultaneously schmooze a client, discuss tonight's Knicks game with his bookie, order his assistant to steal a donut from the traders, and explain to his wife where he had been last night until 4 A.M. – and none will be aware of the other conversations or the nearby pandemonium.

Despite the apparent bedlam, there is a sense of protected order on the floor. Traders and salesmen live harmoniously, safeguarded in their locker-room surroundings from decades of race- and gender-related legislation, social regulation, and informal workplace changes. There are a few minorities and women on most trading floors, but many of them wear janitors' overalls or very short skirts. The only evidence of any socially progressive act is an occasional toppling stack of empty yogurt cartons.

My training class at First Boston had been representative: predominantly white males from Harvard, Yale, and Oxford or from wealthy families. One white male trainee was bound for San Francisco, two white males were bound for Philadelphia, one white male for Chicago, and a dozen or so white males each for New York and London. Evidently First Boston had been unable to find a white male who was fluent in Japanese, so it had hired a native Japanese woman for the Tokyo office.

Of the thirty-seven trainees, thirty were men. As far as I could tell, First Boston had not hired *any* people of color to work in the U.S., although – in the firm's defense – many of the trainees were quite tan. Of the seven female trainees, some already had proven

6

to be successful First Boston employees for several years and only now were permitted to participate in the training program; others were new to First Boston but looked as if they had been pulled off the cover of *Elle*. First Boston had safely navigated the treacherous waters of affirmative action and political correctness, with impressive results: more than 80 percent men, mostly white; a few Asians working abroad; no African or Hispanic Americans; and only seven women.

Investment banks selected female employees with special care. Several salesmen had stressed to me the ever-important "babe factor" in interviewing and hiring. From their perspective, female trainees were either dependable servants or ravishing starlets. In either case, the women promised to be a pleasure for the men to work with; just in case they weren't, banks often hindered their advancement by preslotting them into the least desirable jobs. In fact, many of the female hires in First Boston's training program were "asked to leave" within months after the program began and did leave, although several sued the firm, at least one successfully.

First Boston was so plagued with harassment and discrimination problems that it hired a consultant to train the salesmen and traders not to sexually harass female interviewees. But the training was hopeless. Much to the horror of the middle-aged female consultant, during one training session, a male employee opened a mock interview by asking the prospective female employee, "So, babe, do you want to fuck?"

The smarter females turned the locker room mentality to their advantage, and not merely by displaying their goods in tight dresses and leather pants. One saleswoman I met willingly put her sex life on public display. Early in the morning, a gaggle of salesmen would encircle her to hear her tales of debauchery from the previous night. No one cared if she embellished the stories a little, and I certainly will not forget the description, in exquisite detail, of the "perfect blow job" she had given one lucky guy after he bought her an expensive dinner the previous night. After hearing this story, one salesman told me, "Now *that* woman has a future at this firm."

The head of the sales department had a rotating harem of sec-retaries, one of the longest lived of which was a six-foot blond goddess whose job was to wear as few clothes as she possibly could and walk laps around the floor. She did this with extraordi-nary verve. The interweaving of her one-woman fashion show with the pandemonium of billion-dollar bond trading was heady stuff. And when *that* wasn't sufficiently entertaining for the boys, a manager would pay a junior female employee to perform some obscene act on the trading floor. One senior mortgage trader paid a notably attractive sales assistant $500 to eat, slowly and care-fully, a large pickle covered with hand lotion. A throng of traders admired her as she performed the feat, accepted the cash, and then puked violently all over the trading floor.

I suppose it is a bit of a character flaw that I beheld the finan-cial orgy of a trading floor with such desire. But I did. The trad-ing floor was my home. Fortunately I knew if I left First Boston for Morgan Stanley, I would not lose the feel of the trading floor. My environment would change about as much as that of a gold-fish moved from one bowl to another.

My interviews with the derivatives group at Morgan Stanley went smoothly, and I struggled not to seem too eager. The group was called DPG – short for Derivative Products Group. One man-ager mumbled something about "First class business in a first class way." Another said he thought much of DPG's growth would be in emerging markets, my area. He promised that if I came to Morgan Stanley, I would be invited to an important derivatives gathering, coming up in April 1994, called "F.I.A.S.C.O." I had heard of it and wanted to go, but I knew that when a salesman at an investment bank promises you something, there is virtually no chance it will ever happen. Still, I was hope-ful because I knew he was one of the group's leaders, and he was rumored to be the father of the event.

Several salesmen focused on how many "bars" they made. To derivatives salesmen, a "bar" is not a place to go for drinks. A "bar" is a salary, a huge salary, with a long line of zeros, at least six of them. On Wall Street, you never said, "I make a million dollars a year." You said, "I make a bar." Lots of DPG employees made bars, often several. Of course, I, too, wanted to make bars, and by the end of the day I was salivating.

I desperately wanted to be a part of Morgan Stanley's money-making machine. I prayed, *Please, please let me work here!* The firm's derivatives group was my dream job. They made more money than anyone on Wall Street, they hired the smartest people, and they sold the most innovative derivatives.

Although the trading floors looked the same, in at least one critical way Morgan Stanley's was vastly different from First Boston's: It made more money. That was a big difference. To me, the DPG trading floor looked like a pot of gold.

While I was waiting to hear if DPG would hire me, I considered the differences between First Boston and Morgan Stanley. First Boston's relative poverty suggested deeper problems. If you think two seemingly prestigious investment banks with similar trading floors couldn't be too different, let me try to explain a few of the contrasts.

First Boston was a bank of the past, of the 1980s. It became clear to me that First Boston was second rate the first time I tried to locate its building. The firm's majestic address was Park Avenue Plaza, and I had been told the building was between 52nd and 53rd Street. I assumed that meant it actually was *on* Park Avenue.

However, as I walked up and down Park Avenue, I couldn't find it anywhere. Finally I asked a passing businessman if he knew where Park Avenue Plaza was. He laughed and pointed west. The building wasn't on Park Avenue; you couldn't even see it from Park Avenue. The 150-foot walk between Park Avenue and the firm's entrance was my first taste of the small but real gap between First Boston and other top banks.

The building, if you can find it, represents the failures of 1980s urban planning as much as First Boston itself represents the failures of 1980s investment banking. The forty-story skyscraper, built in 1981, resembles a giant green-glass aquarium, propped vertically between two older and shorter gray bookends. The ostentatious lobby has a thirty-foot ceiling, sheets of deep green marble, a roaring waterfall, massive silver pillars, and numerous boutiques, including a coffee shop, an upscale newsstand, and a swanky Swiss chocolatier. The lobby was a perfect milieu for wealthy 1980s bankers hurrying to work.

Unfortunately, as many of you may know, the wealth of the 1980s sometimes came with a price. According to the security guards at Park Avenue Plaza, the developers of the green-glass aquarium, in negotiating the right to build the gaudy structure, originally had agreed to preserve the lobby as an indoor natural park, complete with real grass and trees. It soon became clear that this plan was ludicrous, and much of it was abandoned. However, a few trees had already been planted in the lobby, and they continue to struggle to stay alive in the hostile indoor environment. The grass floor was marbled over and still is. Today, the only remaining nod to urban planning is the overwhelming presence of homeless people. Because the lobby is a regulated public space, the security guards can't throw loiterers out. As a result, even though First Boston's somewhat-less-wealthy 1990s bankers didn't have to step through a freshly mowed lawn on their way to the trading floor, they did have to bypass clusters of bums. (First Boston recently relocated, to an even less-prestigious address downtown.)

In contrast, Morgan Stanley's building was prime real estate, in Rockefeller Center just across from Radio City Music Hall and overlooking the famous Rockefeller skating rink. The firm's lobby was simple and clean. Most importantly, it was easy to find.

Morgan Stanley also had a newly designed logo, a modern Mercator-style map of the world, which loomed large against the First Boston boat. Morgan Stanley's public relations campaign included glossy print advertising with global themes; any recent explosions or disasters had been kept out of the financial press. So many salesmen and traders had left First Boston for Morgan Stanley that they now were calling the firm Second Boston. Morgan Stanley was a truly global firm, with offices throughout the Americas (Chicago, Houston, Los Angeles, Menlo Park, Mexico City, Montreal, New York, San Francisco, and Toronto), Europe (Frankfurt, Geneva, London, Luxembourg, Madrid, Milan, Moscow, Paris, and Zurich), Asia (Beijing, Bombay, Hong Kong, Osaka, Seoul, Shanghai, Singapore, Taipei, and Tokyo), and elsewhere (Johannesburg, Melbourne, and Sydney), and the firm's aggressive leaders, President John Mack and Chairman Richard Fisher, were planning to expand the firm's global presence and to increase total worldwide employment to more than 10,000. The non-U.S. offices were generating a growing portion of the firm's profits and new jobs. Of course, First Boston – er, CS First Boston – also had proclaimed to have offices throughout the world, but it was closing some of them and firing people in droves.

The fraternity antics also seemed more muted at Morgan Stanley. During my visit, I hadn't seen any sales assistants throwing up or traders having their heads shaved on a bet or secretaries parading the floor in skimpy dresses, all of which were prominent at First Boston. I *had* noticed several copies of *Guns & Ammo* magazine and G. I. Joe dolls scattered on the trading desks, but the bottles of scotch and pornographic magazines were stashed inside desk drawers. Morgan Stanley *was* Morgan Stanley, after all; it would have been unimaginable for anyone to suggest changing the firm's name.

To be fair, I should mention that First Boston hasn't always been a cut below. For several decades, beginning in the 1940s, Morgan Stanley and First Boston were of comparable elite status. After World War II, when the newly formed World Bank began borrowing to finance post-World War II reconstruction, Morgan Stanley shared the limelight with First Boston, and the two firms alternatively received top billing on World Bank prospectuses. Much, but not all, of First Boston had deteriorated since then, and the firm could claim superiority over Morgan Stanley in only one pathetic area: elevators.

11

First Boston had allocated an entire bank of sleek lifts to the traders and salesmen, who, like me, hated early-morning delays. The elevators were roped off from the public and protected by a line of security guards. They resembled those on the starship *Enterprise,* except they were slightly faster. When I arrived at the Park Avenue Plaza aquarium every morning, an elevator was always waiting. I would tap an enormous rectangle labeled FIXED INCOME, and *whoosh,* I would be on the trading floor. I had to admit, Morgan Stanley's unguarded and slow elevators were a disappointment by comparison.

One of the biggest differences between First Boston and Morgan Stanley at the time was in derivatives expertise. You've undoubtedly heard of derivatives by now, from newspaper and magazine articles and from televised news reports, about the billions of dollars recently lost on them. Derivatives have even been discussed on *60 Minutes.* But what are they?

Many people at First Boston didn't know. Although my group – emerging markets – was hugely profitable, with $30 billion of annual trading volume, and was first in various emerging markets rankings, with $10 billion of recent stock and bond issues, even we had developed a serious weakness in derivatives. By 1993 other banks had begun selling huge emerging market derivatives deals. Morgan Stanley in particular was the new leader, selling more than half a *billion* dollars of Mexican derivatives alone, along with billions of dollars of other structured derivatives. Waves of profitable derivatives deals were rolling by First Boston, and my group had missed the boat. When several salesmen and researchers – including my group's former intellectual leader and senior salesman – left First Boston for other derivatives groups, the emerging markets derivatives group at First Boston was left with only one person: me.

At the time, I wasn't exactly a derivatives guru. I had attended law school, not business school, and the knowledge I had acquired, mostly from reading academic treatises, was useless on a fast-paced trading floor. Nor had my training courses at First Boston helped much (although I had received the highest score in their training program).

I knew a derivative was defined as a financial instrument whose value is linked to, or derived from, some other security, such as a stock or bond. If you've read anything at all about derivatives, you've probably seen that definition. If you've recently purchased shares in a company or mutual fund that invested in derivatives, you might know them by an alternative definition: financial gizmos that suddenly become worthless and then appear on the front page of the *Wall Street Journal*.

Whatever your current knowledge, in the next few pages I will tell everything you need to know about derivatives to understand the tactics of Morgan Stanley's derivatives group, including much of what I already had learned by February 1994, when I was trying to move to Morgan Stanley. I will do you the favor of omitting many of the complex topics you might find in a derivatives treatise, topics bearing frightening names such as modified duration, option adjusted spread, put-call parity, bond basis, and negative convexity. My advice, even to investment bankers reading this book, is don't spend even one minute thinking about these concepts. They will not make you any money – ever. And if you believe more intimate knowledge of these concepts might make you a well-rounded person, you'd better keep that belief to yourself, especially if you work on a trading floor. The only way to become well rounded on a trading floor is by eating fattening foods. Of course, if you can use knowledge of complex derivatives mathematics as a smoke screen to hide important facts from your clients, fine. But if you actually want to acquire knowledge that has no monetary value, forget it. You're in the wrong business.

Later, I'll educate you as to how Wall Street has made, and continues to make, huge amounts of money on derivatives by trickery and deceit. First, though, you need some background information. Learning about derivatives today poses the same problem I faced in February 1994: Only a handful of derivatives salesmen know the closely guarded secrets of how derivatives are actually used, and those elite few have no reason to share secrets worth millions of dollars with me or you. Derivatives insiders often won't even tell their colleagues the most valuable secrets. One reason I wanted to move to Morgan Stanley's derivatives group was that they seemed to know more of these secrets. Even for me as a derivatives salesman at First Boston, it was almost impossible to learn the details of the most profitable derivatives deals on Wall Street. Imagine how difficult it still must be for journalists and regulators, who can learn only what the derivatives insiders are willing to tell them. Now you understand why you haven't heard this story before.

I don't blame anyone in Morgan Stanley's derivatives group for not sharing these secrets. As you'll see shortly, some of the more questionable practices have the potential to generate serious problems for some of these people. At a minimum, their clients would not be pleased to hear how they were duped. Even if there were no negative repercussions to divulging these secrets, why share the wealth? If a golden goose arrived at your doorstep and began laying golden eggs, what would you do? Call the press? Share the eggs? No, you would hide them from the world.

Let me start with the most basic question: What are derivatives? Again, here's the standard definition: A derivative is a financial instrument whose value is linked to, or derived from, some other security, such as a stock or bond. For example, you could buy IBM stock; alternatively, you could buy a "call option" on IBM stock, which gives you the right to buy IBM stock at a certain time and price. A call option is a derivative because the value of the call option is "derived" from the value of the underlying IBM stock. If the price of IBM stock goes up, the value of the call option goes up, and vice versa.

Most finance textbooks will tell you there are only two types of derivatives: options and forwards. However, although these books will explain options and forwards in detail, they don't exactly make it easy. For example, even one of the simpler-to-read books,

Options, Futures, and Other Derivative Securities, by Professor John Hull, a well-known derivatives consultant who hosts expensive corporate conferences, has several excruciatingly difficult passages on derivatives, many of which he warns you about on the back cover: "Complete treatment of numerical procedures, Monte Carlo simulation, the use of binomial lattices, and finite difference methods." If that doesn't deter you, try flipping through pages of tiny Greek symbols and rows of formulas and graphs. And if you're still considering purchasing the book, look at its price tag: $76. Instead of reading Hull's book, think about options and forwards in terms any derivatives salesman would appreciate: Corvettes.

An option is the *right* to buy or sell something in the future. The right to buy is a "call option"; the right to sell is a "put option." So if you knew several new Corvettes would be arriving at a car dealership in a month, you might pay the dealer $1,000 now to reserve a Corvette for you to buy at a certain price, say $40,000. When the cars arrived, you would have a call option – the right but not the obligation – to buy one for $40,000. Because you owned a call option, you would want the price of new Corvettes to increase: if the price increased to $50,000 your option to buy a Corvette for $40,000 would be worth about $10,000. Also, with a call option, your downside is limited. If the price were to drop to $30,000, you could simply let the dealer keep your $1,000 (called the option premium) and buy the Corvette for the lower price.

The other type of derivative – a "forward" – is an *obligation* to buy or sell something in the future. This obligation is called a future if it's traded on an exchange, but the concept is the same. Suppose you knew you wanted to buy a new Corvette, but you didn't want to pay $1,000 for an option. Instead, you could enter into a forward obligation to purchase the Corvette for $40,000 in a month. When the new Corvettes arrived, you would be obligated to buy one for $40,000 even if the actual price were lower. As with a call option, you would want the price to increase. But with a forward, your downside is no longer limited, so you *especially* wouldn't want the price to drop. Even if the Corvette's price were to drop to $30,000, you still would have to buy it for $40,000. Despite this downside risk, there's at least one good reason to buy a forward instead of an option – you would save the $1,000 option premium.

Options and forwards are traded on all kinds of financial instruments, including stocks, bonds, and various market indices. Some are traded on organized exchanges throughout the world. Others are traded only in privately negotiated transactions, called over-the-counter, or OTC. Exchange-traded derivatives are more highly regulated, more liquid, and more dependable than OTC derivatives. To get information about an exchange-traded derivative, you can simply look in the *Wall Street Journal* or call a broker. In contrast, you might *never* be able to discover certain information about an OTC derivative unless you worked in the derivatives group at an investment bank.

All derivatives are combinations of options and forwards. Much activity in the derivatives market – including the trades I will tell you about – involves combining different options and forwards and selling them in packages. The most difficult aspect of creating these packages is calculating how much each component is worth. These calculations are the one element of derivatives sales that truly resembles rocket science, and mistakes can be catastrophic.

I knew very well how painful such mistakes could be. If you ever decide to buy derivatives, I hope you never have an experience similar to the one I had. It involved another bank you may recognize as a derivatives culprit: Bankers Trust.

Years earlier, I had been interviewing for a job at Bankers Trust, known on Wall Street as "BT." Bankers Trust recently has acquired quite a reputation for selling exploding derivatives to unsuspecting clients, and the firm has been reprimanded by regulators and sued by numerous clients. However, years ago, when I was struggling to get a job on Wall Street, BT was relatively clean.

BT had one of the top sales-and-trading training programs on

Wall Street. It was a sophisticated, highly quantitative bank, and anyone who made it through BT's rigorous training was guaranteed success. All over Wall Street, salesmen and traders with BT experience were making bars. I had felt good about BT and was optimistic about my chances there. I was confident that if I could get a job there, I would become rich.

At the time, BT wasn't yet known as the bank where – according to one infamous derivatives salesman – they "lure people into that calm and then just totally fuck 'em." To most of the world, this was still a secret. I had assumed that BT was in business to make as much money as it could. Had I known BT's approach to clients was to "totally fuck 'em," my favorable view of the bank might have changed. Perhaps it would have improved.

In any event, I remember very well my first interview at BT. It was my very first interview for any job on Wall Street. The personnel director led me through the glassed-in reception area to the bond trading floor. I had never seen a trading floor in person, and I surveyed the bustling place in awe. It was filled with blinking trading screens and clamoring salesmen. The noise was deafening. Almost everyone was screaming, either into a phone or at someone else nearby. The atmosphere was electrifying, and I was nervous.

I noticed one bespectacled guy poking a Hewlett Packard 19BII turbo calculator at me. The personnel director said he was a derivatives trader and walked away. I extended a sweaty hand.

I followed the silent trader into a plush window office and sat. He stared at a row of green, blinking Telerate screens reporting up-to-the-second prices of various financial instruments, then picked up the phone and mumbled some numbers and coded language I didn't recognize. I watched the BT trader for a few minutes until I was no longer merely nervous. I was terrified. His eyes darted across the screens, and he seemed oblivious to my presence. I couldn't understand a word he was saying. My mouth was dry, and I couldn't swallow. I scanned the room for a water cooler.

The trader finally spoke to me. He dispensed with small talk, ignored my résumé, and simply proposed to sell me a derivatives trade. I listened carefully as he described the terms. As I understood it, the trade was a mixture of forward derivatives trades on Treasury bonds. I knew the forward trade was a contract to buy Treasury bonds at a set future time and price. If the trade moved against me, I would be obligated to pay him an amount of money based on a complex formula.

I thought about the forward trade. It was an over-the-counter trade, so its price would not be quoted on any of the trading screens. I could find the value of the underlying Treasury bonds on a Telerate screen, but it would be up to me alone to use those values to calculate the price of the trade he was proposing. I was wary. Potentially, this trade was incredibly risky. As with the Corvette forward trade, if I committed to buy these bonds at a set price and that price dropped, I could lose a lot of money.

Still, I understood in principle how to value the components of the trade. The trade was leveraged, meaning I would have to multiply the value of each component by a leverage factor. The leverage factor was simply a number you multiplied times the specified size of the trade to determine gains and losses, not unlike the doubling cube in backgammon. For example, with a leverage factor of 10, a $1 million trade really was worth $10 million. I would need to calculate the value of the forward contracts I was buying, and then subtract the value of the forward contracts I was selling. After subtracting, if the resulting value was greater than zero, I would make money from the trade and should do it. If the value was less than zero, I should say no. Simple?

The derivatives trader asked me if I wanted to do a $10 million trade. I glanced at the green, blinking Telerate screens to check the Treasury bond prices and did some quick calculations. He told me I had one minute. I eyed his Hewlett Packard 19BII turbo calculator anxiously, then thrust my sweaty hand into my pocket, searching in vain for my own calculator. Nothing. It was still sitting on my desk at home. *Damn!* My adversary pointed at the paper and pencil on the desk next to me. I mulishly shook my head. No primitive pencils and paper for me. I needed to impress this guy, and I thought I could perform these calculations in my head. I checked the blinking screens again and crossed my fingers. He raised an eyebrow. I tried to clear my throat, and when it wouldn't clear, I prayed that it at least would produce a sound. "OK."

He stared at me coldly. "You're done." The words hung in the air like clouds. "You're done" is trader's lingo, used when a trade has been executed. If someone tells you "You are done," quite simply, you are done. There's no getting out of the trade. Your word is your bond, so to speak. So I was "done" for $10 million. That was fine. I thought I had made money on the trade.

He proposed another $10 million trade, same terms. I felt confident about my previous calculations, and the numbers on the blinking screens had not changed much. I eyed his turbo calculator a little less nervously and nodded. He stared back and frowned. "You're done." I was still nervous, but I was virtually certain I had made money on the first two trades. I tried to appear sanguine.

The trader shifted in his chair and proposed a slightly different trade for $100 million. I stared at the screen, then glanced at the paper and pencil. For the first time, I began to wonder about my previous calculations. Could I have made a mistake? I didn't think so. But I wasn't sure about the effect of the slight change the trader had made. Although the new trade was larger, its terms were similar to those of the two previous trades – assuming the market had not changed in the past few seconds. I looked at the blinking numbers on the screen, and I thought they had moved in my favor. But I could no longer remember precisely what the numbers had been a minute ago. Because of the leverage factor, even a small mistake would cost me millions. I stared again at his turbo calculator and paused. I felt just confident enough to nod again, and I did.

For the first time the trader smiled. "You're done," he said. My mind began to wander back to the previous trades.... .

The trader interrupted my thoughts. "Same trade, one billion dollars." His voice was firm and confident. I sank in my chair.

Apparently, I *had* made a mistake. Now I was faced with a

19

choice. Either I admitted I couldn't understand the trade – and risked being rejected as a novice with limited derivatives proficiency – or I guessed.

Today, as I look back on my decision, I know that the amount of money I was about to lose may not seem that surprising. Eventually several derivatives buyers would lose even more than I lost that day. But back in 1992, most people, including me, thought derivatives were relatively safe. You could still pick up a newspaper and not find one article about an individual who had lost a billion dollars on derivatives. It was well before Robert Citron of Orange County lost a billion dollars, Nick Leeson at Barings Bank lost a billion dollars, Toshihide Iguchi at Daiwa Bank lost a billion dollars, and Yasuo Hamanaka at Sumitomo Corporation lost *two* billion dollars – all on derivatives. It was before companies with long, foreign-sounding names like Metallgesellschaft lost a billion dollars on derivatives. It was even before George Soros lost ... well, he only lost a half billion dollars on derivatives, but it was before that, too.

It was early fall 1992, and I was about to become the very first person to lose a billion dollars on derivatives.

I looked at the trader and nodded that, yes, I would accept the terms of this trade.

The derivatives trader removed his glasses and gave me one last, "You're done." He pointed his finger at the door. "Congratulations, you just lost one billion dollars. That will be all."

I was stunned and could not respond. *That will be all?* I was shattered.

I stumbled out of the office and wandered back to BT's trading floor, where I stared in disbelief at the blinking screens. Had I really just lost a *billion* dollars? I tried to think about the mathematics of the trade and the effect of the leverage factor. What would my friends say? It had gone so quickly. I was worried, and rightly so. A billion dollars was a lot of money to lose.

I tried to cheer myself up. After all, I hadn't *really* lost a billion dollars. I tried to put the loss in perspective. The financial mar-

kets traded *trillions* of dollars daily. The size of the entire derivatives market in 1992 was $40 trillion. The foreign exchange mar-
kets alone traded about $1 trillion a day. Nobody got upset about
a lousy $1 billion loss these days, did they?

I had to admit, my first interview at an investment bank had
not exactly gone well. Earlier I had wondered how anyone could
make so much money selling options and forwards. And if Wall
Street was making so much money on derivatives, who was *losing* money? Now I had firsthand knowledge of precisely how one
person could make, and another could lose, a billion dollars on
derivatives. I had learned some important rules to live by.

First, there are winners and losers in every derivatives trade,
and you didn't want to be a loser, especially one who lost a billion dollars. Second, I needed to be able to make quick and complex calculations with great facility, preferably in my head. Most
people, including the majority of employees at an investment
bank, didn't need the ability to perform such feats, but if I were
to succeed in derivatives, I did.

To help me along the road to making bars, I needed to master
one more concept essential to understanding derivatives, and
closely related to the calculations the BT trader had asked me to
perform: present value. "Present value" is the value of a payment,
expressed in today's dollars. For example, the present value of
$100 to be received today is $100. However, the present value of
$100 to be received in a year is less than $100. In general, the
present value of an amount to be received in the future is less
than the present value of the same amount to be received today.

You probably have some understanding of this notion, at least
its most basic terms, from the maxim "A bird in the hand is worth
two in the bush." Some people think this means a bird in the hand
is more certain, and therefore more valuable, than two in the
bush. To an investment banker, this maxim means that the present
value of one bird to be received today is greater than the present
value of two birds to be received in the future. Believe it or not,

this concept is critical to understanding derivatives, so before we move on to Morgan Stanley, here's what you need to know about present value.

Although an enormous body of finance scholarship is built around bond mathematics and present value, the basics are actually very simple. The essential issue in valuing stocks and bonds, and the essential issue in finance generally, is this: A dollar today is worth more than a dollar tomorrow. That's it. Why is a dollar today worth more than a dollar tomorrow? That answer, too, is easy. Put a dollar in the bank today, and tomorrow you'll have more than a dollar. Or, if you only need a dollar tomorrow, you can deposit less than a dollar, say 99 cents, today. The interest you earn is composed of a "real" return (say, 3 percent) plus an inflation component (usually a few percent). The interest rate varies, based on when the money will be paid. Under normal circumstances, the longer the term, the higher the interest rate.

If you understand these basics, you can understand much of modern finance theory and most of how the bond and derivatives markets operate. If you don't understand it right away, don't worry, you're in good company. Many fund managers and corporate CEOs had only a limited understanding of the bond and derivatives markets until very recently. Even President Clinton reportedly admitted surprise when he discovered the importance of – in his words, according to one source – a bunch of "fucking bond traders." Allow me to explain the most important concepts.

For valuing bonds, the precise question is: How much more is a dollar today worth than a dollar tomorrow? Suppose you have the choice between receiving $100 today and receiving $100 in one year. Obviously, you'd choose the $100 today. But what if the choice is between $100 today and $106 in one year? The answer then depends on what interest rate you could earn during the next year. If the one-year interest rate is 8 percent, you would prefer the $100 today because it would be worth $108 in one year. On the other hand, if the one-year interest rate is only 4 percent, you would prefer to have $106 in one year because $100 today would only be worth $104.

To compare $100 today with $106 in one year, we must express them both in the same terms. This is done using the concept of "present value." We simply ask, "What is the value of each today?" The value of $100 today is easy – $100. What is the value of $106 in one year? If the one-year interest rate is 6 percent, the value of $106 in one year also is $100 today because $100 invested today at 6 percent will be worth $106 in one year. Using the 6 percent rate, we "discount back" the $106 in one year to its value today: $100. The 6 percent rate is called the discount factor. If the discount factor, or interest rate, were higher – say, 8 percent – then $106 to be received in one year would be worth less than $100 today. Similarly, if the discount factor were only 4 percent, then $106 to be received in one year would be worth more than $100 today.

To calculate the price of a bond, we simply think of the bond as a series of cash flows, just like the $100 payments in the previous paragraphs. In fact, a one-year bond with an annual coupon of 6 percent is *exactly the same* as a payment of $106 in one year. At the maturity of the one-year bond, the bondholder would receive his principal ($100) plus interest ($6), for a total of $106. Most bonds pay interest twice a year, but the idea is the same. For example, to value a ten-year bond with a 6 percent coupon, simply calculate what each of the interest payments and the principal repayment are worth today, in terms of present value. The sum of these individual values is the bond's total value.

Put in terms of the bird maxim, for a bird in the hand to be worth more than two birds in the bush, assuming an interest rate of 6 percent, you must not expect to catch the two birds any time in the next twelve years. That's about how long it takes an amount growing at 6 percent per year to double, and that's too long for most birds. Thus, present-value concepts demonstrate the wisdom of an age-old maxim. But you probably knew what it meant already.

A more advanced course in finance would include not only

present value, but also two other concepts: duration and convexity. The bird-bush metaphor doesn't work very well for these concepts, and when business school students – and most salesmen and traders – hear either of these two words, they run screaming. There's no need to run. Even if you work at an investment bank, you should forget about mastering these concepts. Just remember this:

"Duration" tells you how risky a bond is. The greater the duration, the greater the risk. For example, a ten-year bond has greater duration – and greater risk – than a one-year bond. That's it.

Mathematically, of course, duration is more complicated than this. It's the length of time until you receive the average present value-weighted cash flow, and is itself a derivative (in calculus terms), of the partial differential equation that describes the price behavior of a bond. Most bond salesmen forgot this definition long ago, if they ever learned it. In simpler terms, think of a bond as a series of blocks – each representing a single cash payment – laid out along a seesaw, moving in time from left to right. Most of the blocks (coupon payments) are short, and the block to the far right (principal repayment) is much taller than the others. The duration of the bond is the length to the balancing point of all the blocks, at the fulcrum.

"Convexity" is an incredibly complex topic far beyond the scope of this book. All you need to know about convexity – in fact, all that 99 percent of people who work on a trading floor know about convexity – is this: Convexity is good. The more convex a bond is, the more money you will make on it when interest rates change. This explanation works for the bizarre term "negative convexity," too.

Here's a final examination question for you: If convexity is good, what do you think about "negative convexity"?

If you answered that negative convexity is bad, you are correct. Congratulations. You now know enough to begin selling derivatives.

Back at First Boston, I, along with everyone else, was pacing through the last interminable week before bonuses were paid. Soon thereafter many employees would quit. Most investment banking employees are rational economic actors who know that once they've received a bonus payment, they'll have to wait an entire year for another. If you were planning to leave a firm, you never stayed more than an hour or so past bonus time if you could help it. Otherwise, according to the math of the trading floor, you were basically working for free. Most salesmen and traders thought this way because their salaries – usually around $75,000 to $100,000 – were only a fraction of their total annual compensation, including bonus. I thought this way, too. If I could get an offer from Morgan Stanley, I planned to quit the instant after I deposited my bonus check.

Finally, just a few days before bonus day, Morgan Stanley made me an offer I couldn't refuse. I said I would accept the offer immediately after First Boston paid bonuses. I knew I couldn't accept the offer on the spot because if I did and First Boston discovered it, I might not receive my bonus. Every smart employee of an investment bank knows the bank will go out of its way to screw employees who plan to leave for a competitor. So I kept my plans quiet and waited until February 15.

Bonus day at First Boston is known as the Valentine's Day Massacre, and its employees view themselves as serfs subject to the bloody rite of the firm's relatively meager bonuses. By the time bonuses are paid, most salesmen and traders are so infused with greedy, revolutionary fervor that no matter what amount the firm actually pays them, they automatically think they have been screwed. I was intrigued by this odd phenomenon. Could a salesman who received several million dollars really be irate?

Sure enough, by 9:30 A.M., the cavernous trading floor echoed with the angry protests of surly salesmen and testy traders who, minutes earlier, had received checks ranging from several hundred thousand dollars to several million. Even the lowest-paid employees received a significant multiple of the average income of an American family. But perspective is not one of Wall Street's

25

qualities, and the firm's employees were mad as hell.

"Man, I got fucked. They fucked me again. Can you believe it? Did you get fucked?"

"Yeah, I got fucked."

The normally jovial salesmen were so angry, and morale was so low, that whenever an underpaid employee did quit First Boston, he or she would receive a standing ovation from the entire trading floor. The loudest applause would be for salesmen leaving for Morgan Stanley, and there would be more than a few of those.

On bonus morning I took my check to the Citibank branch around the corner from the Park Avenue Plaza aquarium, joining a line of hundreds of disgruntled First Boston employees. You might assume First Boston would have been sophisticated enough to pay its employees by instantaneous "direct deposit." However, the stingy firm needed to pinch pennies, and the firm's managers knew that if they paid us with physical checks, we'd have to deposit those checks in person. That might take a day or so. Meanwhile, the firm would earn the interest on our bonuses. Remember "present value"? For employees with big bonuses, even one day of interest was worth a lot. In aggregate, the interest was worth a fortune. First Boston knew all about the bird in the hand, and, as a result, the line was out the door.

When I returned to announce my departure, I was in good company. Several other salesmen had announced they were leaving, and senior management was deciding whether to offer them more money or let them go. This was a standard Wall Street ritual. You obtained an offer from another bank, then used that offer to try to persuade your current employer to give you a raise. It's the only way to get ahead at an investment bank, and senior managers, though furious when you do this, will think you are a loser if you do not. It's not uncommon for a new salesman or trader to multiply his starting salary by as much as *ten times* in a few years, using such negotiating tactics.

My bosses pressured me to stay. They said the firm would increase my compensation dramatically, although they also noted it would take a few days to confirm this in writing. I said I was walking out of the firm within the hour. One manager offered to write me a personal check for $20,000, in case First Boston ultimately balked at increasing my pay. I told him I was flattered but that I would make many times that amount at Morgan Stanley. In Morgan Stanley's derivatives group, $20,000 was cab fare. An average employee there generated $20,000 in fees *per day.*

Fortunately one of the managers from Morgan Stanley had prepared me for this onslaught, warning me that my bosses at First Boston would persist in trying to persuade me to stay. He had suggested that if I used the words "better opportunity," they would back down. I was waiting for the right moment to try those words. When the sales manager again offered to whip out his personal checkbook, I finally said: "The offer from Morgan Stanley is a *better opportunity.*"

He stopped in his tracks. Those two words – "better opportunity" – are Wall Street code for "more money than you can possibly pay me." I recommend them highly to anyone trying to cut short a negotiated exit from a sales-and-trading job. When I spoke those words, like magic, the managers gave up.

The sheer brutality of Wall Street is never clearer than when senior managers finally realize an employee is going to quit. There are no farewell dinners. No one sheds a tear. Cordial working relationships evaporate. Friendships forged out of necessity on the closely knit trading floor are terminated immediately.

I hadn't expected sad good-byes, but nevertheless I was surprised that my colleagues reacted with such anger. One salesman made a few kind remarks and admitted he was a little jealous of my move. One trader said he would call me next week. But most of my colleagues, including my immediate bosses, were hostile. Not only did they instruct me to leave the firm immediately, they sent for a security guard to escort me out.

I was especially surprised to discover that a search was among the exit procedures at First Boston. Certainly, an exit search wasn't without justification – investment banking employees commonly looted a firm's documents and computer files before leaving for another firm – however, smart employees usually did this several days, if not weeks, before leaving. Apparently, past First Boston employees had been dumb enough to try pilfering files on their last day of work. Fortunately my briefcase was squeaky clean. I gave my identification and firm credit cards to the security guard and left. My days in the second tier were over.

2

The House
of Cards

I considered taking a lengthy vacation between jobs, but Morgan Stanley wanted me to start right away. I asked for only one weekday off, as a quick breather.

Omitting the between-job vacation was fine with me. I remembered the disaster the last time I had taken even so much as a weekend vacation between jobs, when I left my judicial clerkship in New York for First Boston. Although that Friday had been the thirteenth, I still felt lucky. So lucky, in fact, that I withdrew all my savings from the bank and flew to Las Vegas. Was there a more appropriate way for me to spend my last weekend before beginning work on a trading floor?

That trip, the odds had been in my favor: I had practiced counting cards and could count well enough at blackjack to give me a slim edge over the casino. The basic premise of card counting is that the player can beat the house when there are more high cards than low cards remaining in the deck. If you increase your bets when more low cards have been dealt and more high cards remain, you'll have an advantage over the dealer. I planned to have an advantage, and I planned to win.

I had fine-tuned my card-counting strategy during discussions with people I knew from First Boston. They also counted cards and had bragged about their after-hours limousine trips to Atlantic City and the huge sums they won playing blackjack. After a typical day at First Boston, shiny black limos lined up outside Park Avenue Plaza to shuttle traders, salesmen, and sometimes clients as well, on joyrides – first to a Manhattan steakhouse for dinner, then to several bars for drinks, then to gentlemen's clubs to meet special friends, and, inevitably, on a late-night pilgrimage south to the Boardwalk. Several salesmen claimed they often won enough to subsidize the female escorts – sometimes professionals, sometimes attractive sales assistants – who often went along for the ride.

My trip to Vegas was far less swanky, and I was alone. But it was early in my career, and I was interested in subsidizing only one person: me. The trip began auspiciously. Within several hours at one casino I had won nearly a thousand dollars. My strategy was simple: Bet $5 when there were more low cards in the deck, and bet several hundred dollars when there were more high cards. By switching my bets and counting cards, I obtained a narrow advantage over the casino. Blackjack is the only casino game in which the player can consistently beat the house, and it was the only game I played. As I continued winning, the pit bosses began watching me more carefully. They get nervous about *anyone* counting cards, regardless of betting size. Even saving a few hundred dollars a day would pay their salaries. One guy looked over my shoulder and counted the cards along with me. Another tried to distract me with questions. Finally, one of the managers asked me to leave the casino.

I was ecstatic. The authors of the card-counting books had boasted about being thrown out of casinos. But I never imagined I, too, could be ejected for counting cards. I now was one of the proud few.

Unfortunately, my ecstasy was short-lived. At the next casino my luck reversed, and I quickly began losing nearly every hand. My continuing losses were baffling, but I believed in my strategy and persevered. I carefully tracked the dealt cards, shifting my bets up and down as planned. I waited patiently for my luck to change, confident that if I kept counting cards, in the long run I would prevail. I ignored the advice of the dealer, who, after watching me lose a fortune, said I should quit and get some sleep. I ignored the advice of the famous economist John Maynard Keynes, who said, "In the long run, we're all dead."

For me, the long run was actually quite short, and after an hour or so, I was dead. I had lost nearly all of my money. I could barely afford one last $3.99 prime rib dinner and a cab to the airport. Friday the thirteenth hadn't been so lucky after all.

Given this experience, I was happy to have only one day between jobs. I didn't want to press my luck again, so I avoided the temptation of even a day-trip to Atlantic City. I would have plenty of chances for more serious gambling at Morgan Stanley.

Morgan Stanley has been the preeminent global investment bank since the firm opened its offices for business on September 16, 1935, in a flower-banked room at 2 Wall Street. Oddly, the creator of Morgan Stanley was not a person, but a law. In response to the speculative bubble of the 1920s, the 1929 Crash, and the Great Depression, Congress enacted the Glass-Steagall Act of 1933. Glass-Steagall addressed the public concern about the comingling of the commercial banking and securities businesses, and it required U.S. banks to choose one business or the other. When J. P. Morgan & Company, a private bank and a member of the New York Stock Exchange, opted to remain a commercial bank, several J. P. Morgan employees split off to organize a securities firm. Thus, Morgan Stanley was born.

Since the 1930s Morgan Stanley has been in the "bulge bracket," the term for the half-dozen investment banks who capture most of the highest-fee investment banking business. Over time, various firms have entered and exited the bulge bracket, like characters in a long-running play. Most of the early stars faded (Dillon, Read; Kuhn, Loeb) or died horrible deaths (Drexel

Burnham Lambert). Of today's headliners, many are recent (Goldman, Sachs; Merrill, Lynch; Salomon Brothers; Donaldson, Lufkin, Jenrette). During the six-decade history of investment banking, only Morgan Stanley has played a leading role since the beginning.

Initially, it wasn't clear whether the Morgan legacy alone would support a world-class securities firm. The firm's first partners were anxious and described the early years as "going out into a rough sea in a little tiny rowboat." But by the late 1930s their anxiety was gone, and the tiny rowboat had become a steel-hulled luxury liner. Morgan Stanley quickly grew into *the* blue-blooded, "white shoe" investment bank, an accolade it shared with no other. The firm's antique mahogany desks and polished dining rooms reflected its low-risk business, conducted with the most reputable clients and largest industrial corporations, in railroads, utilities, telephones, autos, oil, and mining. For decades Morgan Stanley controlled the underwriting of new securities issues and insisted on sole managing the biggest deals.

The firm's conservative culture continued into the early 1970s, when it still did not employ a single salesman or trader. In 1974 *Business Week* called Morgan Stanley "still the most prestigious of the investment banking houses." The firm had built a sturdy relationship-oriented business, based on its impeccable reputation as a straight shooter. As esteemed money manager Sanford Bernstein once said, "If Morgan Stanley is in it, that means we're kosher." By the 1970s Morgan Stanley, white shoes and all, had become the rabbi of investment banking.

However, while the firm sailed along cautiously, more aggressive banks – especially Salomon Brothers and Goldman, Sachs – began making more money. This was a serious problem for Morgan Stanley. In investment banking, cash conquers all. A bank's goal was to make money, not to preserve its chastity. If Morgan Stanley could outearn rivals by capitalizing on its stellar reputation, fine. But if less-reputed banks were generating more cash, Morgan Stanley was doing something wrong.

The firm needed a change. In an article in *Institutional Investor*, Parker Gilbert Jr., the firm's chairman from 1984 to 1990, stated that "Morgan was essentially the same firm – about the same size and in the same line of business – from 1935 to 1970."

The transformation began in the mid-1970s, as Morgan Stanley answered its competitors' successes, tentatively at first, by modernizing with new armaments. First it hired a gunnery unit, led by Barton Biggs, a money manager *Institutional Investor* had described as "the kind of gunslinger you could introduce to your daughter." Then the firm promoted an ambitious young partner and ex-Navy commando, Bob Greenhill – known as "the ultimate samurai" – to a senior banking slot. Greenhill has been described as the "field marshal" for Morgan Stanley's first hostile battles. According to Morgan expert Ron Chernow, a cartoon on Greenhill's wall depicted Al Capp's Fearless Fosdick – the square-jawed detective famous for shooting customers while he searched for a can of poisoned beans – riddled with bullet holes and captioned MERE FLESH WOUNDS. Greenhill and Richard Fisher, Morgan Stanley's chairman, had been friends since business school, and they embarked on the radical planning study that would become the blueprint for Morgan Stanley's future.

However, for many years Morgan Stanley's planning stalled, and its new weapons lay dormant as the firm stubbornly refused to take on significant risks or "unsavory" clients. It felt the painful effects almost immediately. By the early 1980s Morgan Stanley had lost first place in many "league tables" – the rankings of banks in various business categories – and was missing the swelling wave of 1980s takeover profits. The firm desperately needed a new philosophy to match its munitions.

The pivotal point came in early 1985. Cigar-chomping Ronald Perelman, now a billionaire but then a small-time takeover artist, was trying to use his newly acquired firm, Pantry Pride, to purchase much larger Revlon. Perelman had made it clear that whichever bank represented him in his battle against Revlon would receive enormous fees.

Morgan Stanley would not likely be that bank. Revlon was one of an elite class of long-established household names, often called "house accounts," that Morgan Stanley previously had not risked alienating. Also, the Revlon deal would involve "junk" bonds, risky below-investment-grade debt Morgan Stanley previously had refused to sell. Having rejected such risky business for years, the firm was barely qualified to jump in now. Its recent foray into junk had flopped, producing a $10 million loss on one failed deal. In contrast, aggressive Drexel Burnham Lambert and its now-infamous leader, Michael Milken, were capturing hundreds of millions in junk bond fees and more than half the junk market. For the first time in six decades, Morgan Stanley was being dragged off center stage.

The Revlon deal would both save and revolutionize the firm. The deal was the brainchild of Eric Gleacher, Morgan Stanley's head of mergers and acquisitions and another of the firm's new weapons. Gleacher had been a rifle platoon commander in the Marines, and his take-no-prisoners approach convinced Perelman to use Morgan Stanley in addition to Drexel. The Revlon deal went well, and Morgan Stanley collected nearly $25 million in fees.

Revlon was only the beginning. Now that Morgan Stanley had tasted the forbidden fruit of increased risk and easier money, it hungered for more. The firm made another $25 million in the largest and riskiest deal in Wall Street history, the $25 billion leveraged buyout of RJR Nabisco. Although the deal had required enormous amounts of work and involved huge risks, the $25 million fee was a record for a single transaction. The partners became greedier as they shifted to higher-risk, higher-profit activities. They also began depending more and more on sales and trading.

Morgan Stanley had been privately owned since the 1930s, and the partners had resisted "going public" – selling shares to other investors – for decades. But now, the lure of profits from selling stock was irresistible. In March 1986 the firm's partners finally cashed in. When Morgan Stanley completed its first public offering of common stock, many partners, including Chairman Dick Fisher, walked away with more than $50 million each. They had changed the firm's character, irrevocably. Morgan Stanley's new client list included not only Perelman, but also T. Boone Pickens, the corporate raider from Mesa Petroleum, various arab sheiks, even the Teamsters. Within a few years, the firm had climbed back on top, its white shoes permanently stained but once again with the highest return on equity of any investment bank.

Now fully armed, Morgan Stanley had recaptured its star status, albeit in a remarkably different role. The financial world was shocked by the House of Morgan's sudden character change. Morgan Stanley a strumpet? A Jezebel of junk? A demimondaine of debt? Martin Lipton, the famed corporate lawyer, allegedly asked, "How can you guys be getting in bed with Drexel?" But it was too late. The deed was done, and the remade Morgan Stanley could not be shamed away.

With the floodgates of risk open, by the time I arrived in mid-February 1994, any evidence of the old, stodgy Morgan Stanley had been washed away. The new firm was a turbo-charged profit machine, generating great risks and even greater profits and winning the battle of the bulge brackets, mostly because of its new powerful sales-and-trading operation. By 1994 sales and trading was driving most of the firm's revenues, and its engine was fueled by derivatives.

Although my new group, known as DPG – for Derivative Products Group – employed only a few dozen people, it was a major hub at the firm. DPG was centered between the firm's two core businesses: the Investment Banking Division (IBD) and the Fixed Income Division (FID). My first observation at Morgan Stanley was that the most difficult part of working there would be memorizing all the damn acronyms. Even Morgan Stanley itself and the firm's various subsidiaries had abbreviated names: MS,

F. I. A. S. C. O.

MS Group, MSCS, MSI, MSIL. Nearly every group, product, and activity at the firm had its own acronym. For the first few months, new employees were like kindergartners, struggling to learn their ABCs. So far, my brimming bowl of Morgan Stanley's alphabet soup included DPG, IBD, and FID. Soon there would be more.

IBD, the Investment Banking Division, was the firm's traditional backbone of corporate finance (raising money for companies) and mergers and acquisitions (arranging for companies to buy other companies). IBD had been around forever and was a constant, consistent source of profit. In IBD, young associates spent twenty-hour days preparing "books," the bound presentations senior bankers flipped through during meetings with corporate executives. You took a job there at your peril. After several years preparing these flip books, you either would be fired or promoted, assuming you still were alive. After several more years you would be allowed to carry the books to meetings, and at some point you might even be permitted to speak. Several of my friends had entered the business slaving as flip-book boys. Many of them still were. I wanted to steer clear of IBD.

I felt much better about FID, the Fixed Income Division, also known as "sales and trading." Younger and smaller than IBD, FID housed the trading floor and all of its antics. The firm had created FID in 1971, and even after twenty-plus profitable and growing years, it had only 900 employees, less than 10 percent of the firm. FID employees sold and traded bonds, including government bonds, junk bonds, mortgages, and emerging markets debt. FID salesmen and traders took huge risks, and FID profits were much more volatile than those of IBD, but when Morgan Stanley had a really good year, it was because of FID.

FID was on the trading floor, where there were no flip books. A new sales-and-trading associate had only three tasks: (1) Feed your boss, (2) withstand abuse, and (3) learn. This job was more demeaning than investment banking, but the hours, usually only twelve to fourteen a day, weren't bad. Jobs in sales and trading

36

were on a much faster track. Within a few months you could be the person actually selling or trading bonds. The job was risky, and if you made a mistake, you could be fired. But if you made money for the firm, you would be paid extremely well.

Like most derivatives salesmen, I was an avid gambler and more attracted to FID than IBD. Fortunately, I wouldn't have to make a choice. The firm had placed the derivatives group at the intersection of these two core business – and for good reasons. Derivatives were making the firm a lot of money, and the derivatives salesmen needed and deserved as much access and support as they could get. DPG had the benefit of direct ties to both the old-boy network of the investment bankers and the risk-taking expertise of the salesmen and traders. For convenience, DPG was centrally located just off the fourth-floor elevators on prime real estate, near the center of Morgan Stanley's massive bond trading floor.

There was another reason to structure the derivatives group as an internal "joint venture" between the firm's two most powerful divisions. By sandwiching DPG between these factions and allocating a share of the derivatives profits to each, management hoped to dampen conflict and ease infighting at bonus time.

I knew from First Boston that bonus disputes between these two areas are contentious, and the gulf between investment banking and sales and trading is as wide as any ocean – and similarly unbridgeable. Investment bankers are conservative, cultured, slow-moving men (and a few women) who advise corporate executives about which country clubs they should join; their favorite phrase is, "How extremely interesting." Salesmen and traders are wild, cunning, aboriginal creatures who advise money managers about deceiving their bosses and finding new strip bars; their favorite phrase is, "Fuck you." Investment bankers eat fruit. Salesmen and traders eat meat, preferably fried meat. By law, there is a barrier – called a "Chinese Wall" – between the two sides that prevents them from discussing certain business issues. In reality, the Chinese Wall is superfluous; the two sides are located on different floors and are perfectly happy to speak to each other only once a year, when they meet to argue about bonuses. Those bonus confrontations can be like the meeting of matter and antimatter.

The elders of Morgan Stanley remembered well how, after the Great Depression, J. P. Morgan & Company had been divided into separate banks. More recently, other firms suffered from internal political struggles, and several had split up, failed, or merged with other firms as a result. Morgan Stanley needed to manage any internal disputes about derivatives so that hopefully the House of Morgan would not be divided yet again. The future of the firm depended on derivatives, and the future of the derivatives group depended on cooperation within the firm.

The history of DPG, like the history of derivatives, is not well known, even at Morgan Stanley. Most people there have heard of DPG because the group is such a huge moneymaker. However, few employees, including me, realized how new the group was. DPG did not exist before 1990. In fact, Morgan Stanley didn't even sell many types of derivatives until a few years ago. Previously, the firm's limited derivatives activities had been scattered throughout the bank, and overall profits from such sales had been relatively low.

In fact, although certain types of derivatives have existed for thousands of years – farmers used forwards to hedge and the ancient Greeks used options to speculate – most derivatives innovation has occurred in the past decade, and most of the derivatives Morgan Stanley was selling in 1994 were new. The majority of derivatives DPG sold – including structured notes and interest rate swaps, which I will describe in detail later – didn't exist before 1980. Once Wall Street began creating these derivatives, their use and popularity skyrocketed. But the most profitable derivatives, including those I would sell, were invented after the Reagan years.

In its early days DPG made money by capitalizing on the firm's recent change in character. The group sold risky, leveraged derivatives to some of the firm's less reputable new clients, often wealthy individuals from the Middle East and East Asia. In the early 1990s a few DPG clients lost significant amounts of money on derivatives, but Morgan Stanley had kept those losses quiet – and even those clients who lost money kept coming back for more.

The year before I arrived, DPG had arranged hundreds of derivatives transactions and had raised more than $25 *billion* of funding for clients. The group's new products included derivatives with names I'd never even heard of – Dollarized Yield Curve Notes, Discrete Payoff Bull Notes, Constant Maturity Treasury Floaters, Prime–LIBOR Floating Rate Notes, Oil Linked Notes, and Real Return Bond Strips – and acronyms I could not possibly track.

As the group's products evolved, so did its clientele. No longer merely oil sheiks and real estate tycoons, the expanded client base ranged from large conservative companies and state investment boards to the most aggressive hedge funds and mutual funds. The salesmen had learned to adapt to market changes, shifting tactics weekly, sometimes daily, depending on which trades were the most profitable.

In two years the seventy or so people I worked with in DPG generated about a billion dollars in fees. We weren't permitted to keep *all* the money. Because of the firm's "joint venture" arrangement, employees throughout the firm also enjoyed the profits from the group's derivatives sales. Still, there was plenty left over to pay the DPG salesmen, who claimed to be the highest paid employees at the firm.

These were heady days at Morgan Stanley. No one seemed to care about how risky many of the hundreds of derivatives deals were. No one seemed to care about whether clients actually understood what they were buying, even when the trades had hidden risks. The group simply continued to pile trade on top of trade. Year by year, client by client, trade by trade, the venerable House of Morgan was building a precarious house of cards.

Four senior managing directors, aptly known as the Gang of Four, ran my group. They were multi-multimillionaires and were among the most powerful – and feared – men in the derivatives business. They struggled to maintain a low profile for themselves and the group's business, and for the most part they succeeded. Even at Morgan Stanley these four men were not particularly well known.

The Gang of Four consisted of: Bidyut Sen, the group's mastermind in New York; Steve Benardete, a politically connected New Yorker and former treasurer of the key derivatives lobbying group, ISDA – the International Swaps Dealers Association; George James, head of the London office; and Paul Daniel, leader of the booming East Asian offices, headquartered in Hong Kong.

The Gang of Four had spent most of their careers at Morgan Stanley and were all so rich now that their seven-figure bonuses were important only for competitive reasons. Each wanted to be paid more than his peers, not necessarily because the money was relevant to day-to-day life, but because it would signal that he had beaten the others. The money itself meant very little. What's another few million when you have fifty already? One member of the Gang of Four said he lost much of his 1994 bonus – millions of dollars – when he bet wrongly that the U.S. dollar would appreciate versus the Japanese yen. He was upset about betting wrongly. But he didn't seem to care about the millions he lost, any more than he would have cared about losing a few hundred dollars at the horse track.

Although based in New York at first, DPG's management and control were moving outside New York along with the rest of Morgan Stanley, part of the firm's "globalization" strategy. New York historically had been the focus of DPG's efforts, but London was gaining ground. George James from London had a reputation as a straight shooter and was regarded as the brainiest of the Gang of Four, although many suspected this was primarily because of his smart-looking tortoiseshell glasses. Paul Daniel from Hong Kong was the thin, youthful, rising star of the Gang of Four who controlled the most territory and was best known among senior management. Daniel was one of the firm's tallest employees, and he especially towered over the diminutive New York managers, each of whom was well under six feet.

Beyond London, the new blood of DPG was in East Asia, especially in the Tokyo office, run by Jon Kindred, a ruddy-faced pit bull manager responsible for tens of millions in fees. Not yet a member of the Gang, Kindred, for his seniority level and age, was the most powerful person at Morgan Stanley.

It appeared that the two New York members of the Gang of Four were on the way out. Steve Benardete didn't complain about his loss of stature and power within the firm, and he seemed to prefer his new, limited role. He still managed a portion of the New York derivatives trading desk, but it looked like he was spending more time schmoozing officials in Washington than generating trading profits. Benardete was by far the shortest member of the Gang of Four, but if he had a Napoleon complex, it had subsided long ago. He was a genuinely nice guy. Once, when I hadn't been paid my salary for nearly a month due to a payroll system glitch, and accounting finally paid me in cash instead of by check or direct deposit, Benardete offered to let me keep the large stack of cash locked in his office safe until I could deposit it at a bank the next day.

Bidyut Sen was slightly taller, but he suffered from the full-blown Napoleon complex. A middle-aged Indian with a jet-black goatee, Sen resembles the devil in physical appearance. He has a creative, brilliant mind and was an avid gambler and gamer, especially at chess. Many years ago Sen's gaming skills made him a derivatives superstar. He had been involved in the derivatives markets as long as anyone on Wall Street, well before many of the derivatives we were selling had been invented and certainly since I had heard of derivatives. He could recall details of the first cross-currency swap transaction, in 1981, between the World Bank and IBM. Although dozens of managers at Morgan Stanley claimed credit for inventing various types of derivatives, whenever there was a doubt, most of the DPG salesmen gave the credit to Sen.

Sen had developed a fearful reputation and was renowned for his periodic fits of rage. Nearly every DPG employee could tell stories about being humiliated by Sen with loud, public harangues. In the early 1990s, as control of the group began to slip from Sen to other managers, including those in the firm's London and Tokyo offices, his fits of rage became more frequent. Throughout 1994, during my first months at the firm, his eruptions were as predictable as those of Old Faithful. The more control Sen lost, the angrier he became.

Unfortunately, the loss of control also led Sen to lose interest in applying his creative mind to derivatives. Throughout 1994 he was seldom seen in his appointed spot in the center of the trading floor or even in his posh window office, one of the few offices directly adjacent the trading floor. When he *was* present, he usually played computer chess all day, stopping only occasionally to scream at someone for being stupid and incompetent or to make a market in some sports gambling event. Sen continued to gamble, and he became somewhat animated during the World Cup and the NCAA Final Four Basketball Tournament, buying and selling bets on different teams and even creating exotic derivatives bets based on the performance of different groups of games. But he rarely became excited about the group's business. As far as I could tell, he did almost nothing to earn the millions he received every year, apart from occasionally yelling at some of the other managers.

A few people found his tirades amusing, but nearly everyone in DPG began to resent his bipolar approach. Sen sometimes tried to be kind to his colleagues, especially new employees, and he was especially nice to me – at least at first. But his oscillations between meanspiritedness and inattentiveness ensured that as long as he remained in the group, he would be feared but not loved.

In the upcoming months I would learn more about DPG's history, but early on I learned about one derivatives trade that I think exemplifies the group's business. This particular trade, and its acronym, were among the group's most infamous early inventions, although it still is popular among certain investors. The trade is called PERLS.

PERLS stands for Principal Exchange Rate Linked Security, so named because the trade's principal repayment is linked to various foreign exchange rates, such as British pounds or German marks. PERLS look like bonds and smell like bonds. In fact, they *are* bonds – an extremely odd type of bond, however, because they behave like leveraged bets on foreign exchange rates. They are issued by reputable companies (DuPont, General Electric Credit) and U.S. government agencies (Fannie Mae, Sallie Mae), but instead of promising to repay the investor's principal at maturity, the issuers promise to repay the principal amount multiplied by some formula linked to various foreign currencies.

For example, if you paid $100 for a normal bond, you would expect to receive interest and to be repaid $100 at maturity, and in most cases you would be right. But if you paid $100 for PERLS and expected to receive $100 at maturity, in most cases you would be wrong. Very wrong. In fact, if you bought PERLS and expected to receive exactly your principal at maturity, you either did not understand what you were buying, or you were a fool.

PERLS are a kind of bond called a structured note, which is simply a custom-designed bond. Structured notes are among the derivatives that have caused the most problems for buyers. If you own a structured note, instead of receiving a fixed coupon and principal, your coupon or principal – or both – may be adjusted by one or more complex formulas. If you haven't heard of structured notes, just wait. They are one of the largest and fastest growing markets in the world. Estimates of the size of the market range from hundreds of millions to more than $1 *trillion* – almost $10,000 for every working American.

Morgan Stanley's derivatives salesmen made millions selling PERLS to investors throughout the world. PERLS buyers came from everywhere – the Middle East, Japan, even the state of Wisconsin – and included well-known companies and public funds as well as clandestine enterprises and wealthy individuals. These investors had little in common except that each of them would pay Morgan Stanley enormous fees, and many would lose a fortune on PERLS.

I discovered there are two basic categories of PERLS buyers; I call them "cheaters" and "widows and orphans." If you are an eager derivatives salesman, either one will do just fine. Most PERLS buyers – the cheaters – were quite savvy, using PERLS to speculate on foreign currencies in ways other investors had never even dreamed might be possible. With PERLS, investors who were not permitted to bet on foreign currencies could place such bets anyway. Because PERLS looked like bonds, they masked the nature of the investor's underlying bet. For example, one popular PERLS, instead of repaying the principal amount of $100, paid the $100 principal amount multiplied by the change in the value of the U.S. dollar, plus twice the change in the value of the British pound, minus twice the change in the value of the Swiss franc. The principal repayment was linked to these three different currencies, hence the name Principal Exchange Rate Linked Security. If the currencies miraculously aligned precisely – and the probability of that was about the same as that of the nine planets in our solar system forming a straight line – you would receive exactly $100. But more likely you would receive some other amount, depending on how the currencies changed. If you understood what you were buying, you hoped to receive a lot more than $100, although you knew you could receive a lot less. If the foreign currency rates went the wrong way – if the dollar and pound zigged while the franc zagged – you could lose every penny.

In a clever but somewhat dubious marketing pitch for PERLS, DPG salesmen often bragged that the investor's "downside was limited to the size of the initial investment." These words appeared as boilerplate throughout Morgan Stanley's marketing documents and almost always generated snickers from the salesmen. One of the ironic selling points of PERLS – and many other derivatives my group later sold – was that the most a buyer could lose was everything.

Morgan Stanley, in contrast, had nothing to lose. The firm would profit regardless of what happened to the various rates because it would hedge its foreign exchange risks in separate transactions with other banks. At the same time the firm would charge the investors millions of dollars in fees. PERLS were much more profitable than a typical banking deal. An average investment banking fee for a normal medium-term bond was less than half a percent. So for $100 million of bonds a bank might make a few hundred thousand dollars. By contrast, in 1991 Morgan Stanley charged more than 4 percent for its multiple-investor PERLS. For $100 million of PERLS that would be $4 million of fees. Not bad. And for some deals, the fees were even higher.

Because PERLS were complex foreign exchange bets packaged to look like simple and safe bonds, they were subject to abuse by the cheater clients. Although many PERLS looked like bonds issued by a AAA-rated federal agency or company, they actually were an optionlike bet on Japanese yen, German marks, and Swiss or French francs. Because of this appearance, PERLS were especially attractive to devious managers at insurance companies, many of whom wanted to place foreign currency bets without the knowledge of the regulators or their bosses. PERLS were designed to allow such cheater managers to gamble in the volatile foreign exchange futures and options markets.

But there were other types of PERLS buyers who lacked the training and experience to understand them at all. They looked at a term sheet for PERLS, and all they saw was a bond. The complex formulas eluded them; their eyes glazed over. The fact that the bonds' principal payments were linked to changes in foreign currency rates was simply incomprehensible. These are the buyers I call widows and orphans. These are the buyers salesmen love.

Some PERLS buyers had no idea that the bet they were making by buying PERLS typically was a bet against a set of "forward yield curves." Forward yield curves are a basic, but crucial,
concept in selling derivatives. The most simple "yield curve" is
the curve that describes government bond yields for various maturities. Usually the curve slopes upward because as the maturity
of a government bond increases, its yield also increases. You can
think about this curve in terms of a bank Certificate of Deposit:
You are likely to get a higher rate with a five-year CD than with a
one-year CD. A yield curve is simply a graph of interest rates of
different maturities.

There are many different kinds of yield curves. The "coupon
curve" plots the yields of government coupon bonds of varying
maturities. The "zero curve" plots the yields of zero coupon government bonds of varying maturities (more about zero coupon
bonds, also known as Strips, later). The coupon and zero curves
are elementary, and you can find the quotes that make up these
curves every day in the business section of most newspapers. The
Wall Street Journal also includes a summary of daily trading activity in such bonds in its Credit Markets column.

But the most important yield curve to derivatives salesmen is
one you won't find in the financial pages – the forward yield
curve, or "forward curve." Actually, there are many forward
curves, but all are based on the same idea. A forward curve is like
a time machine: it tells you what the market is "predicting" the
current yield curve will look like at some point *forward* in time.
Embedded in the current yield curve are forward curves for various forward times. For example, the "one-year forward curve"
tells you what the current yield curve is predicting the same
curve will look like in one year. The "two-year forward curve"
tells you what the current yield curve is predicting the same
curve will look like in two years.

The yield curve isn't really predicting changes in the way an
astrologer or palm reader might, and as a time machine, a
forward curve is not very accurate. If it were, derivatives traders

would be even richer than they already are. Instead, the yield curve's predictions arise, *almost* like magic but not quite, out of arbitrage – so-called riskless trades to capture price differences between bonds – in an active, liquid bond market.

I can explain this more easily by an example. Suppose the one-year interest rate is 5 percent and the two-year interest rate is 10 percent. This is a very steep yield curve. Suppose you want to put $100 in savings away for two years. You can either (1) lock in 10 percent for two years, or (2) lock in 5 percent for one year, and wait to see what rate you can earn during the second year. Which would you do? If you lock in 10 percent for two years, and the one-year interest rate stays the same at 5 percent, you are better off. But if you lock in 10 percent for two years, and the one-year interest rate soars to 50 percent, you are worse off. What is the one-year break-even rate? In other words, how much would one-year rates need to increase before you earned the same return with either strategy? The answer – about 15 percent – is the one-year forward rate for one year. That is, the current yield curve is predicting, based on current trading between one and two year bonds, that in one year 15 percent will be the one-year rate. The actual rate in one year might be 15 percent, or it might not. The 15 percent rate is *implied* by current rates. There are elaborate formulas for calculating all the forward rates for every maturity and for deriving an entire forward curve, but the analysis is no more difficult than the above example.

If the above discussion wasn't clear, just remember this: If today's yield curve is flat, the forward curve is flat. If today's yield curve is steep, the forward curve is higher and steeper. In a way, the forward curve simply *stretches or magnifies* the shape of the current yield curve. And if you don't believe what the forward curve is predicting, then derivatives allow you to bet against the forward curve.

Forward curves are an incredibly powerful and important concept in derivatives trading. If you don't understand forward curves and you work at an investment bank, the derivatives salesmen and traders are probably laughing at you. If you don't understand forward curves and you're a normal person investing in *anything* other than stocks and bank CDs, you're probably being screwed by someone who does understand them.

PERLS were a gold mine for derivatives salesmen with clients who didn't understand forward curves. Because of their complexity, PERLS were much higher-margin than normal bonds, and if a salesman could convince a client it was buying a normal low-risk bond when it really was buying PERLS, the salesman could make an exorbitant commission. Given the choice between selling PERLS and selling a normal bond, you always sold PERLS. So what if an unknowing client actually was placing a leveraged foreign exchange bet when it thought it was just buying a AAA bond? If its principal was repaid, the client would never know the difference. And if its principal wasn't repaid, well ...

The downside risk made longer-maturity PERLS especially attractive to sell. Selling a five-year PERLS to a widow or orphan buyer meant you didn't have to worry about the repayment of principal for five years – an entire career on Wall Street – and even then there was a decent chance the buyer would have bet correctly and made money. Not even a widow or an orphan will complain about receiving $200 instead of $100 at maturity.

I don't mean to suggest that all derivatives salesmen sold PERLS to widows and orphans. But certainly some did. And many more salesmen tried to sell bonds similar to PERLS. The combination of simplistic appearance and complex fundamentals made PERLS a potentially lethal mix.

I have heard many stories about salesmen selling PERLS to widows and orphans, but this one, which I heard just after I arrived at Morgan Stanley, is my favorite:

A few months after one successful salesman sold a stodgy insurance company an $85 million string of PERLS it obviously did not understand, a senior treasury officer from the company called the salesman to find out how much the PERLS the company had bought were worth. The officer had assumed they still would be worth $100 – or perhaps $99.99 or $100.01 – and was incredulous to learn that the bonds already had plummeted to a fraction of their original value. The conversation the salesman relayed to me went like this:

"But how did we lose so much money on this bond already? It's only been a few weeks. And it's a government agency bond, for God's sake. My boss is going to kill me."

"Well, you know, the various currencies reflected in the principal redemption formulas have depreciated significantly against the U.S. dollar since you bought this security several weeks ago. Also, time decay and volatility changes in the foreign exchange markets have decreased the value of the options embedded in the PERLS."

"What? Tell me again – in plain English this time. What does all *that* mean?"

"It means you made a big foreign exchange bet, and you lost."

At this point the company officer was flustered. "Foreign exchange bet? What the hell are you talking about? We didn't bet anything, and we shouldn't have lost anything. We didn't make any foreign exchange bet. We're an insurance company, for God's sake. We aren't even allowed to buy foreign exchange."

"Well, when you buy PERLS, you take foreign exchange risk. That's why you were getting an above-market coupon on the bond. I told you that. I warned you. You just don't remember. I tried to explain this formula to you. Come on, why did you think you'd be getting such a high coupon if you weren't taking any risk?"

The officer was dumbfounded. "Oh, my God. You mean to tell me *we* were taking the foreign exchange risk? I thought *you* were taking the foreign exchange risk."

This salesman had earned a giant commission on this PERLS trade, and he laughed uncontrollably at his story. I laughed, too. When he finished his story, he asked me if I knew what it was called when a salesman did what he had done to one of his clients. I said I didn't know. He told me it was called "ripping his face off."

49

"Ripping his face off?" I asked, wondering if I had heard him correctly.

"Yes," he replied. He then explained, in graphic, warlike detail how you grabbed the client under the neck, pinched a fold of skin, and yanked hard, tearing as much flesh as you could. I never will forget how this salesman looked me in the eye and, with a serious sense of pride, almost a tear, summed up this particular PERLS trade.

"Frank," he said, "I ripped his face off."

3
Playing Dice

Although Morgan Stanley has the service trademark rights to the name "PERLS," many investment banks have copied the basic idea, in different types of structured notes. In fact, I first learned about derivatives similar to PERLS long ago at First Boston, and I remember it very well. It was early in my career, and I thought of myself as a pretty big gambler. I thought the First Boston managers who wagered thousands of dollars in various bets every day were *huge* gamblers. I was stunned to discover that a group of unlikely gamblers in the high-stakes world of structured notes made our betting seem penny-ante.

I was sitting with First Boston's "nondollar sales" desk, a small group located near foreign exchange trading. The nondollar desk was appropriately named: The salesmen sold bonds denominated in pounds, francs, yen, marks – anything but U.S. dollars. Many of the bonds were issues managed by First Boston. The investment bankers upstairs were good at convincing companies and governments to issue bonds denominated in different currencies, and this desk sold all those bonds, with one notable exception. The nondollar desk didn't sell nondollar "crap" – that was reserved for my group in "emerging markets."

I was talking to one of the salesmen about a Thai trade their desk was selling, a tantalizing new derivative with a mouth-watering name: the Thai baht-linked structured note. This trade was a delicacy for the salesmen, although it could be poisonous to their clients. It paid a huge sales commission and carried incredible risks. The nondollar and emerging markets desks had battled over the right to sell this juicy trade – it arguably was both nondollar and emerging – and my desk had argued that Thailand should be classified as emerging, even though Thailand and the other Asian "tiger" countries actually were highly rated credits, comparable to most European countries. We had lost. Now I was on reconnaissance, exploring this foreign derivative on a foreign desk.

If normal Thai bonds weren't risky enough to be emerging, this one certainly seemed to be. The trade apparently had something to do with the currency of Thailand, called the baht, and although it sounded like a bond, it wasn't issued by the government of Thailand or any Thai company. I thought I heard one of the salesmen say it was issued by a government agency of the United States. Could I have heard him correctly? What interest did a U.S. agency have in the currency of a faraway poor country whose greatest impact on the U.S. was its cuisine?

I pestered the salesman with intermittent questions about the trade, and finally he threw a stack of paper at me, including a copy of an information packet explaining the Thai trade. I thanked him. This derivative trade was complicated, so the packet was long, about a dozen pages. I was confident it would explain the trade.

This packet was my first up-close view of a real live derivative, and I scanned it anxiously, as if it might explode in my hands. If you were a client considering buying derivatives from First Boston, these are the pages you would have seen. The packet began with background materials describing Thailand's economy and included some fancy graphs and tables depicting Thailand's economic growth, inflation, and foreign exchange reserves. The heading on the packet said: FIRST BOSTON STRUCTURED NOTES, then prominently, just below: ONE YEAR THAI BAHT BAS-KET-LINKED NOTE. It looked impressive. At the end of the packet was a "term sheet," a two-page listing of the indicative terms and conditions of a proposed trade.

I noticed each page of the packet was labeled clearly at the top: FOR INTERNAL USE ONLY and CONFIDENTIAL. I remembered hearing one of the salesmen order his assistant to fax the packet to all of his accounts. I wondered whether it had been appropriate for him to send out an internal-use-only confidential document.

I read on. At the bottom of each page, in tiny, barely legible print, was a lengthy disclaimer written in impenetrable legalese. As far as I could interpret the language, it fed the reader two bitter blanket warnings: (1) that all of the information in the packet likely was wrong and should not be relied on, and (2) that First Boston probably has a secret relationship with someone else involved in this trade so that if you buy it, you are likely to be screwed.

Why did this packet need such an extensive disclaimer? It seemed strange. On the one hand, these pages were confidential internal documents. On the other hand, the disclaimer would be relevant only if the packet were sent outside the firm. What was going on?

I was getting my first taste of the wink-wink, nod-nod close relationship between the trading floor and the legal department. That close relationship allows an investment bank to perform a neat – and profitable – trick: make money by ripping off clients even though the bank knows in advance that some clients will lose money on the trade and sue. To this end, disclaimers served a critical purpose by protecting the firm from these suits.

Imagine you are a lawyer at First Boston, and you know the salesmen will be sending pages peppered with First Boston's name to their accounts. What do you do? One solution is to paste those pages with protective labels and disclaimers – as many as you can and as broad as you can make them – so that when clients who buy the derivatives and later lose money sue First Boston, you can claim numerous defenses: The selling documents obviously weren't intended to be sent out or relied on; in any case, there was an adequate disclaimer; or, in part because of the disclaimers, sales of this derivative weren't entitled to the protection of U.S. securities laws.

First Boston's use of these labels and disclaimers was remarkable. This was summer 1993, well before any of the major derivatives losses. Yet First Boston was *already* expecting trouble from these derivatives and anticipating lawsuits. Why was the firm doing this now? I quickly learned that, if nothing else, when it came to covering their asses, First Boston's management was smart. Very smart. And, of course, as we know now, after billions of dollars of derivatives losses throughout the world, they were right.

From a salesman's perspective, he may as well have been selling exploding Ford Pintos. A salesman cared only about making the sale, not about the damage it might cause later. All derivatives salesmen knew that eventually some of their trades would blow up, and some of their clients would then go up in flames. If the losses really got ugly, you always could quit the firm. If you had a reputation for selling dangerous high-margin derivatives, it would be easy to get another job.

From the firm's perspective it was important to make as much money up front as possible on these trades. Take out a big fee, plant the time bomb, walk away, and wait. Of course, after the explosion the derivatives losers would sue, but as long as the firm had made enough money up front and could defend the lawsuit adequately, it would be fine. The important message I took from the disclaimers was this: *The way you made money selling derivatives was by trying to blow up your clients.*

I examined the two-page term sheet. It said this trade was a one-year bond with a guaranteed annual coupon payment of 11.25 percent. That was a huge coupon, especially given that the bond was issued by a U.S. agency. U.S. agencies are virtually risk-free, and a normal bond issued by one would pay a coupon of maybe half that much. What was the catch?

The formula for principal redemption said the return of the amount you originally invested was linked to the difference in one year between the value of the Thai baht and a "basket" of currencies. This basket was composed of approximately 84 percent U.S. dollars, 10 percent Japanese yen, and 6 percent Swiss francs. If in one year the baht and the basket had changed by the same amount, you would get all of your principal back. So if you bought $100 million of this derivative, and the baht matched the basket, you would receive a whopping $11.25 million coupon plus $100 million in principal, an enormous total return. However, if the changes in the baht and the basket did not match exactly, you might get less than your entire principal amount back; you might even get zero.

Was there any reason to expect the baht to match the basket? First Boston said yes. Thailand had a "managed currency," which meant its central bank, the Bank of Thailand, adjusted the daily value of the baht based on certain variables, including the value of Thai foreign trade. First Boston had designed this basket to duplicate the formulas they believed the Bank of Thailand was using to manage the baht. Although the Bank of Thailand kept those formulas top secret, First Boston claimed it had discovered them.

If First Boston was right, you would earn the cool, calm 11.25 percent and never realize you had been in the eye of a storm. However, if the Bank of Thailand zigged when you thought it would zag, you would be swept into a monsoon and wiped out. This trade was a perfect example of the tactic cited by the infamous BT salesman: "Lure people into that calm and then just totally fuck 'em." (After a few years in that calm, investors were stunned in July 1997, when the Bank of Thailand announced it was abandoning the formulas, and the baht – together with its associated derivatives – immediately collapsed.)

You might have some questions about this derivative. Who was buying it and why? Were they just speculating, or did they believe First Boston had discovered a secret formula? And if this trade was such a good bet, why was First Boston offering to sell the trade, rather than taking the risks itself? Was First Boston taking the *other* side of this bet, or were they hedging somehow? Why were U.S. government agencies involved in this trade, issuing bonds linked to a complex formula based on how the Bank of Thailand managed its currency? And most importantly, how much money was First Boston making on the sales of these derivatives?

I asked one of the salesmen a few of these questions, starting with, "Who buys these things, anyway?"

No answer. The salesman refused to tell me. I thought the buyers might include hedge funds, the swashbuckling traders who placed big, sophisticated bets in nearly every market. I mentally ticked off a list of the most sophisticated private hedge funds. They had names like Quantum or Tiger or Gordian Knot. I decided to pester the salesman until I got an answer.

"Is it Quantum?" Quantum, originally started by financier George Soros, was now the largest hedge fund in the world. Quantum and Soros had made (and lost) billions speculating on foreign exchange rates.

"No way. Are you kidding me?" It was a stupid question. The top hedge funds were much too sophisticated to buy this trade from First Boston. They could place such bets on their own, without paying First Boston's hefty fees. Whom did that leave?

"Other investment banks?"

"No again." A second stupid question. Another bank, such as Morgan Stanley or Goldman Sachs, was more likely to be selling the trade than buying it.

"How about mutual funds?" I knew the big funds played in emerging markets derivatives. Could Fidelity or Templeton be a buyer?

"Nope."

"Commercial banks?"

"No."

I was running out of choices. I pressured the salesman to admit who was buying the Thai baht trade.

"Look, I'm not going to tell you any names, but if I tell you who the main categories of buyers are, will you leave me alone?"

"OK." I could badger him for names later.

He said, "State pension funds and insurance companies."

"*What?*" I was shocked.

He just smiled.

"Really?" I asked him. I couldn't believe it. "*State pension funds and insurance companies?*"

The salesman simply nodded. He said state pension funds were among the biggest buyers of structured notes, of which this Thai trade was but one example. Generally the list of structured note buyers included the State of Wisconsin and several counties in California, including Orange County, although the salesman noted that this Thai trade was small and unusual and that state pension funds and insurance companies typically bought other types of structured notes.

State of Wisconsin? Orange County? That seemed ridiculous. Why were *they* buying these risky derivatives trades? The next thing you know, someone would try to claim Procter & Gamble was a big derivatives buyer.

I asked, "What about insurance companies? They're conservative investors. Why would they buy these structured notes?"

He looked at me as if I were a moron. "Come on. These notes are issued by U.S. government agencies. They're rated AAA or AA, and they're the only way for an insurance company to play the foreign exchange markets. Isn't it obvious?"

Was it obvious? I thought about what kinds of securities an insurance company might buy. Insurance companies were extremely cautious, weren't they? There were strict guidelines limiting the investment divisions of most insurance companies.

The National Association of Insurance Commissioners, the NAIC, kept close tabs on insurance company investments. The NAIC rated investments from 1 to 5, and regulated how much of each category of investment a particular insurance company owned. How could an insurance company get away with speculating on a complex formula linked to the Thai baht and a foreign exchange basket, when for many insurance companies even stocks were too risky? And why would it matter if the structured note had been issued by a U.S. government agency? That might make the bet *look* less risky, but it couldn't mask the very nature of the investment, could it? If the underlying risk was a complex formula linked to the Thai baht, wouldn't the regulators know that?

The answer, amazingly, was no. In fact, that was the major reason – perhaps the only reason – why a U.S. agency was involved in the trade at all. When the regulators looked at this trade, they didn't see "Thailand." They didn't see "baht." They didn't see the complex formula or the "basket" or the complicated charts and graphs. All the regulators saw was that the note was a one-year AAA note issued by a U.S. government agency.

These notes struck me as an incredible abuse of the U.S. government's borrowing power. The U.S. Treasury borrowed money directly by issuing Treasury bonds. In addition, various federal government agencies (with names such as Ginnie Mae, Fannie Fae, Sallie Mae, and Freddie Mac) were permitted to borrow money backed indirectly by the promise that the U.S. Treasury would repay the debts.

For a structured note buyer, it didn't matter what these agencies actually did. They might collect student loans or pool residential mortgages. For the regulators, all that mattered was that the agency's promise to repay them was an implicit promise by the U.S. Treasury, and how could a note issued by a government agency and backed by the U.S. Treasury be risky? The great irony of this scheme was that because structured note buyers were willing to pay extra to place these bets through U.S. agencies, the agencies could borrow money at a lower rate than the U.S. Treasury itself.

The regulators would not discover the hidden risks – the dangerous Thai bet cloaked in red, white, and blue – until much later, and only then if the buyer lost money. I was astonished. Wall Street was full of gamblers, and investment banks often were compared to the casinos just south of Manhattan, on the boardwalk in Atlantic City. However, at least that kind of gambling was licit. I had discovered a shadier part of investment banking that mirrored the gambling institutions in Atlantic City *before* gambling had been legalized; the sign on the door might say GOVERNMENT AGENCY, but you knew that inside a craps game was going on.

Morgan Stanley also was running a pretty good game at the time, but before my new bosses in the derivatives group would let me play, they required that I submit to a thorough cleansing process. When you move from one bank to another, the new bank usually requires that you complete a preliminary series of interviews, much like the sterilization process you might expect a real rocket scientist to complete before entering a laboratory.

I attended two key debriefing sessions. First I met with a group of the firm's lawyers. They admonished me not to discuss any secrets about pending deals. If I had stolen documents from First Boston, I should destroy them. There was a process I would have to follow before calling on clients I had known at my previous job. Morgan Stanley and First Boston had experienced recent problems related to employee defections, and Morgan Stanley was being especially careful, although I was surprised that no one mentioned anything about Morgan Stanley's confidential information. Various salesmen and traders previously had brought stolen documents, software, and clients from one of the firms to the other. I knew about one especially sore spot, involving a much-hated manager at First Boston who previously had been a much-hated manager at Morgan Stanley and who had been

59

accused of stealing clients and proprietary information when he left Morgan Stanley for First Boston.

I assured the lawyers that I had not stolen anything from First Boston and that they did not need to worry. They seemed to think I was lying. I said I meant it, but they no longer cared. From their perspective, I had been cleansed.

Next I met with four of the DPG managers in New York. These managers soon would become my bosses, my private gang of four. They asked some of the same questions the lawyers had asked, but from an obviously different angle. They didn't seem to question *whether* I had taken documents or software. They wanted to know what I had, or, even more specifically, when they would receive copies.

"What do you know about these clients?"

"Where is your client list, and who is on it?"

"Whose business did you bring with you?"

When I told them the only material I had taken from First Boston was my personal copy of the North American Free Trade Agreement, they accused me of lying. I assured them that most of the information they were asking about was in my head, but they doubted my memory. As to computer models, I was certain I would able to create new models for the trades we would be doing. However, as to clients, I wanted to be careful. I said I could continue to speak with people I knew, but I couldn't promise they would buy anything. As they continued to probe for information, their disappointment was apparent. Then one of them asked a really important question:

"Where is that craps game, anyway?"

I had created a computerized craps game during a few slow weeks at First Boston and listed this craps game on my resume when I was interviewing at Morgan Stanley, to show I was serious about gambling – one employee told me that the game had been a significant factor in Morgan Stanley's decision to hire me. When I told them I hadn't taken even the craps game from First Boston, they became furious.

I had to admit, the game was impressive. It was complete with what looked like a green-felt layout and two red dice that appeared to spin. The computer automatically calculated the payouts for different bets and kept a running tab of "P&L" – profits and losses – for up to eight players. If you wanted to hide the game from someone, you simply touched a key, and the craps layout was replaced by a bond mathematics spreadsheet.

I remembered how, when the salesmen and traders at First Boston discovered my craps game, all work on the trading floor ceased. One senior salesman forced me to bankroll the game, and for weeks I administered the craps program throughout the day as various eager gamblers stared at the spinning red dice, screaming at me when they lost. The running tabs I kept became as complex as the group's trading ledger. I also remembered how my personal finances had been in the balance.

Remarkably, everyone at First Boston had trusted me not to rig the game, which I easily could have done. They knew, and I knew, that, if discovered, rigging a craps game would have ruined my future on Wall Street. I considered rigging the game, of course (any self-respecting derivatives salesman would at least consider it), but I rejected the option when I imagined the story spreading throughout First Boston: "Can you believe that kid? I mean, I'd expect a salesman to lie – about bond prices, maybe – but for God's sake, a *craps game?* Isn't anything sacred?"

I remained honest and told myself that the house has the advantage in craps, that because I was playing the house, in the long run I would win. However, I had learned about the long run the hard way, on my earlier trip to Las Vegas, and, once burned, I was less than confident. When the betting volume increased, I insisted I could no longer bank the game. It was too time consuming – and too stressful. Besides, I was unlikely to become a star in the derivatives business simply by running a craps game. I copied the dice program onto several floppy disks, passed them out, and got out of the gaming business.

Foolishly, I didn't take a copy when I left First Boston. I

suggested to one of my managers that I could call a former colleague at First Boston, who probably would give me one. The manager was not impressed.

At first I didn't mind it if my private gang of four thought of me as someone with business ethics, even though many of my colleagues thought the term was an oxymoron. These four managers would be the four most important individuals to my career at Morgan Stanley. I wanted them to think I was smart, not sleazy. At least not right away. I would have plenty of time, if I wanted, to squelch any impression that I was a guy who played by the rules.

My private gang of four consisted of two managing directors and two "principals," the job title just below managing director. The hierarchy at Morgan Stanley was: managing director, principal, vice president, associate, analyst, secretary. There was no senior/junior distinction among vice presidents or associates. I was an associate as were most employees less than four years out of graduate school.

Compensation roughly matched job title. On average, managing directors made several million dollars, principals made close to one million, vice presidents made a half million, and associates made several hundred thousand, with wide ranges within each job title. The salaries of DPG employees typically exceeded those of similar rank elsewhere in the firm. The salaries of analysts and secretaries throughout Morgan Stanley were referred to as mere "rounding errors." (On Wall Street, compensation less than $50,000 was rounded down to zero.)

I now was twenty-seven years old, still several years younger than the average Morgan Stanley associate, most of whom had worked between college and business school. Associates were typically in their late twenties and early thirties, vice presidents were in their mid-thirties, and principals and managing directors could be as old as forty. Promotions to the next level took two to four more years. Anyone well over forty who had not retired, quit, been fired, or been assigned a senior executive position was "put out to pasture" in one of the many divisions at Morgan Stanley we called "retirement homes."

My ultimate boss was Bidyut Sen, the chess-playing member of the real Gang of Four. During my tenure at Morgan Stanley, most of my interaction with Sen would involve gaming and gambling, not client business. Occasionally I would watch him play computer chess. More often we would place bets on sporting events. Perhaps most importantly, he later took on a portion of a large bet I had made on the NCAA Tournament (we lost). Other than gaming and gambling, Sen did very little for or to me. He often hovered around my spot on the trading floor, but I was one of the few fortunate people in the group he rarely orally assaulted.

My other managing director was Marshal Salant, who re-ported to Sen. Salant was a short, rotund Harvard Business School graduate and a native New Yorker. He claimed he had been slim as a youth and an avid runner as recently as business school, but his marathoning days clearly were over. A steady decade-long diet of cash and nonphysical activity had placed Salant firmly in the class of men whose ties struggle to reach their belts but never quite make it. Despite his sedate lifestyle, Salant was far more active in the derivatives business than Sen, and he played a much more important role in DPG. Salant was quick with numbers – with some help from a now-ancient Hewlett-Packard 12C calculator – and was renowned for his wildly gesticulating left arm. He would wait during a heated meeting for the right moment to use his left. When there was an appropriate pause, he would begin his windup, grabbing a legal pad and a pencil and extending his arm Sandy Koufax-like, until suddenly he fired off a series of fastball diagrams that would ex-plain away any opposing argument. Salant was one of the few managers at Morgan Stanley who did not have much of a temper. Unfortunately he also lacked the charisma necessary to inspire his troops, even as a dependable relief pitcher. So although the

F. I. A. S. C. O.

other derivatives salesmen appreciated his relatively mild manner and strong arm, Salant was neither feared nor loved.

The other two members of my private gang of four were more junior "principals," which meant they were only millionaires, not multimillionaires. These two principals would be my direct bosses during my life at Morgan Stanley. To the extent any part of my experience on Wall Street stuck to me, it was because of these two. I spent most of my day, every day, within a few feet of them. They were as different as two people possibly can be.

I will do these two principals the favor of referring to them by nickname only. Each nickname is fitting.

First there is Scarecrow. When I met Scarecrow during my interviews, I didn't know of his reputation nor his many colorful nicknames, of which Scarecrow is one of the more innocuous. He earned the name Scarecrow by wandering the floors of Morgan Stanley repeatedly whistling "If I Only Had a Brain." Nevertheless, he was a reasonably effective leader. He led by example, and over time this tune caught on. In 1994 a visitor to Morgan Stanley's sophisticated trading floor was likely to see a line of salesmen staring at flashing bond quotes on their computer screens, oblivious to the irony of the happy melody they were whistling.

Scarecrow was the exception to the rule about putting over-aged employees out to pasture. Although he wouldn't tell anyone how old he was, the consensus bet was at least forty-five. He had been stuck at the rank of principal forever, yet he still worked on the trading floor. Management couldn't justify promoting him, but neither could they permit him to leave. Soon I would learn all about Scarecrow, but after just a few hours with him, I suspected that one reason the derivatives managers had retained him, despite his years and lack of skill, was he was just so damn entertaining. After I left the firm, Scarecrow finally was put out to pasture, outside the derivatives group, and he has enough career problems now without having his name plastered throughout this book, so I will respect his privacy.

I will wait to tell you my other principal's nickname. It's

64

enough now for me to say that this nickname and this person are a bit unusual. I learned her nickname at the same time I learned the acronym for Morgan Stanley's most explosive and clandestine class of derivative – including the single most profitable transaction in the history of the firm – which she was involved in creating and selling. This bellicose woman still thrives at Morgan Stanley. She is ably climbing the management ladder and probably would not suffer from having me name her. However, I'll withhold her real name, too, but for a different reason: fear.

As to Scarecrow, he was a gun-toting strip-joint connoisseur who kept a bottle of scotch in his desk and walked the trading floor, cigar clenched, telling obscene – and, I must admit, usually very funny – stories and jokes. Scarecrow often would take me aside and explain that he lived by two simple rules. First, perception is reality. Second, trust but verify. Each of these rules, he was proud to say, he had learned during the most enlightened period in the history of the United States – 1980 to 1988 – from the most enlightened man alive during that period. Scarecrow believed Ronald Reagan was God, and at Morgan Stanley he wasn't alone.

Fortunately for Scarecrow, by 1994 he had managed to position himself in the hottest profit area on Wall Street: Latin American derivatives. Scarecrow even gave a high-profile presentation on Latin American derivatives at an investor conference, although I later heard from a participant that the presentation had not been at all impressive. Impressive or not, in February 1994 Mexico was the hot profit area, and Scarecrow was my boss. I planned to do the best I could.

4

A Mexican
Bank Fiesta

I n early 1994 Mexico was hot. The U.S. had recently passed
NAFTA – the North American Free Trade Agreement – and
bankers were racing south to Mexico City. The Emerging Markets Traders Association said 1993 trading volume was $1.5 trillion, double the previous year, and Latin American derivatives were the fastest growing portion of the derivatives market. Monthly trading of Latin American derivatives had increased to a face value of $25 billion in 1993 from $3 billion in 1992. Every major American bank wanted to skim some of the anticipated flow of money between Mexico and the U.S. All the largest U.S. banks were preparing applications to set up Mexican branches. Many banks, including Morgan Stanley, already had teams working in temporary offices in Mexico.

With my experience at First Boston, I was practically a Latin American derivatives veteran. Morgan Stanley had hired me and one other associate to expand its commanding Latin American derivatives presence. Latin American bonds were quickly becoming one of the most important parts of the trading floor. Scarecrow was charged with leading our Latin American derivatives efforts.

I should take a moment to describe the layout and hierarchy of a trading floor, so you can understand where Latin American derivatives fit. They are more prominent than you might think.

The shape of authority on the trading floor depends heavily on how much money a particular group is making. For the past several years, the most desirable jobs by far on Wall Street have been in derivatives groups, and those groups have usually ruled the floor. In general, if you aren't in derivatives, the closer you are to government bond trading – the hub of the bond trading floor – the better. Surrounding the trading of government bonds, known as govvies, are the middle-tier jobs, including foreign exchange, mortgage trading, and corporate bonds. Less desirable jobs may not even be on the trading floor. Equity sales is bad. Private client sales may be worse. One of the worst jobs, for example, is selling money market instruments in Philadelphia, assuming the firm still has a Philadelphia office, which many do not.

The worst jobs of all are in the municipal bond department. "Munis" are bonds, usually tax-exempt, that municipalities, states, or other local governmental entities issue to pay for roads, education, sewers, and so forth. Munis can be found in the backwaters of the trading floor and the wasteland of investment banking. Before I took the training examination at First Boston and was told, "You'd better do well on the exam ... or else," I knew very well what the "or else" meant: *or else you'll end up in munis.*

Fortunately I had not ended up in munis, and my area, emerging markets, was near the top of the trading floor hierarchy. You may know what "emerging markets" are; if you do, it's a tribute to Wall Street marketing. Bond salesmen are very clever at inventing deceptive names for risky bonds to make them seem more desirable. One example is the ill-favored "junk bond" of the 1980s, which is now euphemistically called a high yield bond. Another example is emerging markets.

Bonds issued by so-called Third World countries such as Mexico, Brazil, and Nigeria had been called Third World debt until

the Third World debt crisis, when they became known, more accurately, as crap. After the crisis, billions of dollars of this debt
were owed to U.S. commercial banks, who were eager to get rid
of it. Unfortunately there were no buyers.

In the late 1980s U.S. Treasury Secretary Nicholas Brady au-
thored a plan to mix this crap together with valuable U.S. bonds
and create a more attractive paté of restructured Third World debt
that, it was hoped, someone would buy. Brady modestly named
this tasty blend a Brady Bond. Unfortunately, Brady's name
alone did not convince investors the bonds were palatable, and
the Brady market stalled.

The entire market needed a sexy new appealing name. The
Third World debt salesmen had plenty of ideas. First, they tried
"less developed countries" debt, but the implications of "less developed" were too negative. Then came "LDC" debt and the hope
that potential buyers might not remember the abbreviated *L* stood
for "less." However, that attempt failed, too. After all, this was
before Kentucky Fried Chicken's pioneering switch to KFC.
Today's consumers of fast-food poultry can be fooled; 1980s
investors could not.

Next the salesmen tried "developing nations" debt, which almost caught on but was still tied too closely to "less developed."
Finally one ingenious salesman suggested "emerging markets."
Everyone excitedly agreed, and departments all over Wall Street
were renamed. For example, my group at First Boston first had
chosen the name Emerging Countries Capital Markets Group
(ECCM), and then – after an unbelievable amount of haggling
with management and a close, nail-biting vote – changed its
name again, in the name-changing spirit of CS First Boston, to
the more-streamlined Emerging Markets Group (EMG). Most
other banks called the area simply emerging markets.

It wasn't clear what "emerging" meant, or how these markets
might "emerge." Still, it sounded awfully good, and it helped
cloud the fact that the emerging bond an investor bought actually
was a Peruvian loan that hadn't paid any interest since the 1800s.

I hadn't planned to be in emerging markets derivatives, and I wasn't exactly an obvious choice. I didn't speak any foreign languages, I had no international experience, and I had limited knowledge of Latin America, the most important emerging market. In fact, I hadn't even known the emerging markets group existed at First Boston until I asked one of my early interviewers what area he thought would be the hottest during the next few years. He told me, "Emerging markets," and I asked the personnel director if I could interview with them – whoever they were.

The best piece of advice I ever received was from one manager who suggested I could become an expert in emerging markets simply by telling people I was an expert in emerging markets. Over time I would fill in the gaps. Amazingly, this advice proved correct, and after a very short stint in the business, even employees in Morgan Stanley's DPG, including Scarecrow, regarded me as an emerging markets derivatives guru. I wasn't about to dissuade them. As long as emerging markets, especially in Latin America, continued to be powerful and profitable, I liked my position there.

Until March 1994 most of Morgan Stanley's Mexican derivatives deals had been directed at getting U.S. institutions to buy Mexican government bonds. That strategy had generated millions in profits. Plenty of that business remained, but now, if the firm was to dominate all emerging markets derivatives, it needed to shift gears.

At the time, many U.S. bankers regarded the Mexican banks as cash piñatas and were eager to smash them open. Mexico had protected its state-owned banks from foreigners for decades. The Mexican government began privatizing its banks in 1992, but it permitted only Mexicans to own banks and continued to impose severe restrictions on foreigners. While the U.S. was assembling an army to keep illegal immigrants from crossing the Rio Grande, Mexico had built its own, much more effective, banking border patrol. It was easier for a Mexican farmworker to cross

---

into the U.S. than it was for a U.S. bank to cross into Mexico.

Still, U.S. banks knew that if they could break through this protective shell, they could reap billions in profits. One reason the Mexican markets were so profitable was that Mexican regulators permitted the two dozen locally owned banks to charge high interest rates and maintain wide profit margins. Mexican authorities also prohibited foreign banks – other than Citicorp, the only active foreign bank in Mexico – from lending Mexican pesos or providing other peso-denominated products, and from establishing foreign currency or securities-trading operations in Mexico. The result was a Mexican bank fiesta: Mexican banks were among the least competent in the world, yet the wealthiest Mexicans were in banking.

The only U.S. bank to attempt to bat down the profitable Mexican banks was Citicorp, and it had failed miserably. The largest U.S. bank in Mexico since the 1920s, Citicorp had only 800 employees and six branches in the entire country. Its greatest claim there was the introduction of a Diners Club credit card. The 1980s Mexican debt crisis had brutalized Citicorp more than any U.S. bank, and its reaction to the multibillion-dollar Mexican debt restructuring had been similar to that of a tourist in Mexico who drinks the water. Since 1992 regulations had eased somewhat, and even Citicorp had managed to digest $8.8 billion of foreign investment recently channeled into Mexico. But Citicorp's unpleasant experience had ruined the appetites of many U.S. banks.

The DPG salesmen, including Scarecrow, said Citicorp and other banks had approached the Mexican market from the wrong perspective. We didn't view the Mexican banks as piñatas ready to be broken. These banks weren't our enemy, and if they *were* piñatas, they weren't even close to full yet. Years of profits had fattened the Mexican banks a little, but recent changes, including NAFTA, had made foraging for banking profits in Mexico more competitive. Our plan was to fatten the banks some more. If these banks were still hungry, we should feed them, not fight them. An easier path to a Mexican bank's wallet was through its stomach.

What would we feed the Mexican banks? Obviously, it should be high margin and high volume. We wanted to make as much money as we could. It should be addictive, too, so the banks would gorge themselves. Once the banks were bloated and couldn't eat another bite, it would be easy to bat them down. Then, at the appropriate moment one little nudge could cause the entire obese Mexican banking system to topple like Humpty Dumpty.

By 1994 Morgan Stanley was in a position to feed the Mexican banks anything it wanted. During the previous year, the firm had achieved legendary status after it successfully completed its first "PLUS Notes" transaction. "PLUS" was another acronym – for Peso-Linked U.S. Dollar Secured Notes – and since March 1993 PLUS Notes had been the rage in Mexico. PLUS Notes were Mexican derivatives denominated and payable in U.S. dollars, and offered both Mexican banks and U.S. buyers an investment they never imagined was possible.

The firm's first Mexican derivatives transaction – the $500 million PLUS Capital Company, Ltd., known in the market simply as PLUS I – had been pathbreaking and was cited in countless seminars as a nearly perfect derivatives deal. Though this deal may seem too esoteric for the average individual investor, it isn't. In fact, if you owned a mutual fund in the past five years, especially one that invested internationally, it's very likely that you owned a piece of either this Mexican deal or one just like it.

The saga of PLUS I began in early 1993, when the Mexican banking equivalent of Citicorp, Banco Nacional de Mexico, known as Banamex, asked several U.S. investment banks whether it could remove some undervalued and illiquid inflation-linked bonds from its balance sheet without actually selling them. That was a difficult request. Banamex wanted to exchange the bonds for cash so that it could invest in something else, but it didn't want to sell the bonds because it would have to book a loss from the sale.

These inflation-linked bonds were called Bonos Ajustables del
Gobierno Federal – more commonly known as Ajustabonos
(translated literally, "adjustable bonds") – and were peso-denominated obligations of the United Mexican States, the Mexican
government. The bonds' payments were adjusted for increases in
inflation, as measured by a Mexican cost-of-living index, in the
same way U.S. Social Security payments are tied to the U.S. Con-
sumer Price Index. The Ajustabonos' principal amount increased
every thirteen weeks, based on a formula that included the value
of the increase in an inflation index published by the Central
Bank of Mexico. Ajustabonos had seemed like a good idea when
Mexican inflation rates were above 100 percent, but by 1993 inflation was nearing single digits, and few investors – not even
Banamex – wanted to own Ajustabonos anymore.

It appeared that Banamex was looking to do the impossible:
sell bonds into a market that didn't want the bonds, without having to admit publicly that it was selling them. According to Banamex Senior Vice President Gerardo Vargas – known at Morgan
Stanley as Blades for the dark sunglasses he sported to meetings
– Banamex had been looking for a U.S. bank to complete the
Ajustabonos trade for a long time, but most banks had said that
"this idea could not be executed or sold and gave all kinds of ex-
cuses." Of all the derivatives groups on Wall Street, only Morgan
Stanley's DPG said it could accomplish this impossible mission.

Depending on whom you ask at Morgan Stanley, about four
dozen managing directors claim credit for the PLUS Notes idea.
One manager who is especially quick to take credit – and, in fair-
ness, deserves much of it – is Marshal Salant. Salant, with his
adept left-handed diagramming, has built a derivatives empire at
Morgan Stanley by solving problems like the one posed by Banamex. Salant stalks the trading floor, armed with his calculator, a
pencil, and detailed technical knowledge of derivatives minutiae.
In the world of nerdy derivatives salesmen, Salant is the king.

But even Salant and his troops faced major obstacles to
completing the Banamex transaction, the first of which was

convincing someone to buy the Ajustabonos. Mexican buyers were out of the question; they, like Banamex, were trying to un-load the bonds. Many buyers in Europe were suspicious of Latin America generally and were unwilling to take on Mexican risk. Although some U.S. and Asian buyers were willing to buy into Mexico, they needed bonds that were both rated investment-grade (BBB or better, on a scale from AAA down to D) and de-nominated in U.S. dollars. Unfortunately, these two qualities didn't coexist. All the Mexican investment-grade bonds, includ-ing Ajustabonos, were denominated in pesos; all the Mexican bonds denominated in U.S. dollars were below investment grade. To sell Mexican bonds to U.S. buyers, Salant and his army of "rocket scientists" would need to find the holy grail of Mexican bonds: an investment-grade-rated Mexican bond denominated in U.S. dollars. The challenge was difficult, but if DPG could create such a bond, it could establish a new billion-dollar market.

There were good reasons why a bond with both qualities didn't exist. The credit rating of sovereign debt generally depends on the debt's currency denomination. Mexico, like many countries, borrowed money in various currencies, including Mexican pesos and U.S. dollars. Mexico's peso credit rating was high because it could simply print more pesos to pay off its peso debts. On the other hand, its U.S. dollar credit rating was low because it would have to generate hard currency to pay off its U.S. dollar debts. Mexico couldn't print U.S. dollars. Because it was easier and cheaper for Mexico to repay in pesos than in dollars, buyers of Mexican debt believed Mexico was more likely to repay peso debts than dollar debts. The credit rating agencies also knew, quite rightly, that Mexico's fragile economy might not be able to generate enough hard currency to repay its large and growing U.S. dollar debt. As a result, Mexico's peso debt was rated AA-, a very high rating, just below the AA ratings of many large U.S. companies and the AAA rating of the U.S. government. In con-trast, its U.S. dollar debt was rated below investment-grade, in the BB junk bond range.

I sometimes questioned the accuracy of these ratings, but U.S. buyers followed them religiously. The DPG salesmen knew that many U.S. buyers were permitted to buy only investment-grade U.S. dollar debt, which at this point did not exist in Mexico. We also knew that many U.S. buyers liked Mexico and were beginning to crave Mexican bonds. This knowledge helped DPG focus its approach to Banamex's problem. If DPG could create a new Mexican derivative backed by Ajustabonos that U.S. buyers *could* buy, then, risky or not, they *would* buy. We weren't alone in this view. Vincent Bailey, portfolio manager at BEA Associates, a New York money-management firm that managed $3 billion in Latin American funds, said that when Latin American derivatives are sold, "Mostly it's done for people who can't buy the actual securities because their guidelines don't allow it."

DPG needed a little magic, and some financial alchemy, to create the new derivatives. The first trick was to split the Ajustabonos into two pieces. The most basic way to do this was to form a new company to buy the Ajustabonos and then have the company issue two new securities linked to the Ajustabonos. To create such a company without incurring the wrath of Mexican and U.S. regulators, Morgan Stanley looked to sunny Bermuda. Bermuda was known as a haven for all kinds of dysfunctional financial behavior and money laundering, first by drug dealers, then by the Mafia, and last by investment banks, including Morgan Stanley. Getting into bed with Drexel in the 1980s had pushed Morgan Stanley down a slippery slope. Now the firm was operating in Bermuda and behaving like the mob.

Bermuda would protect DPG, but only at a price, and DPG had to play by Bermuda's rules. First, Morgan Stanley hired several politically connected Bermuda lawyers to incorporate a special Bermuda company. These lawyers would serve on the company's board of directors and provide crucial political contacts while the company was issuing its special bonds. Next, to avoid negative tax consequences, Morgan Stanley needed to find an appropriate charitable institution to purchase the company's stock. Bermuda law required that the owner of the new company's stock be a qualified tax-exempt entity. Fortunately, Morgan Stanley discovered The Capital Trust, a Bermuda charitable trust whose beneficiaries were the Bermuda High School for Girls, Saltus Grammar School, Lady Cubitt Compassionate Association, and the Bermuda Foundation. Morgan Stanley, through its investors, would give the charitable trust the $12,000 required to purchase the company's stock.

Finally, the newly formed company had to obtain the permission of the Bermuda Monetary Authority to issue $1.5 billion of bonds backed by the Ajustabonos. The $12,000 stock had been created merely to satisfy a Bermuda technicality. It was this company's new bonds, not the stock, that Morgan Stanley was planning to sell to investors. To get permission for the company to issue these bonds, Morgan Stanley – again through its investors – had to commit to pay $1,600 per year to the Bermuda government. From an outsider's perspective, these payments looked like kickbacks. Overall, Morgan Stanley's actions were barely distinguishable from those of a drug kingpin seeking an appropriate tax haven to launder money. In fact, later that year the PBS television show *Frontline* would expose the use of off-shore tax havens by both money launderers and Wall Street alike. (I discussed the show with Scarecrow, who said he was flattered by the comparison.) Morgan Stanley was taking precisely the same steps drug dealers took to evade U.S. regulators. The only real difference between the actions of a drug kingpin and those of Morgan Stanley was that $12,000 of drug money rarely found its way to a charity for Bermuda schoolgirls.

Once the Bermuda regulatory details were under control, Morgan Stanley would need to arrange with at least one of the ratings agencies to receive an investment-grade rating for the new Bermuda company's bonds. There are two primary ratings agencies, Moody's Investor Services and Standard and Poor's, and numerous secondary agencies. I always found Moody's analysts to be more intelligent and creative than analysts at any other agency. However, when you really needed a rating, there was only one choice: Standard and Poor's, known as S&P.

It might surprise you that private entities can pay for their credit ratings. Most people assume that credit rating agencies are principled and accurate, and that S&P in particular is above reproach because it is at least partially accountable to the federal government. Certainly S&P and Moody's Investors Services are two of the premiere ratings agencies in the United States, and the Securities and Exchange Commission regulates each as a Nationally Recognized Statistical Ratings Organization. However, it's also true that although ratings agencies once provided information about particular debt issues without charging the issuer of the debt, today – and for the past two decades – such agencies have been collecting credit rating fees from issuers, simply for telling investors what credit rating they assign that issuer's debt.

A rating isn't cheap, either. Fees typically range from $30,000 on up, more for large and complicated deals such as PLUS Notes. Because S&P also had to preserve its reputation, for some deals you simply could not buy a rating. For a while these Bermuda bonds appeared to be one of those deals, and it looked as if Morgan Stanley might not be able to obtain an investment-grade rating at any price.

Although Morgan Stanley tried to persuade S&P that the new company's bonds were entitled to a rating of AA-, the same rating as the Ajustabonos, there were problems with Morgan Stanley's argument. The company's bonds would be issued in U.S. dollars, and similar Mexican U.S. dollar bonds carried much lower ratings. Morgan Stanley argued that because the underlying Ajustabonos were denominated in higher-rated Mexican pesos, the bonds really were Mexican peso bonds, not Mexican dollar bonds. However, from an investor's perspective, the bonds looked like U.S. dollar-denominated bonds, and S&P's ratings of U.S. dollar-denominated Mexican debt were much lower than AA-.

Morgan Stanley offered two key concessions that persuaded S&P to give the new bonds a AA- rating. First, the company would issue two classes of bonds, and S&P would rate only the much safer of the two. Banamex would keep the riskier unrated class of bonds, to serve as a cushion to protect the safer bonds, providing greater assurance that the rated bonds would be repaid in full. The company would also purchase some U.S. Treasury bonds, as additional protection. The safer, rated bonds were the bonds actually called PLUS Notes.

Second, Morgan Stanley also agreed that the company would commit in advance to execute a foreign currency transaction in which Morgan Stanley would convert the peso payments on the Ajustabonos into U.S. dollars. S&P must have been suspicious that Morgan Stanley would try to market these new bonds as denominated in U.S. dollars, not pesos. As a compromise, S&P required that Morgan Stanley advertise the new bonds with a caveat. The Offering Memorandum for the bonds had to include a disclaimer: "This rating does not reflect the risk associated with fluctuations in the currency exchange rate between Dollars and New Pesos." With this warning, and a huge fee, S&P finally was satisfied and agreed to rate the new bonds AA-.

With this compromise, Morgan Stanley had satisfied the needs of the potential buyers of these bonds. However, that was only half the battle. Now the firm needed to address the seemingly impossible request from Banamex, that it be able to "sell" the Ajustabonos to the company without actually selling them.

The ingenious solution to this problem depended on the un-rated class of bonds Banamex would retain. Amazingly, it was based on Generally Accepted Accounting Principles, or GAAP. The basic idea was that if you own a company, you include all of the assets and liabilities of that company as part of your own assets and liabilities. If by retaining the second unrated class of bonds Banamex could be treated as the owner of the Bermuda company, it could consolidate all of that company's assets and liabilities, including *all* the Ajustabonos. This ownership worked a neat trick. Because Banamex would own the company that owned the Ajustabonos, from an accounting perspective, it still would own the Ajustabonos even if it received cash for them.

I was amazed by the power of this trick. If Banamex retained bonds that represented 20 percent of the Ajustabonos, it would not have to treat the sale of the bonds to the Bermuda company as an actual sale. That 20 percent would represent the *real* equity of the company, and the $12,000 sliver of equity held in part by the Bermuda High School for Girls would become irrelevant. The sale would be treated as a transfer, merely part of a complex financing. Banamex's 20 percent ownership of the Bermuda company would allow it to avoid recognizing a sale, and Banamex could "sell" 80 percent of its Ajustabonos without generating the accounting loss it had feared.

Moreover, because Banamex's bonds would not be paid until after the safer, rated PLUS Notes had been paid, the PLUS Notes appeared far less risky. A prospective buyer of Mexican debt who was concerned about the effects of a depreciating peso now would be protected against a 20 percent decline. This extra cushion of collateral became known as "overcollateralization." For example, if you started with $100 worth of Ajustabonos, the PLUS Notes would be repaid in full even the Ajustabonos dropped to $80 because Banamex ate the first $20 of losses. The PLUS Notes' overcollateralization – actually slightly more than 20 percent – was extremely attractive to prospective buyers, and they flocked to the deal. The Mexican peso might depreciate, but it couldn't drop more than 20 percent, could it?

These PLUS Notes were an exciting security that previously had not existed in the marketplace: They were rated AA-, they paid a high interest rate in U.S. dollars, and they were protected by a 20 percent cushion. For a large conservative buyer, such as a big-name mutual fund, PLUS Notes became the perfect entrée into Mexico.

PLUS Notes proved so successful for Banamex and other clients that Morgan Stanley eventually sold more than $1 billion worth, in ten separate issues with maturities ranging .from six to twenty-one months. Morgan Stanley even claimed "Peso Linked U.S. Dollar Secured Notes" as a protected service mark to prevent other banks from copying the name. The buyers were a virtual Who's Who of the investing community, including the largest U.S. investment funds (Alliance, Scudder, TCW, Merrill Lynch Asset Management, Van Kampen), numerous insurance and pension companies (Cigna, AFLAC, Arco), the largest Japanese and European companies (Alps, Hanwa, Aoyama, Olivetti), and even the State of Wisconsin. One odd fact about derivatives was that whenever you sold a new one, some stray state investment board always seemed to tag along.

The most surprising aspect of PLUS Notes was not how much these funds and companies liked them; it was how little they told their investors and shareholders about the nature of the investment. Often there was no requirement that a fund or company describe in detail its investment in PLUS Notes, other than to disclose that they were AA- bonds issued by a Bermuda company. As a result, many mutual fund owners, pensioners, shareholders, and even a few Wisconsin residents had no idea what the funds and companies they owned were buying. PLUS Notes enabled certain fund managers to hide many of their Mexican positions from investors. They allowed supposedly low-risk funds who could only buy highly rated U.S. dollar bonds to invest in Mexico, even though their underlying investment really was a Mexican peso-denominated bond. They allowed even the State of Wisconsin to bet on the Mexican peso.

What would Joe and Mary investor do when they learned the short-maturity AA- bonds listed as "PLUS Notes" in their retirement portfolio actually were Mexican peso-backed inflation-linked derivatives issued by a Bermuda tax-advantaged company? What would Wisconsin dairy farmers do when they discovered the Badger State was speculating south of the border? What would you do when you realized your retirement savings, which you had assumed was safely tucked away in a highly regarded mutual fund, was being invested in PLUS Notes? The only thing you could do was get angry because you probably wouldn't learn about your investment in Mexico until it was too late – after you had lost money. Because of their high rating, PLUS Notes were a permissible investment, and your mutual fund wouldn't have to tell you much about them. It was astonishing, but as long as the Mexican peso didn't collapse, you might never know your retirement money was being gambled on Mexico.

These Mexican trades opened my eyes like a midmorning *cerveza*. Morgan Stanley had left First Boston in the dust. The firm's derivatives group had made a fortune on PLUS Notes. And the party was just beginning.

In March 1994 I was becoming more involved in the group's business decisions and working on some exciting trades. Having met most of the people in the group, I was beginning to network with other parts of the trading floor. Morale at the firm, and especially in the derivatives group, was high. The previous year had been extraordinary, and the firm had recently paid record bonuses. March was a time for celebrating – and for spending money. The derivatives group held its annual conference on the Cote d'Azur. The entire firm held an extravagant sales conference at the Breakers resort in West Palm Beach, Florida.

This annual sales conference perfectly captured the mood at Morgan Stanley. During the day, the firm's most senior management presented elaborate slide shows full of good news and optimistic projections. At night, the salesmen engaged in various acts of debauchery. Management apparently was aware of the celebratory mood, so one night they had the hotel build a massive "Morgan Stanley Sports Bar" in a large ballroom. At one end of the room were about 10,000 bottles of beer. At the other end of the room were dozens of sporting games, every indoor sport you could imagine: basketball "pop-a-shot" machines, air hockey, Ping-Pong and billiards tables, even indoor football and baseball. (I was hit by several wild pitches.)

The evening included a bizarre postdinner poetry reading by a senior managing director. His poem concluded:

The one thing you knew at the end of the night,
Was that Morgan Stanley was always right.

This poem seemed to inspire the troops, and within the hour several large salesmen were playing tackle basketball in their suits and throwing pool balls at defenseless junior employees. This event again demonstrated the stark contrast between sales and trading and investment banking. As one salesman proudly declared that night, "I bet those fucking bankers are sipping fucking cognac and playing fucking bridge right now."

After the sports event, Scarecrow rounded up a group to travel to his favorite hardcore strip joint in the area, Mr. T's. The previous year one woman had traveled to Mr. T's with Scarecrow and a group of drunken salesman, and she never recovered from what she had witnessed. This year only men were allowed. Scarecrow knew details about clubs not only in Southern Florida, but throughout New York and even in the Midwest, where he had been raised. I once heard him discuss in great detail with one midwestern client a personal local favorite called Art's Performing Center. Even Mr. T's paled in comparison to Art's.

When the salesmen returned from Mr. T's in the early-morning hours, I tried to lure several of them into a poker game. I was eager to relieve some of the wealthier managers of their most recently acquired bonus compensation and I found a few of the more aggressive salesmen from California in the hotel lobby. They were piling on top of each other and climbing all over the plush sofas. One of the salesmen periodically dry humped several of the others. When I suggested a poker game, he screamed and tried to dry hump me, too. I am not a big fan of dry humping, especially when the humper weighs more than 230 pounds.

I was saved by a hotel employee who said Peter Karches, the head of sales and trading, had requested that we retire to our

81

rooms. Karches was our respected leader, and everyone obeyed. But as we walked down the hallway, one of the California salesmen said he had a deck of cards and two bottles of scotch, and we bolted for his room. Five of us played poker in that room for several hours, and it was nothing short of astonishing that I only won several hundred dollars. One salesman flipped on the Playboy Channel, stood inches from the television, screamed profanities, and hardly glanced at his cards. Another salesman bragged about the female clients he had bedded. The others badmouthed their wives. None of them paid close attention to the card game. I listened politely, offered an occasional encouraging word, and continued to shuffle the deck. I suppose I should feel guilty about taking their money. But I don't.

The next morning the conference disbanded. Most people caught early flights, but I wanted to stay to play a round of golf and scheduled a later flight. I had spoken to several salesmen the previous night about golf and assumed I would have no trouble finding a foursome, but when I arrived at the pro shop, no one was there. I waited for a while but finally decided to play alone.

The course was deserted, which seemed odd for a Sunday afternoon, but I was playing well and didn't mind spending some time by myself. After a few holes I noticed a caravan of golf carts on the back nine. Several dozen carts were circling wagon-train style around a group of players. I wondered if they were celebrities and drove my own cart closer to check it out.

I couldn't believe my eyes. Hooters, the restaurant chain, had gathered its most attractive waitresses for a corporate golf outing. Each of several men had purchased a beautiful scantily clad twenty-year-old female golf partner at an auction – women unmistakably chosen to uphold the Hooters corporate image. That explained my colleagues' absence from the pro shop. They had spotted the Hooters women earlier and abandoned golf for a round of ogling, circling the Hooters tournament in their electric carts as bond salesmen of the wild west. I laughed and drove back to the fourth hole to finish my round.

As my group continued to make money on PLUS Notes deals throughout 1994, I began to crave the sensation of ripping someone's face off. At First Boston I had never actually ripped a client's face off, and I certainly had not blown up anyone. Now, as I watched Morgan Stanley's derivatives salesmen in action, I began to like the idea. Scarecrow and others encouraged me.

Morgan Stanley carefully cultivated this urge to blast a client to smithereens. It was no surprise that I had caught the fever so soon. Everyone had caught it, especially the more experienced managing directors. My bosses were avid skeet shooters, constantly practicing at their private skeet shooting clubs, gathering for weekend hunting trips, and even traveling together on safaris and dove hunts throughout Africa and South America. When they screamed, "Pull!" they imagined a client flying through the air.

This killer attitude went all the way to the top of Morgan Stanley. The lead gunman was John Mack, the firm's brash president, known as Mack the Knife, who had acquired a reputation as a leader who thrives in battle. Large and athletic, a former football star from a small town in North Carolina, Mack is an imposing presence, with or without a shotgun.

Mack was harsh but loyal, especially to the salesmen and traders. In a previous job, as head of sales and trading, when other divisions had threatened his turf, he reportedly barred entry to the trading floor. If he saw frolicking or slacking on the trading floor – even reading the *Wall Street Journal* at 8 A.M., for example – he would tell the salesman or trader, "I see that again and you're fired."

Getting his job as president of Morgan Stanley had been a struggle, and Mack was there to stay. Years earlier, he had ousted former president Robert Greenhill in a palace coup while Greenhill was on the ski slopes entertaining clients. Greenhill had not been a pushover; his tightly knit group of loyalists had earned the nickname Branch Davidians. Nevertheless, after a bitter contest, Mack had won, and Greenhill's group, like the Waco, Texas, cult, was out.

Mack was a charismatic leader, charming as well as intimidating. One Morgan Stanley manager described him as "the best salesman I've ever seen." He scheduled informal lunches with all of the lowest-level employees at Morgan Stanley, in groups. His office had two glass canisters filled with candies and a gumball machine, to encourage colleagues to stop by and chat. Mack was worshipped for his patriotic addresses to the firm as well as his inspiring locker-room pep talks. Even the most hard-hearted of Morgan Stanley's managers were moved by Mack's most stirring speeches. He had given many of them goosebumps, and even made a few cry. Mack seemed adept enough to resolve just about any conflict. When the trustees of socialite Doris Duke's $1.2 billion estate needed someone to step in and settle the brawl over her estate, including accusations of murder, whom did they ask? John Mack.

In aggressively seeking his goal of global dominance, Mack also deserved credit for the amount of money Morgan Stanley was making. In just a few months DPG had made more on PLUS Notes than I ever had imagined we would make at First Boston. Bonuses were up dramatically, and hundreds of employees were making bars. The two cochairmen of the firm made more than $5 million a year ($10 million, more recently), and each was already worth more than $100 million. The derivatives managers made millions each, and everyone, including me, had six-figure incomes. Meanwhile, First Boston's employees still were waiting in line to cash their meager checks.

Ten years earlier Morgan Stanley had decided to change its philosophy, and the newly aggressive firm was the investment banking star of the 1990s. Once again, Morgan Stanley, just blocks north of the Broadway theater district, was playing all the best parts – the disciplined Merchant of Venice *and* the usurious Shylock – while First Boston, a half mile east and struggling to find work, was playing Gobbo the clown.

This kind of aggressive fervor was new to me. I had never belonged to a militia before. Even in its training program, First

Boston had not been nearly as warlike. The salesmen at First Boston might have played practical jokes on their clients, but they certainly hadn't discussed firing shotguns at them or blowing them up or ripping their faces off. In contrast, Morgan Stanley was a savage cult. I marveled at how quickly the firm had seized on such a fierce creed.

5
F.I.A.S.C.O.

I n the derivatives world, Tuesday, April 12, 1994, is a day that will live in infamy. On that day the first significant derivatives losses were announced. The salesmen in DPG were so elated by our recent good fortune, we barely even noticed at first.

The first public announcement was that Cincinnati-based Gibson Greetings, Inc. – the third largest U.S. maker of greeting cards – had lost $20 million on what it called an unauthorized interest rate swap with Bankers Trust. Gibson had hinted at these losses a month earlier, when it quietly disclosed a $3 million loss.

The loss sent shock waves through the financial world. William Flaherty, Gibson's chief financial officer, had tried to slough it off, saying, "We decided this is a nonoperating issue and we won't be commenting further." However, the stock market disagreed. Gibson's stock was down more than 8 percent on April 12. The company's law firm, Taft Stettinius & Hollister, said it was investigating the swaps but wouldn't comment. One of Gibson's directors, Anthony Wainwright, reportedly claimed the swaps were "illegal," and CEO Benjamin Sottile stated in a press release, "The company should never have been put in a position like this, as we relied on Bankers Trust to advise us on these transactions. We are presently evaluating legal alternatives." The rumor was that Gibson was preparing to sue Bankers Trust.

BT released a brief statement saying its trades with Gibson were "legal and proper." It appeared, surprisingly, that tiny Gibson Greetings had been trading swaps for a long time. According to Gibson's 1993 annual report, the company had a $96 million swaps portfolio even then, up from $67 million in 1992. Gibson wasn't as adept at swaps trading as it was at making greeting cards, and its swaps trading returns had been less than spectacular. At the end of 1993, it had lost $1 million.

As the facts unfolded, I learned that in early 1994 Gibson had purchased two new swaps from Bankers Trust, and it was those swaps that caused the damage. In one swap Gibson had bet, wrongly, that LIBOR, the interbank interest rate set in London, would not rise above 3.9 percent. For each basis point (hundredth of a percent) rise, Gibson would lose $72,000. In the other swap Gibson had bet, again wrongly, that the difference between the yields on a Treasury note maturing in 2005 and a swap with similar maturity would not narrow. For each basis point that difference narrowed beyond 33.5 basis points, Gibson would lose $746,000, subject to a maximum when the difference fell to 20 basis points. BT estimated Gibson's loss on these swaps at $19.7 million. The company said its maximum potential loss on the swaps was $27.6 million. No one commented on what the purposes of these swaps had been. No one explained how either of the bets Gibson had made could even conceivably be connected to making greeting cards.

That same day, April 12, 1994, the second derivatives loss was announced. Procter & Gamble Company, the 157-year-old household products maker, said it would take a $102 million charge to close out two losing interest rate swaps, also with Bankers Trust. P&G's loss was the largest derivatives loss ever reported by a U.S. industrial company. Chairman Edwin Artzt admitted, "Derivatives like these are dangerous and we were badly burned. We won't let this happen again." P&G also hinted it might sue Bankers Trust. In a conference call, P&G's chief financial officer, Erik Nelson, told analysts the complexity of the swaps violated P&G's derivatives policy. He contended that the company's policy calls for "plain vanilla-type swaps" and that "there are no other swaps of this type in our portfolio and there never will be again." It wasn't clear who, if anyone, at P&G was responsible for the loss. P&G treasurer Raymond Mains, who had been in charge of the derivatives portfolio, was quietly moved from the treasurer's office to a "special assignment."

BT released another brief statement, this time saying senior P&G officials had been kept informed about the swaps and that it had "strongly and formally" urged P&G to unwind the swaps as interest rates started to rise, but P&G officials had rejected BT's recommendations. BT's defense would be difficult because it was known for selling the most complicated derivatives. I had learned of the bank's reputation the hard way, when I lost a billion dollars during a job interview there years ago. BT had been among the first banks to sell exotic options and swaps, pioneering many complex leveraged derivatives. More than a decade previously, BT had decided it couldn't compete with bigger banks for individual customers, so it shed some of its branches and focused on trading securities and providing financial advice to large corporations. The bank had made a fortune selling these instruments to clients such as P&G; its wealth of riches made it an easy target for complaints by securities regulators and by customers who lost money. After P&G disclosed its loss, BT issued a halfhearted statement that the swaps had been a relatively small part of P&G's portfolio.

Like Gibson Greetings, P&G had been trading derivatives for a long time, albeit in much larger numbers. P&G's 1993 annual report disclosed that it held $2.41 billion of off-balance sheet derivatives contracts on June 30, 1993, up from $1.43 billion in 1992. In fact, by 1994 P&G's derivatives trading was so large that by purchasing P&G stock, you were betting more than that detergent sales would rise, you were also betting that U.S. and German interest rates would fall. P&G shareholders would bear the costs of these trades. Although April 12 should have been a good day for P&G stock – quarterly earnings, without the derivatives losses, were up 15 percent – the stock market punished P&G for the losses, and its shares closed down.

A salesman that Morgan Stanley recently had hired from another bank said he had made millions selling exotic derivatives to Procter & Gamble. He claimed he had made $2.5 million on one trade with P&G and that P&G had purchased something called a "quantoed constant maturity swap yield curve flattening trade" – whatever that was. He couldn't believe P&G claimed it didn't understand derivatives, and other salesmen concurred. Bidyut Sen said the P&G situation was like "a man who goes out on a date with another man dressed in drag, and he gets in bed and complains his date is a man." He called P&G "fucking idiots" and advised us to short their stock.

The two announcements drew immediate responses from other companies. On April 14 DuPont treasurer John Sargent reassured company executives that DuPont's derivatives policy was not intended to turn a profit. Colgate-Palmolive Company issued a statement that it had a "firm policy to reduce financial risk, rather than trade financial instruments for profit." And Scott Paper Company CFO Basil Anderson said P&G may "taint the legitimate use of derivatives" and that Scott used a computer system "that keeps track of our entire portfolio on a minute-to-minute basis."

A few other companies were accused of overexposure to derivatives. David Garrity, an analyst at McDonald & Company, even called the Big Three automakers "basically banks masquerading as manufacturing companies" because of their financing subsidiaries. Chrysler Financial Corporation, a unit of Chrysler, had $1.5 billion of interest rate swaps and $535 million of currency swaps, and parent Chrysler had another $1 billion. Even Goodyear Tire & Rubber Company had a $500 million derivatives portfolio. I wondered who *didn't* own derivatives.

As it turned out, there had been plenty of warnings about potential derivatives losses. In a January 1992 speech, E. Gerald Corrigan, then president of the Federal Reserve Bank of New York, had warned that a series of large derivatives losses could lead to a domino effect, throwing the financial system into crisis. Corrigan said he intended his warning "as a shot across the bow, and it's become the shot heard around the world."

Months later, the same Corrigan would be firing blanks. After Goldman Sachs, Morgan Stanley's archrival, hired Corrigan as an international adviser, his warnings cooled. By April 1994 he was heard disparaging his previous statements: "Derivatives, like NFL quarterbacks, probably receive more credit and blame than they deserve. Defense is always the name of the game." Even without Corrigan's presence, other members of the Federal Reserve Board, including Governors Susan Phillips and John LaWare, continued the warnings.

Just before the April 12 losses, members of the Securities and Exchange Commission repeatedly had warned of the potential for disaster. Commissioner Carter Beese had cautioned that the "clock is ticking" for the derivatives market, citing Bankers Trust's 1993 annual report, which listed derivatives positions of almost $2 *trillion*. Commissioner Richard Roberts expressed concern that "some derivative products are being marketed more for the fat profit margin they make available to the securities firm than for their suitability to the customer." Former SEC Chairman Richard Breeden issued similar warnings, and current Chairman Arthur Levitt told the Public Securities Association, "We take this issue very seriously. And we will do our best to make sure brokers take it seriously, too." On April 11 Comptroller of the Currency Eugene Ludwig joined the warnings about "designer derivatives."

Michael Lipper of the fund-tracking company Lipper Analytical Services said that the warnings applied to mutual funds, too; 475 of 1,728 stock, bond, and balanced funds had invested billions in derivatives, yet such holdings "magically seem to disappear" the day funds have to file statements with shareholders. Although mutual funds are forbidden by government regulation from using leverage to buy securities with borrowed money, the Investment Company Institute, a Washington-based mutual fund trade group, announced that mutual funds not only held derivatives worth $7.5 billion (2.13 percent of total assets), they owned $1.5 billion of the special derivatives called structured notes, of which PERLS was one type. For example, Fidelity Investment's $10 billion Asset Manager fund had $800 million invested in structured notes in the last quarter of 1993, including leveraged bets on Finnish, Swedish, and British interest rates. One note, based on Canadian rates and leveraged thirteen times, had gained 33 percent the previous year; in the first four months of 1994, that same note plunged 25 percent. What was worse, the mutual fund trade groups didn't even seem to know about the purchases of PLUS Notes.

Of course, up until April 12, 1994, there were plenty of voices defending derivatives against the regulators, as there are today. A Fidelity vice president for operations development in Boston said, "Asset Manager is designed for people who are relatively conservative." Joanne Medero, a law partner at Orrick, Herrington & Sutcliffe and former general counsel of the Commodity Futures Trading Commission, went on record as saying, "I do not believe there needs to be more regulation, based on my belief that markets are not made more efficient by intense market regulation."

By the time the first losses were announced on April 12, Congress was ready. That same day, Democratic Representative Henry Gonzalez, then chairman of the House Committee on Banking, Finance and Urban Affairs, released derivatives legislation he had been preparing. His bill included a proposal to study whether Congress could tax derivatives speculation and a law making "improper management" of derivatives illegal. Democratic Representative Edward Markey and others joined the fray. Markey's office announced that he "has been concerned about

how the market has expanded from sophisticated financial intermediaries and Fortune 100 companies toward smaller and less
sophisticated end-users, either corporations or municipal governments." On April 6, Markey had asked the SEC to study derivatives more carefully, noting his concern about the increasing
connection between derivatives and recent swings in the stock
and bond markets. Republican Representative Jim Leach warned,
"One has to be very concerned about the size of contracts per the
size of the company," and said the "whole board of directors is
accountable." Gonzales summarized the congressional approach
to this hot political issue: "Instead of waiting for catastrophe to
strike, we should show American financial leadership and take a
proactive stance."

The next day, April 13, the House Banking Committee called
Budapest-born George Soros, manager of the $10 billion-plus
Quantum Group of Funds, to testify about the dangers of derivatives. Soros is, if not the world's smartest expert on derivatives, at
least the world's richest one. Quantum has been recognized as
having had the best investment performance record in the world
during its twenty-five-year history.

Soros said the explosive growth of derivatives presented special
dangers to investors: "There are so many of them [derivatives], and
some of them are so esoteric, that the risks involved may not be
properly understood even by the most sophisticated of investors."
He said some derivatives appear to be designed to enable institutional investors to take gambles that they otherwise would not be
permitted to take. For example, some bond mutual funds were buying synthetic securities with ten to twenty times the amount of risk
those funds are allowed to take. He warned that "some other instruments offer exceptional returns because they carry the seeds of
a total wipeout." He also warned of a meltdown, in which regulatory authorities would have to intervene to protect the integrity of
the financial system. He concluded on a somewhat upbeat note by
saying that he saw "no imminent danger of a market crash."

However, not even Soros could persuade Congress to pass any

laws, and ultimately these proposals failed. Soros, Gonzales, Leach, and others were up against stiff competition. In the past two election cycles alone, legislators received an estimated $100 million in contributions from banks, investment firms, and insurance companies.

It was apparent that there would be more derivatives disasters. Robert Baldoni, managing director of Emcor Risk Management Consulting, said that there were "smoke signals in the distance that there will be new rules on disclosure of derivatives," and until Congress acts, "people with very good institutions will do bad transactions that are not well understood in the company." On April 13 Paul Mackey, an analyst at Dean Witter Reynolds, said, "There are going to be a lot of companies screaming bloody murder about derivatives before long. Procter & Gamble won't be the only one."

I remember how all these announcements swept across the Morgan Stanley trading floor. Gibson Greetings? Procter & Gamble? Had *we* sold the derivatives that exploded? The answer appeared to be no. Bankers Trust was the main culprit. We had dodged a couple of bullets – at least for now.

As predicted, other losses were announced soon thereafter, and throughout April 1994 the losses multiplied. Dell Computer in Austin, Texas, announced a derivatives loss that, despite its spokeswoman's plea that the loss was "not even on the same playing field as someone like Procter & Gamble," caused Dell's stock to tumble 12 percent in one day, the second most active stock traded that day. Dayton, Ohio-based Mead Corporation, a paper manufacturer and provider of electronic data services, also announced a major loss. In the upcoming months, a new major derivatives loss would be announced virtually every day. Many of the early victims were household names. Dell? Mead? I couldn't understand how they had lost so much money. When you bought stock in one of these companies, what were you buying? A manufacturing company or a derivatives speculator? How could you tell the difference? In each case, the DPG salesmen vowed that

93

they had not sold any of the exploding derivatives. In each case, rumors bounced throughout the firm, then died. It appeared that Morgan Stanley had dodged these bullets, too.

Curiously, this first flurry of announcements didn't even faze Morgan Stanley's management. If anything, the screams of bloody murder fueled our bosses' aggression. The immediate rallying cry of Morgan Stanley's president, John Mack, was typical of the mercenaries in the derivatives group. Soon after the first losses were announced, Mack told a group of managing directors, "There's blood in the water. Let's go kill someone." The idea was that if our derivatives customers were in trouble, and we could convince them that they needed us – perhaps to "double-down" on their losses – we could make even more money off their hardship. Management salivated at these potential victims, known euphemistically as distressed buyers. As my bosses told me repeatedly during this period, "We love distressed buyers."

However, some of my colleagues and I were beginning to worry. Our bosses' reactions seemed much too optimistic, almost naive. John Mack's instructions seemed reckless. I was not interested in killing someone, and my training in law school led me to think that maybe I should stay away from these "distressed buyers." I thought it would be a better idea to lie low for a while and not propose any new trades for clients who already had lost millions of dollars on derivatives. However, I was not entirely dispirited. I was starting to get excited about the upcoming F.I.A.S.C.O.

The big day was Saturday, April 18, 1994, just days after Procter & Gamble had disclosed a derivatives loss of more than $100 million. Although I had been worried about the size of that loss, and about the prospects for the derivatives business, by the time I woke in the early pre-dawn hours that Saturday, my worries were gone. I was proud to be a new member of the special forces from Morgan Stanley, and I was especially proud to be attending my first F.I.A.S.C.O. Armed with my marching orders from President

Mack, I was headed for the shooting range at Sandanona, a club in upstate New York. Braving the pouring rain, I waited outside for my ride.

An associate of mine, Alexander "Lex" Maldutis, picked me up at my West Village microstudio. Lex was a true "rocket scientist" and a young one at that. Although he claimed to be in his early twenties, I suspected he really was only eighteen. He had attended college at an age when some kids still were learning how to ride a bike. At twenty-seven, I was an old man compared to Lex. I smiled when I saw him driving down Grove Street in an enormous Lincoln Continental Mark VII. He pulled his cruiser up to the curb and swung the massive door open. I complimented him on the car's luxurious interior, and we settled in for the ride up Eighth Avenue. With his Mark VII, we blended in nicely with the Eighth Avenue pimps and prostitutes whose nights were winding down. Our day, on the other hand, was just beginning.

Lex explained how the Mark VII was a great "chick car." I nodded politely. Did I agree? I sensed Scarecrow's powerful influence over Lex as he awkwardly uttered the word "chick." Many of the younger salesmen and traders tried to emulate our elders, especially Scarecrow. But there was something strange about a teenage rocket scientist who had a six-figure income, drove a posh V-8 automobile, and used the word "chick." As I caressed the dashboard, I knew that part of me agreed with Lex. This *was* a great chick car. I imagined Lex cruising the streets with one of the golf-playing Hooters waitresses. Could I afford a Mark VII?

We fell silent for a few minutes, and I wondered how much I had changed in the past months. Had Scarecrow affected me? He certainly seemed to have affected Lex. Scarecrow's influence was pervasive, and I suspected we were becoming more and more like him. I withdrew my hand from the dashboard. Why were two intelligent young men awake before dawn on a dreary April day, excited about sloshing through the mud in the pouring rain so that we could, if we were lucky, pump a few pounds of birdshot into

95

little pieces of clay? What was happening to us? I noticed Lex was wearing freshly pressed wool pants and polished oxblood wingtips, which in a few hours would be thoroughly ruined. I was wearing jeans and boots, which also would be ruined, although at lower cost. I was relieved that at least Scarecrow had not yet persuaded us to wear World War II fatigues.

We drove up Eighth Avenue and crossed to the Upper East Side to pick up two of our bosses, including Steve Benardete, the shortest member of the Gang of Four. Benardete was Scarecrow's frequent hunting companion and told one of my colleagues that he had paid $40,000 for the right to shoot a rhinoceros in Africa. Benardete's spacious East 70s penthouse was a sharp contrast to my 300-square-foot studio. Many salesmen attending the event lived in Manhattan's normally hushed Upper East Side, and it must have looked like a military operation was commencing there. One by one, the odd-looking militiamen emerged into the rain from their opulent East Side apartments, outfitted in new flannel shirts, yellow slickers, and khaki fatigues. Many brought their own polished twelve-gauge shotguns, although our crew did not. Benardete complimented Lex on his car, and we headed north to Sandanona.

During the two-hour drive, we discussed the recent announcements of derivatives losses. I knew Morgan Stanley was involved in litigation related to derivatives the firm had sold to the State of West Virginia's Investment Board. We discussed that case as well as the derivatives purchases of several other state investment boards, including Wisconsin, and a few counties in California. I wondered aloud whether derivatives might be a speculative bubble that was about to pop. Why were such supposedly conservative investors taking on so much risk? We debated whether a California county should be placing huge derivatives bets on interest rates. My bosses said that as long as we were upfront in disclosing the risks, it was none of our business what these clients bought. It was the client's responsibility to assess the risks, and the client's problem if the risky derivatives lost money. Still, they seemed worried.

Our worries slipped away when we arrived at Sandanona, an historic and exclusive private club nestled in the farmlands of upstate New York. The natural landscape of Sandanona is beautiful, and the setting is especially tranquil in the early morning, as the sun rises over the low knolls and through the dense firs. Of course, we weren't there to admire the area's natural beauty. Not with all the shotguns and ammunition. Sandanona also was home to one of the largest outdoor skeet shooting courses in the area; we were there to shoot.

Scarecrow ushered us into the clubhouse. This was an important anniversary for F.I.A.S.C.O., its tenth. A decade ago, F.I.A.S.C.O. was a mysterious acronym at Morgan Stanley. However, as it became clear that the derivatives group's share of Morgan Stanley's profits would continue to grow, numerous salesmen and traders wanted to hop on the derivatives gravy train quickly, before it left the station. They had understood that derivatives, whatever they were, would make them rich. If that required a mysterious predawn trip to Sandanona for the Fixed Income Annual Sporting Clays Outing, and a twelve-gauge shotgun, then so be it. Besides, it was fun. By 1994 F.I.A.S.C.O. had become a legend.

Scarecrow explained the rules. Each group's mission was to ransack and destroy Sandanona. For several hours they would shoot at anything that moved, except possibly each other, although no one would receive points for hitting anything other than skeet. This was no wimpy paintball shooting contest; the guns and ammo were real. We were about to learn the corporate team concept of shooting to kill and experience the ultimate in male bonding (although a few women were present, this being the 1990s and all).

Some salesmen questioned whether F.I.A.S.C.O. was originally Scarecrow's idea. Original ideas may not have been Scarecrow's forte, but on this issue, I must defend him. The clever acronym may not have been his invention, but the idea of shooting at things certainly was. He subscribed to all the major gun, hunting, and recreational shooting magazines and owned enough weaponry to supply the entire firm. The walls of his Connecticut house were decked with swords, guns, and military uniforms. He had a special love for World War II and attended military helmet conventions with some regularity. I will never forget his solitary piece of advice before I left for an extended trip to Tokyo: Visit the Samurai Sword Museum.

A few salesmen wondered whether Scarecrow's military experience was sufficient to qualify him for a job in the derivatives group at Morgan Stanley. Most of the men and a few women who sold derivatives were called rocket scientists usually for good reason: because they had math degrees and enormous, powerful brains. Derivatives salesmen typically played chess or mathematical computer games in their spare time. Derivatives salesmen typically did not shoot things. Scarecrow was the antithesis of the prototypical derivatives salesman. His nickname was apt. He had neither a math degree nor an enormous brain. When Scarecrow aimlessly whistled "If I Only Had a Brain," no one stepped forward to disagree. What, then, was he doing in derivatives?

Over time the salesmen asked that question less and less as they realized why Scarecrow had succeeded in selling derivatives. Ultimately, Scarecrow's military talents proved far more valuable than mere math skills. He and others were able to persuade the rocket scientists that shooting was more effective than thinking. This was the key to Morgan Stanley's new philosophy. As Scarecrow's views proliferated, mathematical theorems were replaced by pseudo National Rifle Association slogans: Derivatives don't kill people, people kill people. When derivatives are outlawed, only outlaws will have derivatives. The traders and salesmen tossed their math journals in the garbage and bought copies of *Sun Tzu* and other military how-to books. The results were favorable. As Scarecrow's ideas about the art of war caught on, the derivatives group started to make some serious money.

As the quick-learning derivatives salesmen began to have more and more violent thoughts, the securities they sold became more violent, as well. In 1986 a typical salesman subscribed to

Time or perhaps *Playboy,* played golf, and sold corporate and government bonds. By 1994 that same salesman read *Soldier of Fortune* and *Guns and Ammo,* shot doves, and sold leveraged-indexed-inverse-floating-dual-currency structured notes. This was no coincidence.

To encourage the younger salesmen, Scarecrow bought a battery-powered commando doll that shouted military responses. He displayed it prominently on the trading desk. Scarecrow called him the derivatives trader of the '90s. Scarecrow would shout various questions about derivatives to the doll and then hold the doll in the air as he pressed the button on the doll's chest. The doll would retort in a deep, disciplined voice, "Yes, sir! Yes, sir!"

I looked at the dozens of sharpshooters assembled for the tournament. They were aggressive hunters. In the early 1990s, when the derivatives business became more competitive in the United States, salesmen looked abroad for victims, especially in Latin America and the Far and Middle East. Senior management ventured abroad on business trips they called derivatives "safaris" hunting large derivatives deals they called "elephants." These managers described prospective sales in terms of hunting down big game, and their derivatives safaris often complemented real hunting trips. One group of senior directors took an extravagant junket to Uruguay to kill doves. They especially loved killing doves. Why? It couldn't have been the challenge. The group paid a Uruguayan farmer who had thousands of doves on his property to allow them to shoot there. One of the managers told me the air was so thick with doves that the hunting resembled a scene from Alfred Hitchcock's movie *The Birds.* Perhaps they enjoyed these trips because the hunting was so easy. It was impossible to miss – almost as easy as selling derivatives. They said hunting trips, along with F.I.A.S.C.O., were intended as target practice for our business. That rationale wasn't offered merely to justify the trips as business expenses. It made sense. Shooting doves or clay pigeons was excellent training for the even more exhilarating real-life kill, when the shrapnel of a complex financial instrument tore through a wealthy, unsuspecting human pigeon.

This mania seemed to be affecting everyone, even the host of F.I.A.S.C.O. and owner of Sandanona, George Bednar. In 1986 Bednar had broken tradition by renting his hallowed grounds to Morgan Stanley for its first F.I.A.S.C.O. After several years of receiving fat fees for F.I.A.S.C.O., Bednar decided to break with tradition again to expand Sandanona from a rugged country shooting course into a posh corporate caterer. Starting in the early 1990s, Sandanona had borrowed huge sums to enlarge and improve its shooting facilities and clubhouse. Bednar began accepting corporate members and extended Sandanona's traditionally limited local membership to wealthy out-of-town clientele. Sandanona became the home of various corporate outings in addition to the annual F.I.A.S.C.O.s.

By 1994 the shooting club's change in philosophy, like the parallel change at Morgan Stanley, was apparent. At this F.I.A.S.C.O., Sandanona employees would be serving us wild game (obviously shot elsewhere) and fine wine in an elegant firelit dining room, part of their newly constructed clubhouse. The money was flowing, and Sandanona, like a buyer of derivatives, had become addicted to a strategy of maximum leverage.

I noticed a certain momentum to F.I.A.S.C.O. and wondered if my appearance at Sandanona this morning could be a coincidence. Was a spinning cyclone around Sandanona mysteriously drawing Morgan Stanley employees closer and closer? Had that cyclone, even as far back as 1986, begun to draw me too? When the first F.I.A.S.C.O. was held, I had just graduated from high school. Did I feel the pull of F.I.A.S.C.O. even then, from Kansas? As more F.I.A.S.C.O.s were held, I graduated from law school, moved to New York, and got a job at First Boston. After the 1993 F.I.A.S.C.O., Morgan Stanley hired me, and I was pulled into the vortex of the firm's derivatives group. Was this all happenstance? Or had I been drawn, inexplicably, to the event?

Scarecrow grabbed me and insisted that I be in his shooting

group. He apparently thought that because I was from Kansas, I would be a good shot. He couldn't have been more wrong. I didn't have the heart to tell him that as a young Boy Scout, I had been traumatized by my repeated failure to pass the requirements for Rifle & Shotgun merit badge, which essentially required that one of every three shots hit the broad side of a barn. I had been mocked by the other Boy Scouts, who, also being from Kansas, were quite familiar with the saying about the broad side of the barn but had never met a person who actually couldn't hit one.

Lex whispered to me that he had heard the officials of F.I.A.S.C.O. would be awarding a special prize for the worst score. I panicked. I grilled Scarecrow for details. He confirmed that, yes, the worst score would receive a prize, and that his (or her) name would be engraved on a not-so-coveted silver trophy called the Krum Kup. The Krum Kup was named after Fred Krum, an incredibly wealthy and powerful managing director at Morgan Stanley, who had participated in F.I.A.S.C.O. one year but furiously had vowed never to return when he discovered that he, too, could not hit the broad side of a barn. As I examined the list of names on the Krum Kup, I imagined my name, engraved there for eternity. I wondered if clicking my boots three times would send me back to Kansas. Scarecrow stopped that thought and told me that of course I had nothing to worry about. Our team was assembling outside. F.I.A.S.C.O. was about to begin.

The actual shooting lasted about two hours, although my embarrassment was so great that it seemed like days. At first the groups attacked Sandanona wildly, filling the air with shot and shattered clay. The woods clamored with the same repeated sequence: a deafening shriek of "*Pull!*" followed by a twelve-gauge blast and a stream of quick, creative profanity. Pull, boom, swear. Pull, boom, swear.

The skeet-shooting course consisted of a dozen or so different shooting stations, and the groups of four rotated through the dense woods, sloshing along muddy paths between stations. After a few rotations, the echoes of shells and swearing doubled, then redoubled. The shooters began gambling feverishly. Pull, boom, pay. Pull, boom, collect. Huge sums of money changed hands with each shot.

Then many shooters began cheating. In the rain it was difficult to see whether anyone was hitting targets. Even if a shooter had hit absolutely nothing – and knew it – if he confidently announced "eight of ten" when he had finished, he might prevail, after some argument, with a score of, say, six. Pull, hit, collect. Pull, miss, lie, still collect.

As the soldiers increased their intake of booze and cigars, the quality of the shooting disintegrated. After a few hours, everyone's priorities shifted from birdshot to scotch and tobacco. Pull, boom, pay, drink, puff. Pull, drink, puff. Drink, puff, drink, puff.

By noon, the salesmen had littered the grounds of Sandanona with liquor bottles, cigar butts, and urine. The tenth F.I.A.S.C.O. had been a success.

As I had feared, I missed nearly everything I aimed at. I tried to blame my poor performance on the conditions. The rain was spattering my glasses, and I couldn't even see the end of my gun. But it was obvious that, rain or no rain, I was a horrendous shot. I had tried closing my eyes while shooting and actually managed to hit a clay then. But after a few rounds the skeet attendants began to eye me nervously. I prayed I hadn't hit one of them, although I couldn't be sure. I had even tried cheating, but that, too, failed.

As we headed for the clubhouse, several salesmen reminisced about previous F.I.A.S.C.O.s. Was it like the good-old days? Apparently not. The quality of shooting had suffered as the event became more popular. After ten years, F.I.A.S.C.O. was a symbol of the firm's new military approach and killer attitude, and everyone was joining the fray. Shooting skeet and hunting game had swept the firm as hobbies of choice; employees had joined gun and hunt clubs in droves; and Morgan Stanley had begun offering skeet shooting, in addition to golf, at its periodic firm retreats.

Although the 1994 F.I.A.S.C.O. had the requisite amounts of

rain, cigars, gambling, and alcohol, a strange nervousness was in the air. As I walked into the clubhouse, one salesman mentioned that Sandanona had been caught up in the easy money of 1993 and overextended its borrowing. Apparently Sandanona was not much different from the most recent derivatives victims. As interest rates rose in early 1994, Sandanona, too, faced increasing liabilities and struggled to meet its large loan payments.

The shooting scores were tallied and announced in the club's luxurious banquet room. Our team finished squarely in the middle of the pack. Scarecrow was third in the individual competition, and a young associate won with an impressive score of 82 out of 100. Most of the scores were in the 50s and 60s. When my score – 35 – was announced, my heart sank. I prayed for someone to have a lower score. *Please, God, at least I didn't kill anyone today.* I nervously counted the number of skeet attendants present and wondered why one of them was missing.

Thankfully, the next score announced was 9, one of the women. She would not receive any gender preference. By 1994 Morgan Stanley was a gender-conscious firm, hiring and promoting female employees and trying to institute various affirmative action policies, both at the entry level and to pierce the glass ceiling. But that was back in New York, not here. This was F.I.A.S.C.O. And at F.I.A.S.C.O., men were men, women were women, and a 9 was a 9.

I was ecstatic. My score wasn't even close to winning the Krum Kup. I, too, had dodged a bullet. Perhaps my shooting had improved since my teenage years. I had sighted that humiliating barn in the crosshairs ... and blown the broad side of it right to hell.

We loaded the Mark VII and waved good-bye to the hosts at Sandanona. They returned our salute, a little solemnly. They may have known then that soon Sandanona would be following the derivatives victims into bankruptcy. Sadly, the 1994 F.I.A.S.C.O. would be Sandanona's last, and the tradition of holding F.I.A.S.C.O. there would end, as Sandanona would be unable to

103

pay its overextended loans. Later in 1994, as Morgan Stanley scavenged the bodies of derivatives victims in search of bargains, a few directors in Morgan Stanley's derivatives group would smell the blood in the water at Sandanona and try to buy the bankrupt shooting range for their personal use, although ultimately they couldn't close the deal.

The Monday after F.I.A.S.C.O., I arrived at work to find that Scarecrow had left on my desk a copy of the April 1994 edition of *Shooting Sports* magazine. He must have thought my shooting skills needed work. The cover was a picture of two of the cutest white bunnies I had ever seen. They were nestled together, cuddling among a stack of shiny, new shotguns. Scarecrow had scribbled above the picture that the bunnies were saying, "Hi, Frank!"

Scarecrow also must have wanted to make it clear to me that I needed to be able to shoot those bunnies right between the eyes, without hesitation. The bunnies were no different from our derivatives customers. When an account called to say hello, I needed to be prepared to blow his head off, if necessary, to make a sale, regardless of how much I liked him or her. As I gazed at the bunnies, I wondered whether the recent burst of derivatives losses had been an accident. A conspiracy theorist could say the losses were part of a planned worldwide attack, and, as I soon would learn, that wouldn't be far from the truth.

When I saw Scarecrow, he repeated to me his message that investment banking is like war, and derivatives salesmen are the special forces. He hoped I had enjoyed F.I.A.S.C.O., but he wanted to be sure I understood its broader message. Scarecrow had seen vicious derivatives battles. Once he had watched an inflamed ex-Navy pilot discover he had purchased a bond that didn't even exist. Scarecrow regarded even a casual sales call as hand-to-hand combat, and he would shout, "We're going in!" before he entered a client's offices. He wanted me to think the same way he did, and F.I.A.S.C.O. was but one part of my training.

According to Scarecrow's view of the world, it was the combination of brains and bullets, not merely rocket science, that had made DPG the most profitable group of people in the world. At another investment bank – such as Salomon Brothers, the renowned jungle of the 1980s – a sharpshooting salesman would have been known as a Big Swinging Dick. But by the 1990s investment banking had changed. Wall Street was no longer merely a jungle, it was a sophisticated hub of modern financial warfare where it wasn't enough for a Big Dick to swing; he had to shoot, too.

As I stared at the cute little bunnies, I thought back to my first big derivatives disaster, and I breathed a sigh of relief. I had never told anyone at Morgan Stanley about how I had "lost" a billion dollars during my interviews at Bankers Trust, and apparently no one had discovered it. In any case, two years had passed since then, and I hadn't really lost a billion dollars. I looked at the two cute bunnies and the weaponry surrounding them. Many defenseless animals roamed around the wilderness of Wall Street. Would a derivatives salesman ever cause one of them to *actually* lose a billion dollars on derivatives?

6

The Queen
of RAVs

Every trading desk has a Mephistopheles, a person whose very presence instills such terror that salesmen and traders run and hide to avoid contact. For more than a decade at Morgan Stanley, John Mack had been the sinister omnipresence, ruling the trading floor with an iron fist. Other investment banks had similar characters. At Salomon Brothers it was a guy called the Human Piranha. At First Boston it was a former green beret who, it was rumored, had literally ripped someone's arm off. At Morgan Stanley it was Mack the Knife.

However, when Mack relinquished the trading floor to become president of the firm, he left a void. Who could fill his shoes? Was anyone mean enough to replace him? Peter Karches, the new head of fixed income, certainly was powerful enough, but he was actually a nice guy, which disqualified him. Bidyut Sen, the leader of New York's derivatives group, received many votes. He looked the part more than anyone, and his fiery temper was legendary. However, Sen's stature at the firm had slipped as business shifted overseas and he spent as much time playing computer chess as on the derivatives business.

Then a radical idea struck. By the 1990s Morgan Stanley had

become much more progressive in its promotion policies, especially compared to First Boston. Morgan Stanley's treatment of minorities was a little spotty, and the firm, like most of Wall Street, had been accused of discriminating against certain minorities. But its track record with women wasn't that bad. By 1994 there were several female employees who weren't secretaries, and unlike First Boston, the firm didn't have anyone traipsing the trading floor in a skimpy skirt. Women even attended F.I.A.S.C.O.

The radical idea was to have a woman take over as head of the trading floor. Women across America were moving into top corporate jobs. There were female ministers and rabbis and even speculation that God was a woman. Did the glass ceiling extend all the way to heaven? If not, how could there be a glass floor above hell? I pondered the question. Could the devil be a woman?

The answer appeared to be yes, and the search began for an appropriate princess of darkness. There weren't many choices. Only a handful of women, many of whom were quite amiable, worked in high-level jobs on the trading floor. Of all the senior saleswomen and female traders, only one was even remotely qualified. She had the right personality, had been promoted rapidly, and was among the highest-paid principals at the firm. Unfortunately, she was my boss. I called her the Queen of RAVs.

The Queen had earned her nickname from the types of derivatives deals she created and sold, called RAVs, short for "Repackaged Asset Vehicles." RAVs (pronounced "rahvs") were well named. A RAV was used to repackage existing securities into new derivatives using various investment vehicles, including trusts and special companies. RAVs were often referred to as black box transactions, because in a RAV you put securities into a trust or company, the so-called black box, and then magically the securities turned into derivatives. PLUS Notes were a type of RAV. With PLUS Notes, Morgan Stanley had repackaged Mexican bonds using a Bermuda company as the black box to issue the new derivatives.

F. I. A. S. C. O.

With "RAV," Morgan Stanley had invented another great acronym. RAVs had caché. Simplistic black box transactions were commonplace; almost every bank and major drug dealer used them, and business publications such as *The Economist* even advertised them. However, Morgan Stanley's RAV was much more complex and therefore seemed like an entirely different kind of deal. It was a brilliant marketing move. Because the deal was called a RAV, it had style.

RAVs were the highest-profile derivatives deals at Morgan Stanley, and they earned the fattest fees at the firm, by far. RAVs were the "elephants" the derivatives managers hunted on their derivatives safaris. A single RAV could generate millions of dollars in fees.

Few people understood RAVs, even at Morgan Stanley. The small RAVs team in DPG ferociously protected its turf. After a few months at the firm, I was invited to work on that coveted team, with a couple of other junior employees. The RAVs team defined hegemony. After a few days on the team, I understood the hierarchy painfully well. If royalty existed anywhere at Morgan Stanley, it was on the imperial RAVs team, and the ruler of the royal family clearly was the Queen of RAVs.

The Queen was no stranger to the ways of the ruling class. Her family had fled Iran just before the Shah was deposed, along with many wealthy and powerful families, and she carried the grandeur and sensibility of pre-Ayatollah Iran. The Queen looked like a pharaohess, with dark eyes and long black hair, her fingers and neck adorned with jewels and gold. She wore dazzling colors, expensive European-styled silk scarves, and suits from the best stores in London. Her thick Farsi accent penetrated even the noisiest parts of the trading floor. She often lapsed into her native tongue, and her English was sometimes flawless and sometimes terrifyingly imprecise, as in: "You're making a mountain out of a mole" or "Let's put a bed to this."

The Queen's temper was white hot, her altercations as intense as any Persian Gulf conflict. Everyone in the group, even members of the Gang of Four, feared her outbursts. And rightfully so. I am pretty good at defending myself in an argument, but the Queen's sharp tongue sliced me to pieces many times. Other members of the RAVs group suffered the same fate. Scarecrow didn't have a chance – Scarecrow lacked a brain; the Queen lacked a heart. I finally understood just how heartless the Queen was when we were discussing dogs just days after mine had died. She said she hated all pets. What kind of a person hates all pets?

The Queen reminded me of an aggressive woman at Bankers Trust who had interviewed me for a sales job years before. I still remember how terrified I was following her across the bond trading floor, stopping when she stopped to bark orders at a sales assistant.

Finally we found an office, and she sat and spat out a quick, rehearsed bullet-point version of her resume. "B.A. finance '80, HBS '85, first in my class, associate here '86, VP '88, MD last year." Luckily, I knew "VP" meant vice president and "MD" meant managing director. I assumed "HBS" was Harvard Business School.

Next, she shot off more bullet points about the types of bonds she sold. My mind wandered as I stared at her. I only vaguely heard the last stream of words out of her mouth: "What would you do with a pile of bricks?"

I was startled, not sure I had heard her correctly. "Pardon me?"

She asked again, "What would you do with a pile of bricks?"

I hesitated, still a little surprised by her question. "What do you mean? Here? Now?" Had she really said "bricks"?

She simply repeated, "What would you do with a pile of bricks?"

I thought for a few seconds. What was the best response to such an odd question? "I don't know. I guess I would build a house."

"Name another thing."

This line of questioning baffled me. What else should I say?

She squeezed the trigger again. "Name another thing."

"Do you mean another thing I would do with a pile of bricks?" I asked.

She continued to stare.

"OK," I said. "Build a road."

She fired back. "Name another thing."

This is bizarre, I thought. I guessed it must be some kind of a game to test me. I was pretty good at games, and law school had trained me, like Pavlov's dog, to respond to this type of inquiry. I relaxed – a little. This might be fun.

I thought I'd try something clever. "If they were yellow bricks, I could build a yellow brick road. You know, I was born and raised in Kansas."

She was not impressed with my Kansas shtick. She ignored it. "Name another thing."

Fine, if she wanted to play hardball, we would play hardball. I retorted. "Build a wall."

"Name another thing."

"Build an apartment building."

"Name another thing."

"Landscape a yard."

"Name another thing."

A long volley ensued. "Build a silo."

"Another."

"Paint them."

"Another."

"Build a baseball stadium."

"What else would you do with a pile of bricks?"

"Grind them to dust."

"Name another thing."

"Throw them through a window."

"Name another thing."

"Strap them to my feet."

"Name another."

"Heat them."

"Another."

"Drop them off a building."

"Another."

"Repair a street."

Amazingly, this battle continued throughout the duration of my interview. She asked the same question, over and over. After twenty minutes I was exasperated, not to mention running out of ideas.

"Another."

I pointed my finger and raised my voice for the first time. "Throw them at that wall." My exasperation was showing.

She raised her voice. "*Another.*"

I couldn't take this anymore. What did she want from me? And what else *could* you do with a pile of bricks?

She must have sensed I was near my breaking point. I pointed and raised my voice again. "Throw them through that computer screen."

She glanced at the computer screen, edged forward in her seat, and raised her voice. "*Another!*"

That was the final straw. I stood up and did something very stupid, something that ensured Bankers Trust – even if it had been willing to hire someone who had just lost a billion dollars – would not hire me. I pointed at her and screamed at the top of my lungs, "*Throw them at your head!*"

She seemed satisfied. She stood, shook my hand with her icy grip, and walked out. She hadn't even bothered to say, "That will be all."

I had learned my lesson about challenging female managers on a trading floor. I rarely talked back to the Queen, and I never raised my voice. She and I developed a cordial working relationship. In the upcoming months we would work on deals related to dozens of different countries, and we would complete derivatives trades from Mexico, the Philippines, and Argentina. We would make a lot of money together.

But the first derivatives trade I did with the Queen of RAVs was a disaster. It was a Brazilian deal called BIDS.

The goal of BIDS had been to create a transaction akin to PLUS Notes, except for Brazil instead of Mexico. BIDS stood for "Brazilian Indexed Dollar Securities." That was a pretty good acronym, and fundamentally BIDS was a sound trade idea. In mid-1994 Brazil's economy resembled Mexico's from a few years earlier. Inflation was high; Brazil's credit rating was low. Brazil's government had issued bonds called NTN-Ds that were indexed to the U.S. dollar in the same way Ajustabonos had been. At the same time, Brazil had imposed restrictions on non-Brazilians owning these bonds. We believed many U.S. buyers wanted to invest in Brazil, and we envisioned BIDS as their opportunity to do so. We would repackage the NTN-Ds through a special black box company to allow U.S. buyers to buy them. DPG was optimistic about BIDS, and we thought the deal could rival PLUS Notes in size and profitability.

In the beginning the Queen and Scarecrow had comanaged work on the deal, but that arrangement didn't last very long. We realized early on that the Brazilian bond market was incredibly complex and restrictive. There were good reasons why no U.S. bank had been able to penetrate the web of arcane Brazilian rules. We hired a Brazilian investment bank and law firm to help us, but the negotiations had been intense and replete with exacting detail. Within a few days the discussions were far out of Scarecrow's league, and he settled for insisting on credit for the acronym.

Scarecrow had worked with the Queen of RAVs before. She was a formidable adversary, and as she became more involved in the Brazilian deal, Scarecrow virtually disappeared. BIDS was closer to real rocket science than anything Scarecrow ever had experienced, and he tired of being humiliated virtually every time he opened his mouth. The Queen wanted this Brazilian deal badly, and she easily muscled control from Scarecrow.

Scarecrow's primary contribution to the deal had been extremely negative. DPG often relied on salesmen from other parts of the trading floor, especially when we were pushing a new product. For BIDS, Scarecrow had invited a dozen or so key salespeople to a Latin American lunch, with tacos, nachos, quesadillas, and a strangely colored guacamole. It was Mexican food, not Brazilian food, but that was close enough. We described the BIDS trade to everyone, and Scarecrow gave a little pep talk. The salesmen ate. The effects of the lunch, which weren't felt for several hours, would ensure that Scarecrow wouldn't be allowed anywhere near BIDS.

I first felt it when I woke early the next morning and barely made the four-yard dash from my bed to the bathroom at the other side of my microstudio. It was clear I had been poisoned. Unfortunately, I couldn't call in sick because I needed to check on the other salesmen, to see how the initial calls to their accounts had gone. Today was an important day for BIDS. I bought some Pepto Bismol.

When I arrived at work, a little late, Scarecrow still wasn't there. I noticed that the trading floor was deserted. Where was everyone? Another tremor struck, and I ran to the bathroom. Later, back out on the trading floor, I asked Scarecrow's secretary where he was. She didn't know. I called him at home. Nothing. I called again fifteen minutes later. He finally answered the phone with a moan.

"Hey, are you alive? *What's the deal?*" I was shouting. I wanted to make him suffer, too.

"I don't know," he whispered.

"Was it the food?" I knew it had been. I thought about all the nachos I had eaten and eyed the distance to the bathroom.

"Tell them all I'm sorry," was all Scarecrow could muster. By now it was late morning, and I still hadn't seen anyone from yesterday's lunch. Scarecrow had wiped out the entire sales force with a food poisoning so bad, I began calling it Scarecrow's Revenge. I ran to the bathroom again but found that all of the stalls were full. I waited in despair. Finally, one of the salesmen emerged with a sickened look.

"I wouldn't use that thing if I was you." He was ailing and angry.

"Thanks a lot for lunch, you asshole," another salesman said. "The whole fucking desk is gone." I held my nose and tried to push my way past him, but he stood his ground. "You tell that bastard he's a dead man!" he yelled. I nodded and disappeared into the stall.

With one meal, Scarecrow had almost killed the Brazilian deal. The Queen was irate. Fortunately, she either had not eaten the lunch or had an iron stomach. She had been at her desk for hours that morning, taking full control of the BIDS transaction. From that day on, I reported to the Queen, not Scarecrow.

We spent more than a month working with lawyers in the U.S. and Brazil to structure the BIDS trade. In late 1993 Brazil had banned one vehicle that allowed investors to lock in fixed returns using stock options. Now, such "option box" strategies were illegal, and most alternative investments faced additional restrictions, including a 5 percent up-front tax and a 15 percent withholding tax on any money earned on Brazilian bonds. Finally we discovered a loophole in Brazil's fixed income mutual fund law that allowed a U.S. investor to buy the bonds and still capture an acceptable after-tax return.

The main problem we struggled to resolve was the risk of runaway inflation. Brazil had an active bond and derivatives market, but U.S. investors had found the market too complex, primarily because of inflation. Brazil had been slower than other countries to emerge from debt restructuring, and spiraling inflation rates had twisted its financial markets into a mess. After years of hundred-percent-plus inflation rates, the country had been forced to index most of its prices to inflation. Now merchants changed their prices at least daily. The cost of a banana or coffee might be higher in the afternoon than in the morning. The same was true of interest rates, which roughly kept pace with inflation. A Brazilian could earn as much interest in a day as an American could earn in a year, although inflation would eat away most of it.

We were having a tough time convincing U.S. investors that BIDS would not expose them to unwarranted risks associated with Brazilian inflation. Theoretically, the returns on BIDS would be 12 percent for one year, an enormous return. However, we couldn't guarantee that the return would be *exactly* 12 percent. It could be more or less, depending on different variables related to the inflation indices, which changed every day. Many investors weren't comfortable with the possibility of receiving less than 12 percent.

The Queen and I attended many of the sales calls in person, to explain these complexities. I traveled to Boston to meet with some of the top U.S. fund managers, including the managers of two of the largest emerging markets mutual funds in the world, Rob Citrone, portfolio manager at Fidelity Investments, and Mark Siegel, vice president and head of emerging markets at Putnam Investment Management. Both of them, as well as dozens of other fund managers, gave BIDS a big thumbs down. The trade was too complicated, and the fees we were charging were too large.

The BIDS deal ended a failure, although it probably would have been worse if Scarecrow had been involved throughout. On the one hand, we were only able to sell $21 million of BIDS in total, mostly because we couldn't pique the interest of U.S. investors. On the other hand, we were able to charge such an enormous fee on the BIDS we actually sold that the group still grossed half a million dollars in profits. Although U.S. buyers weren't interested in BIDS, we had sold a huge portion of the deal to a Mexican bank still enjoying its fiesta and eager to gamble on anything it could find.

After the BIDS deal, I shifted from a seat next to Scarecrow to a seat next to the Queen. I had only moved a few feet across the trading floor, but now I was within the confines of the palace. Scarecrow stayed away. I was one of the deadbeats who hadn't yet paid Scarecrow a $125 gun rental fee for F.I.A.S.C.O., but he sent me an e-mail requesting payment instead of just stopping by.

Times were tough for Scarecrow. His bonuses weren't that large by Wall Street standards, and he said he desperately needed the money to meet his monthly payment on a newly leased Land Rover Discovery. I hoped he was joking about that, but I wasn't sure.

In my new location I would miss Scarecrow, especially his jokes. He told me a farewell joke, just before I switched positions. It was related to the recent McDonald's commercial featuring basketball stars Michael Jordan and Larry Bird as they compete to swish jump shots of increasing difficulty, each time saying, "Nothing but net."

QUESTION: What did Lee Harvey Oswald say to Michael Jordan?
ANSWER: Through the book depository window, over the grassy knoll, off the wrist, nothing but neck.

Scarecrow was not a big JFK fan. I noted that he never joked about Ronald Reagan being shot.

After our tribulations in Brazil, we decided to turn back to our mainstay trades, in Mexico. The Mexican banks were still gambling feverishly, and months earlier the group had completed its second PLUS Notes trade, called PLUS Capital Company II. That $310 million deal was a template for any new PLUS Notes deals. PLUS II had involved Mexican government bonds called Cetes, which were much simpler than Ajustabonos, the bonds we had used in PLUS I. With PLUS II done, the only real work required to complete another PLUS Notes deal was finding a Mexican bank, creating a catchy name, and selling the bonds. That wouldn't take long. I completed my first PLUS Notes deal with relative ease.

First, we found a Mexican bank, Groupo Financiero Serfin, often called Serfin Securities. Its corporate logo, a golden bird engulfed in a circular insignia, resembled the warning symbol for nuclear waste. Many risky derivatives were called nuclear waste, but the derivatives Serfin bought especially deserved the label.

Next, we needed a name, and PLUS III didn't seem very creative. We finally settled on MEXUS, for "Mexican U.S.$ Security." MEXUS could be written as MEXU$, and it sounded like LEXUS. We marketed the trade as the premiere, luxurious Mexican derivative.

Finally, we needed to sell the trade to investors. When we told the salesmen on the international sales desk about the trade, they refused to discuss anything except the BIDS disaster. They chided us about derivatives, called the MEXUS prospectus a "Mexipad," and refused to eat lunch with us, ever again. Still, a deal was a deal and a commission was a commission. They said that they would try to sell the MEXUS bonds, and we were confident they would.

We also tried tapping a new salesforce, the salesmen from Morgan Stanley's Private Client Services, called PCS. PCS was on a different floor – and in a different world. They sold securities to wealthy individual investors and small institutions. In Wall Street lingo, PCS was called retail, although at Morgan Stanley, retail meant high end. If you were worth $10 million or more, you were a potential Morgan Stanley PCS client. Otherwise, forget it.

You cannot understand the meaning of the word "aggressive" until you have witnessed PCS salesmen in action. They inspired an often-quoted phrase at Morgan Stanley: "Sell your mother for a basis point." For many of them the phrase was a gross understatement. I never will forget one conversation I had with a PCS salesman the day after I had learned that Shelby C. Davis, a prominent New York investment banker, had died. I mentioned this to the guy and was surprised to learn that he not only had seen the obituary, but he had already called the executors of the estate, to try to sell them some PLUS Notes.

The Queen and I attended one of the PCS morning meetings to push MEXUS. We briefly explained the trade, and then the PCS sales manager took over. He gave a rousing pep talk, telling the sales force that they would make more money off MEXUS than anything else they would ever sell. The PCS salesforce loved the derivatives group because our trades paid huge commissions. The salesmen were electrified. When one of them asked a somewhat skeptical question about the risks associated with MEXUS, the manager dismissed it as utterly irrelevant. He said there was a "99.99 percent chance" the PLUS Notes would pay off as expected. That sounded a little high to me.

However, no one at Morgan Stanley seemed to disagree. The firm was staunchly pro-Mexico. DPG was advertising it had completed $1.5 *billion* of Latin American derivatives in only a few weeks. Morgan Stanley's researchers were optimistic that the peso would not decline. The value of the peso was important to MEXUS and other PLUS Notes, which fell in value as the peso depreciated. Fortunately, Ernest "Chip" Brown, the firm's research analyst for Mexico, said there was little risk of any downside movement in the Mexican peso. Chip went on record as saying repeatedly, in very strong terms, that the risk related to the peso was that it would go up, not down. If the peso actually went up, then the PCS manager was right – there *was* a 99.99 percent chance that the PLUS Notes would pay off as expected. With such rosy recommendations, and those odds, MEXUS was an easy sell.

Of course, as with most derivatives trades, MEXUS wasn't entirely smooth sailing. At one point, after most of the deal was subscribed, everyone was joking about the time they had discovered at the last minute that they had forgotten to incorporate the special Bermuda company for a similar transaction. Everyone was roaring with laughter about the panic that had ensued. Then we realized that, with all of the focus on selling MEXUS, we, too, had forgotten to incorporate. "Deja vu all over again," as Yogi Berra used to say. We immediately called our lawyers in Bermuda and discovered there was just enough time – assuming the lawyers could find the Bermuda minister of finance. His signature was required on the MEXUS corporate charter before the incorporation process could begin. An hour later the lawyer called us and said he had pulled the minister out of a meeting of the Bermuda Congress to get him to sign our charter. We could incorporate in time.

While we were working on MEXUS, DPG was negotiating with Banamex, the Mexican bank of PLUS I fame, for yet another PLUS Notes deal. Typically, the goal of such negotiations was to lock the client into signing an engagement letter, specifying the parties' responsibilities, the structure of the transaction, timing, and – most importantly – fees. Once an engagement letter was signed, DPG would be in good shape. As a result, there was enormous pressure to obtain a signed engagement letter.

The Banamex negotiations had been difficult. Scarecrow had not been involved, but when he heard we were struggling, he suggested we liven up a negotiating session or two by bringing an Uzi. With all the recent murders and kidnappings in Mexico, as the negotiations deteriorated I thought Scarecrow might be right. The deal was near collapse. When Bidyut Sen heard about our troubles with Banamex, he called us into his office. He was furious. We all knew that technically he still was running the group in New York, and we prepared for one of his periodic tirades.

The Queen, although very much junior to Sen in rank, assumed an air of authority in dealing with him. She tried to calm him, saying we were close to getting a deal. There were two barriers: the size of the note issuance and the level of overcollateralization. We wanted to do a deal of at least $250 million, to make it worth our time and expenses. We also believed our investors would require a cushion of at least 15 percent of overcollateralization, the cushion for the most recent PLUS Notes deal.

As he heard about these barriers, Sen became angry, then apoplectic. He finally picked up the phone and screamed for Banamex's telephone number in Mexico City, to give that sunglasses-wearing Blades, Gerardo Vargas from Banamex, a piece of his chess-playing mind.

When Vargas picked up the phone and said, "Hello," Sen exploded. He skipped the small talk and blurted, "Either you do

$250 million and 15 percent overcollateralization, or you do nothing!" There was a long silence. Blades seemed surprised to hear from Sen at all, and he certainly had not expected such a frontal assault. Blades quietly replied that he had been negotiating with the Queen and others in the RAVs group, and the talks were progressing. He asked if Sen had spoken to any of us about the ongoing negotiations. Sen ignored the question and tried to pressure Blades to agree to the terms, but he wouldn't give. Finally, they hung up.

Sen was livid. He screamed, *"Fuck this business!"* and stormed out of the room. Now the Queen was angry, too. She had been effective in the negotiations thus far, despite their obvious difficulty, and she wanted the deal badly. Banamex was an important client and an excellent source of future business, and Sen had alienated Vargas. She yelled, "If we lose this deal, it's all his fucking fault!" and also stormed out. I was left alone with Marshal Salant, and we just looked at each other and shrugged. We knew the deal was dead.

Sen returned to the one part of his day he seemed to enjoy, other than playing chess: betting on World Cup matches. As he worked on one complex bet involving several soccer teams, he seemed to relax. He said, "I love this game. But it's like Banamex; it probably won't happen because there are assholes on both sides." He took out some aggression on Scarecrow by mocking him when he stopped by to show Sen a list of Brady Bond options in a Latin American magazine.

"The thing that's interesting is this table of option providers," Scarecrow said, obviously having no idea what he was talking about.

Sen said, "Wow. That *is* very interesting. But what does it mean?"

Scarecrow shrugged, retreating to his seat.

When Sen learned that Banamex had refused to sign an engagement letter, he became despondent. He said, "I don't have any reason to be here." I actually felt sorry for him, but I didn't disagree. We discussed one potential solution to the Banamex negotiations that involved Morgan Stanley buying a package of options called a put spread to increase the overcollateralization protection from 15 to 18 percent. However, this idea also failed.

When the group finally tallied our profits from Serfin Securities' MEXUS deal, Sen's spirits recovered slightly. He insisted that more profits were possible and bragged, "By the time this is over, I will be the king of the Mexican market." He even threatened to wear a sombrero to work. Several months later, after the Mexican peso had collapsed, a cartoon would circulate the trading floor depicting a beggar extending a sombrero to collect his change. The caption would read BIDYUT SEN.

Although we made several hundred thousand dollars on MEXUS, my bosses were far from satisfied. The Queen instructed me to shift my priorities away from Mexico. It was time to move to another country. Marshal Salant congratulated me on MEXUS but said it was a "cookie cutter" transaction. I hadn't accomplished anything new. He said the RAVs team needed something innovative, a new idea for a deal capable of generating a $1 million fee. Or more.

Although I was working on several big-ticket ideas, I found my next RAV deal, far away in the Philippines, almost by pure chance. As with many deals my group had done, the idea sprang, unpredictably, from the misery of others. Instead of planning for a series of profitable derivatives deals, it often was better to wait to see who was hurting the most at any particular time, then begin hunting for a new derivatives deal in their vicinity. In this case, the people who were hurting were our colleagues at Morgan Stanley.

Anyone who has visited the Philippines inevitably has only one thought when they confront a return trip: "brownout." Since well before dictator Ferdinand Marcos sullied the Philippines with graft and waste, the country was famous for its brownouts – partial, and frequent, power losses, especially in the capital city of Manila. The lights would dim, and then dim some more, but usually they wouldn't go out. These partial outages occurred a dozen times a day, for periods of up to ten hours.

The main culprit was the 57-year-old Philippines state-owned electric company, the National Power Corporation, known not very affectionately as NPC or Napacor. NPC had been generating frequent power outages since before World War II. The way Filipinos tell the story, before the creation of the graft-ridden NPC, the country didn't have much of a power outage problem. However, as NPC became more powerful following World War II, the outages increased in frequency and length. NPC, a virtual monopoly for much of that time, became the butt of many bitter jokes. For example:

QUESTION: "What did the Philippines have before candle power?"
ANSWER: "Electricity."

For years, even decades, few power plants were built or repaired. Under Ferdinand Marcos's dictatorship, NPC became even more corrupt, although there was some solace in the fact that power shutdowns under Marcos were regularly scheduled. At least the country could plan around the brownouts, which occurred throughout the day like clockwork. However, by 1994 the regularity of the outages, and Marcos himself, were long gone. For most businesses in the new democratic regime, the randomness of the power outages significantly worsened their electricity problems. Brownouts were still just as frequent. The only effect of democracy was to make them unpredictable, too.

Not surprisingly, given its reputation, NPC had a tough time raising capital in the financial markets. Why would anyone lend money to such an incompetent company? The ratings agencies gave NPC below-investment-grade ratings because of the risk that it wouldn't earn enough cash from electricity generation to pay its debts.

The World Bank, as NPC's leading creditor and only benefactor, had agreed to help the company make the transition to private ownership. The World Bank praised the privatization of NPC as one of the few successful such attempts in the developing world. It even agreed to provide a guarantee of principal repayment on NPC's new fifteen-year bond issue. With that guarantee, a buyer of NPC bonds almost certainly would receive its money back in fifteen years, even if NPC went bankrupt, because the World Bank promised to repay.

Morgan Stanley had strong ties to the World Bank and the Philippines, and the white-shoe investment bankers of the firm's Investment Banking Division agreed, as part of maintaining those ties, to underwrite the new $100 million NPC bond issue. Unfortunately they didn't check with the derivatives group first. Even with the World Bank guarantee, investors loathed the new NPC issue. The junk bond trading desk at Morgan Stanley was responsible for selling the NPC bonds, but despite their expertise at selling poorly rated bonds, they couldn't unload NPC.

As the deal was marketed, clients assailed the salesmen with horror stories about power outages. In democratic Manila, the problem had become so endemic that some companies were trying to capitalize on power outages to generate business. Private power generators had become a popular marketing tactic. Stories filtering through to the investment community included a beauty salon with its own generator advertising a "Brownout Beauty Special" (including a facial plus other treatments, even during power outages) and several privately powered restaurants displaying NO BROWNOUTS signs.

The NPC deal went horribly, as expected, and Morgan Stanley's junk bond desk ended up owning much of it. The junk bond traders were hurting. Wanting to get rid of the bonds immediately, before they plummeted in value, they ran across the trading floor to the derivatives group. What could we do? Please, they begged. We had to help them.

The basic problem with the NPC bonds was that even though their principal repayment was guaranteed by the World Bank, the

123

interim fifteen years of interest payments were not. The ratings agencies didn't think the World Bank guarantee was enough to give the entire bond, including principal and interest, a high rating. Consequently, the entire bond received the rating of its lowest common denominator, the NPC interest payments. Without a high rating, many potential buyers simply could not own the bonds.

This was familiar territory for us. DPG had faced the same problem with PLUS Notes, and we had designed RAVs to repackage the bonds and obtain a high rating. Now we needed to find a way to persuade the ratings agencies to give NPC a high rating, too.

I was aware that Lehman Brothers recently had convinced S&P to rate a bond AAA because it had AAA principal and a sliver of AAA interest payments, even though the majority of its interest payments were not AAA. Remember, there are two components to a bond: interest and principal. Usually both had the same credit rating because the same entity was promising to make both sets of payments. However, for the NPC bonds, the interest was junk (NPC), and the principal was gold (World Bank). Lehman's deal had used a type of bond with similar characteristics. I knew it well from my days on First Boston's emerging markets desk. It was called a Brady Bond.

Brady Bonds resembled the NPC bonds in that their principal repayment was backed by U.S. Treasury zero coupon bonds, which were rated AAA. Also, like the NPC bonds, the Brady Bond interest payments were based on the credit of the developing country that issued them, Mexico, Brazil, Nigeria, and others. In other words, the interest payments were junk. The trick Lehman had discovered was that if you put the Brady Bonds into a trust and added some zero coupon bonds with the junk interest payments, you could convince S&P to rate the entire trust AAA. Combining the two was like baking a cake and then adding icing. The cake was crap. But the icing was real chocolate. The icing persuaded the ratings agencies to call a crap cake a chocolate cake.

With the icing, the trust really had three components: junk interest, AAA interest, and AAA principal. S&P required that you state in fine print that the AAA rating only applied to the "real" AAA components of the trust, not to the junk interest payments. Still, for many investors, the fine print didn't matter. For example, although Brady Bonds alone were an impermissible investment for many large investors, including various mutual funds and insurance companies, the trust units were just fine.

The world of zero coupon bonds was a fertile one for derivatives – and for derivatives disasters. Zero coupon bonds, also known as Zeros or Strips, were actively traded at most investment banks, even quoted daily in the *Wall Street Journal*. Strips are named for a U.S. Treasury program that allows investment banks to strip apart or reconstitute the coupons and principal portions of government bonds. A government bond is composed of several periodic payments, each of which represents an individual Strip. Each strip is a zero coupon bond – a single payment at maturity with no coupon payments. At First Boston I had heard great praise of Strips traders who, it was rumored, made $50 million one year. First Boston was known as a Strips powerhouse, and earlier in the year the Bank of England had asked First Boston to look into stripping its government bonds, known as gilts.

I never could understand how the Strips traders at First Boston – or Strips traders anywhere – made so much money. It seemed incredible. The Strips market is extremely liquid, and profit margins generally are low, especially compared with other, more complex, derivatives trades. Massive profits in this market seemed unlikely, unless these guys were trading with a chump, so I assumed the $50 million rumor was false, or at least exaggerated.

What I didn't know then was that one of the Strips traders with whom these guys were trading was named Joseph Jett. Jett was the head Strips trader at Kidder Peabody, and within Kidder's small world, Jett was known as a superstar. According to Kidder's accounting system, Jett was responsible for hundreds of millions in trading profits, so Kidder happily rewarded Jett with several million dollars in bonuses. In 1993 Jett was named Kidder's Employee of the Year.

In the larger world outside Kidder, Jett's reputation wasn't quite as stellar. To put it bluntly, in 1993 many traders regarded Jett as one of the worst Strips traders on Wall Street. His notoriety was recent, and his Wall Street career had been unremarkable before he moved to Kidder. Before Kidder, Jett had worked at both of my firms: First Boston, where he had been a junior-level trainee, and Morgan Stanley, where he had been known only as a low-level oddball and where one day he had been discovered hiding in a closet just off the trading floor. It was only when Jett arrived at Kidder that he blossomed, and he was quickly promoted to managing director and head of the trading desk. To other traders, who had made a fortune trading with Jett, his apparent success at Kidder was inexplicable.

Warren Buffett, the famous investor, has said that if you don't know who the sucker is, it is you. In this case, Kidder had absolutely no idea who the sucker was. Soon after Kidder paid Jett a $9 million bonus, it discovered that Jett's enormous profits were a ruse. Instead of earning Kidder hundreds of millions of dollars, Jett had *lost* Kidder about $350 million. Kidder immediately froze Jett's bonus and fired him. General Electric, which had recently purchased Kidder as part of its foray into investment banking, was less than thrilled with this discovery. It wasn't clear whether Jett, or Kidder's accounting system, was to blame.

The news would only get worse. In the following months, Kidder would disclose millions of dollars of additional losses from: a senior employee who had mismarked swaps positions, a vice-president of bond sales who had incorrectly reported commissions, two government bond traders who had lost money from maintaining unhedged trading positions, and – last but not least – Clifford Kaplan, a twenty-eight-year-old bond derivatives vice president who, Kidder discovered, had not only lost a fortune for the firm, but had also held a second job while he worked for Kidder, a salaried consulting post with a U.S. unit of La Compagnie Financière Edmond de Rothschild Banque. Although Kidder fired each of these employees, only Jett experienced the full fifteen minutes of fame, appearing on various magazine covers, on *60 Minutes,* and – months later – in a lawsuit in the federal district court in Manhattan, each time denying he had done anything wrong.

Kaplan also experienced a few minutes of fame. He had previously worked at Morgan Stanley, where I heard of his reputation for hosting lavish, work-related holidays at vacation homes he claimed he owned in Europe. At Kidder, Kaplan reportedly received a bonus of $500,000, despite two well-reported problems. First, a complex Italian deal called DELS (for derivative-enhanced asset-linked securities) that Kaplan had coordinated lost $1.7 million. Second, Kidder employees discovered while this deal was being marketed that Kaplan lacked the required securities license; according to the *Wall Street Journal,* Kaplan's boss told him to finish the deal and take the licensing test later.

Ironically, Kidder ultimately fired Kaplan, not because of either of these problems, but because Kidder executives finally discovered Kaplan's second job, after the Rothschilds asked Kidder to reimburse certain of Kaplan's credit card expenses, including payment for a fur coat. It was the fur coat that generated Kaplan's brief notoriety. After some hubbub, on June 2, 1994, Kaplan finally responded with a letter to the *Journal,* denying that he had even purchased, much less expensed, the fur coat and claiming Kidder had known about his Rothschilds job all along.

The allegations against Jett were far more serious. How had he lost $350 million? Kidder's accounting system allowed a trader to create bogus profits by buying a Strip and then booking the sale of the Strip at a much higher price. The problem stemmed from the fact that Strips are sold with reference to the face value of the original bond they are stripped from. However, because a Strip is only a piece of that original bond, its value is substantially less than the value of the whole bond. For example, suppose a bond is

127

worth $1,000 and has a $1,000 face value. You might be able to buy a Strip from that bond for $200. The Strip's face value still would be the $1,000 face value of the original bond, but its price of $200 would be at a substantial discount to its face value. Remember present value? The $200 is like a bird in the hand.

Essentially, Kidder's accounting system allowed you to buy a Strip for one price, then sell it immediately for a much higher price, thereby generating a magical "profit." In reality, the Strip was still worth only $200, not $1,000, so the true profit was zero. It wasn't clear whether Jett had been the mastermind behind this accounting glitch or if more senior management had been aware of the false profits, but these two facts were clear: (1) Kidder's accounting system had failed to disclose $350 million of losses from Strips trading, and (2) Jett, before he was fired, had been Kidder's head of Strips trading. It also appeared that some of the $350 million in losses had migrated to First Boston, where it accounted for at least a portion of the $50 million of Strips trading profits.

Although Kidder's problems were made public, what isn't widely known is that the many Strips traders at other banks also fudged their accounting statements to inflate their apparent profits. However, those activities were small potatoes compared to Kidder's. The best Strips traders at other banks could do was occasionally record a higher selling price than the actual selling price for a Strips sale. That would make one day's profits appear greater than they actually were. Although these "mark-up" practices were common, and virtually impossible to detect, they usually only worked for one day. Of course they also were illegal, even if for only a day, although that didn't seem to matter to anyone. In fact, the only reason such practices weren't even *more* common was that most accounting systems caught the losses right away. Traders at First Boston never got away with hiding as much as $350 million in losses. At least, not as far as *I* knew.

I was now about to enter the long-running saga of Strips. I knew Lehman's deal had been quite successful, although I suspected its success was due primarily to its clever acronym. It was called BIGS, for Brady Income Government Securities. Everyone loved BIGS, and Lehman sold more than $100 million of the trade.

I suggested applying the BIGS idea to Morgan Stanley's failed NPC deal. The NPC bonds had a AAA principal guarantee, just like Brady Bonds. If we put the NPC bonds into a trust, together with some Strips, we, too, might be able to convince S&P to rate the new trust units AAA. At least it was worth a try.

At first the salesmen joked about how such a deal was a sham. I didn't disagree. However, many of our derivatives deals arguably had been shams, and as it became clear the idea might actually work, sham or not, the salesmen in DPG became excited. If we could use this bizarre ratings trick to convince Standard & Poor's to give a very risky Philippines investment its highest rating, we could sell the NPC bonds.

It was difficult to claim credit for trade ideas. However, I thought of a way to get credit for this deal, even if I didn't deserve it and even in the face of competing claims by more senior employees. Every RAV, including the trust we would use for the NPC trade, had to have a name. The name of the Bermuda company we had used for PLUS Notes was PLUS Capital Company; the name of the BIDS company was NTN Capital Company. To preserve my role on the NPC deal for eternity, or at least until the bonds matured in fifteen years, I convinced my bosses to name the trust after me. Ostensibly, the name of the trade, FP Trust, stood for First Philippines Trust. But everyone in the derivatives group knew that the FP really stood for Frank Partnoy.

Now that the NPC trade was my namesake, I needed to make sure it succeeded. I was in charge of "keeping the book" for FP Trust. I helped educate Morgan Stanley's salesforce about the trade, kept tabs on clients who were interested in buying, and participated in numerous sales calls. The trade was simple. The NPC bonds paid interest of 9.75 percent. We simply added an extra 0.5 percent of U.S. Treasury Strips (the icing on the crap cake) to bring the total interest payment to 10.25 percent. That was it. The principal repayment was guaranteed by the World Bank, and the bond – or at least *some* of the bond, if you read the fine print – was rated AAA by S&P. We canvassed Morgan Stanley's client base and pitched the deal to nearly one hundred different clients.

I attended a few early sales presentations and was disappointed to discover they weren't going well. A client would seem willing to buy at first, then would say no at the last minute or express interest in a different trade. After I explained FP Trust to one veteran salesman, he arranged for us to meet the president of a large insurance company just up the street. Before we left, I asked him to assess our chances. He leaned back in his chair, smiled, and told me to relax. In a thick, nearly impenetrable Boston accent, he averred, "Let me tell you something, Frank. What I'm about to tell you, it's the most fundamental principle of our business." He paused – for dramatic effect – and said, "If a bond cannot be sold with two hockey tickets and a good bottle of wine, the bond cannot be sold."

That was perhaps the best advice I ever received at Morgan Stanley. The salesman grabbed an attractive female employee from the research department, just for show, and we headed outdoors. We scurried a few blocks up Eighth Avenue to this company's headquarters, where we were ushered in to a large conference room to meet with the president and one of his assistants.

The salesman explained the trade. The president was intrigued but said he hadn't bought any Philippines bonds yet. He was under pressure to "go international" but faced regulatory constraints in buying non-U.S. bonds. He seemed uncomfortable with the trade, and after some discussion he concluded that the Philippines was too far away and that he preferred to buy something closer to home. We had brought neither wine nor hockey tickets, not that they would have helped.

The salesman was disappointed. I knew he didn't necessarily care about FP Trust; he just wanted the commissions from a juicy trade. I also knew there were plenty of other deals closer to home that we could mention to this guy. The other deals didn't carry my name, but they would generate large fees, nonetheless. Years earlier, as a cashier at McDonald's, I had been trained in the art of "suggestive selling." If a customer ordered a cheeseburger and fries, I knew to ask, "Would you like an apple pie with that?" That same strategy worked at Morgan Stanley. If a customer ordered a simple treasury bond, you asked, "Would you like a leveraged derivative with that?" Often the investor said yes – or at least pursued the inquiry.

In this case, if the insurance company didn't want the Philippines, we should offer them another flavor. I asked the president about Latin America. He said he might consider an investment in Argentina. Fortunately, I had brought some of the marketing materials for an Argentina deal I was working on, and I slipped him a copy. He said that the trade looked interesting, and he would get back to us. The salesman winked at me as we said good-bye.

Unfortunately, we still needed to find someone to buy FP Trust. The outlook was bleak. Several clients said they refused to play ratings agency games. One salesman described with dismay how he had pitched the deal to one client. In a conference room, the salesman had written TOP SECRET on a chalkboard and then explained how the rocket scientists from DPG had persuaded S&P to rate this trade AAA. The salesman's closing line was, "Come on, you know you have wood for this trade." "Wood" was a phallic reference to interest in buying a bond. The client responded curtly that not only did he *not* have wood for the trade, but that the salesman could choose from one of four responses to take with him on his way out the door:

(1) Is that fuckhead dick-with-ears Scarecrow
    behind this?
(2) No fucking way; you're making too much
    money on this deal,
(3) Go fuck yourself; why are you asking? and

    (4) I'm going to the insurance regulators to tell
        them about this.

Although more than sixty clients either expressed some interest or gave us specific comments related to the deal, the salesmen
were able to generate real interest from only three investors. Fortunately, one of them was the Teacher's Insurance Association of
America, known as TIAA or just "Teachers." Teachers was a
large and well-respected manager of public-school teachers' retirement funds. Teachers liked FP Trust so much that they agreed
to buy more than half of the deal. Why a bunch of public-school
teachers might want their retirement checks to depend on the
performance of the Philippines state power company was beyond
me. But with Teachers in as a lead order, the two other investors
gladly agreed to buy the remainder.

The most nerve-racking day for any trade, even a trade that
simply involves buying Strips and putting them into a trust, is
the "pricing date." That's the day on which Morgan Stanley
would purchase the Strips and would tell the investor to the
penny how much the FP Trust would cost them. All of this would
happen within seconds, by telephone. Or, rather, by telephones.
We would need to have several phones available on the pricing
date.

Anyone who works on Wall Street has a favorite nightmare
story about telephone mishaps, especially when a deal is being
priced. My favorite is one I heard about a trader who told a young
trainee to watch his phones while the trader went to the bathroom. While the trader was away, a line rang, and the trainee answered it. The caller asked, "So, are we done on $100 million
bonds?" The trainee panicked, and stupidly mumbled, "Yes." The
caller responded, "OK, you're done," and hung up. Of course, the
market for those bonds immediately plummeted, and by the time
the trader returned, he discovered he owned $100 million bonds
at an enormous loss. Needless to say, traders don't like it when
you buy $100 million of bonds for them without permission, es-

pecially when they plummet in value. The trainee was fired on the spot.

Since this incident, most investment banks require new employees to use "training phones," handsets without mouthpieces. The phones – like training wheels on a bicycle – are designed to prevent trainees from hurting themselves during their first few months. They work.

I had graduated from my training program long ago, and all of my phones did have mouthpieces – although on pricing days I sometimes wished they hadn't. Typically, only one person was responsible for pricing a new deal. If you were that person, you monitored several computer screens and talked on several phones, while your managers all stood a few feet behind you and watched over your shoulder. Every few minutes a manager would yell about a number changing or demand to know how much money we would be making. The pressure was intense. More than one young employee, after finishing pricing his or her first derivatives deal, would break down in tears.

I was responsible for the pricing of FP Trust, and fortunately it went smoothly. We bought the Strips, sold them to the trust along with the NPC bonds we already owned, and collected our money. DPG sold $48.4 million worth of FP Trust to only three buyers. I was overjoyed.

I was responsible for calculating the precise fee. A 1 percent fee would have been $484,000. Our goal had been $1 million, and I knew a fee of more than 2 percent would be massive for a transaction with the size and risk of FP Trust. I tallied the fee total carefully, just to be certain. Sure enough, I had closed my first $1 million deal. The total fee for FP Trust was almost $1.2 million.

The only people more ecstatic about FP Trust than the DPG managers were the junk bond traders. They had owned tens of millions worth of NPC bonds and were nervous about having to sell them at a loss. Instead, through DPG, they were able to sell the bonds for a profit. Morgan Stanley's investment bankers were thrilled, too, because they not only had preserved their relationships with the World Bank and the Philippines, they had earned an underwriting commission of several hundred thousand dollars associated with the underlying NPC bonds. Everyone was happy. We had saved the day and made more than a million dollars in the process. Who cared if in a few years the lights went out on all those public-school teachers?

I didn't get the bad news until much later. S&P called to notify me that they would be changing the ratings of several Morgan Stanley derivatives deals, including FP Trust. The deals would retain their AAA rating, but S&P would add an R subscript to the AAA. (R stood for Restricted.) Now, FP Trust would be rated AAA_R. This was awful news. I suppose we should have seen the change coming. More than a year earlier, S&P had announced it would review ratings given to hybrid securities that combined derivatives with traditional debt instruments. At that time a director of S&P had suggested one option would be to add a subscript to certain ratings to indicate that S&P was rating only the issuer's *ability* to repay, not the *likelihood* that it actually *would* repay the full amount. After Procter & Gamble's big loss, derivatives had become a high-profile problem, and S&P was cracking down.

I was devastated. My pride and joy, my derivatives progeny, would be branded forever with a subscript R. Our lucite deal mementos would need to be amended to add this $R,$ now the scarlet letter of derivatives. Even worse, I had to tell everyone else. One clueless salesman asked, "If it's a long-term rating, how could they change it so quickly?" The head junk bond trader was furious. His comments included "Fuck them" and "They should be men about this." I told him every single person I had dealt with at S&P for this deal was female, including the person who actually had rated the deal. He was flabbergasted by that, but said, "Fuck 'em all, anyway."

I thought Bidyut Sen would be angry, but when he stormed into the morning DPG meeting the next day, it was simply to scream that the daily update sheet we were looking at was too lengthy. Sen walked up to me after the meeting and mumbled, "People in this group have virus-eating arms. We must have evolved." I didn't know what to say to that. I simply nodded and walked away. Weeks later, after several more announcements that investors had lost money on derivatives, Sen stood in the middle of the trading floor and yelled, "If there's one more article about derivatives, I am going to die!" It appeared that the recent derivatives disasters were causing my bosses to become slightly unhinged. Even the behavior of normally sane Marshal Salant had become peculiar; he was oddly concerned that former President Nixon's death was "really going to screw up our business."

The only manager in DPG with a firm grip on reality was the Queen, and when I told her the news, her grip tightened – around my neck. She asked me to explain exactly why S&P had given us an R rating for FP Trust. Why had we finally lost in these negotiations? Truthfully, I didn't know – although I assumed it was in part because S&P was right; these bonds really weren't AAA. Several salesmen were listening to see if I had any answer. I wasn't going to lie or make some lame excuse. We were stuck with the R rating, and I didn't have a good answer. So I said, quite honestly, "I don't know."

The Queen exploded. Little did I know then that a cardinal rule of the trading floor was that you never, ever said those trigger words. When I uttered them, the Queen began screaming, inches from my face, that "I don't know" is *never* an acceptable answer. An audience gathered to witness my flogging.

I said that I didn't know you never said "I don't know." That doubly demonstrated my ignorance. On a trading floor you could utter any profanity you wished; any disgusting or vile terminology was just fine. But *those words* were repugnant and revolting. If you even *whispered* "I don't know," you risked a beheading.

The Queen hailed one of the other managers and told him what I had just said. He shook his head with disappointment. I wondered if they were planning to wash my mouth out with soap. My attempts to defend myself were, in retrospect, quite pathetic.

"What if I really don't know? I said 'I don't know' because I really didn't know."

"I don't give a shit what you don't know."

"But if I don't know the answer, what am I supposed to say?"

"Just make something up. It doesn't matter what you say. Just don't ever, ever say 'I don't know' again."

"But I *didn't know.*"

"GODDAMMIT, DON'T YOU EVER SAY THOSE WORDS AGAIN!"

I was learning the hard way that derivatives was a game in which you couldn't afford to slip up, not even once. Even though DPG had made more than $1 million on FP Trust, all the Queen would remember was that I had answered "I don't know" to a question and that the deal was rated R. The positive aspects of the trade already were forgotten. I had been happy to have the trade named after me. But now I wanted to scrub the trade's name clean off my lucite deal memento. FP TRUST was emblazoned across marketing documents and prospectuses, throughout the firm and at dozens of clients. I was inextricably linked to the first R-rated deal in DPG history. I was in a big hole.

I was desperate to begin digging myself out. I must not have been thinking clearly at the time because I returned to Scarecrow for help. What could I do to recover?

Scarecrow suggested we try to copy the Lehman BIGS deal using Brady Bonds. If they could do this deal, so could we. I had never tried duplicating another investment bank's trade verbatim. It should have been a bad sign: We were so short on creative ideas that we were relegated to stealing them from old Lehman deals. In any event, our attempt at plagiarism failed, and I wasted the next month.

We tried replicating the BIGS trade in every possible way. First, we took Brady Bonds, added the extra interest payments as icing, and changed the acronym. The new name Scarecrow settled on was "Credit Enhanced Duration Notes." That was a really stupid-sounding name, and CEDN wasn't exactly a catchy acronym. On the other hand, it was by far the best of Scarecrow's suggestions, which had included "Brady Repackaged AAA Securities Trust" (BREAST), "Brady Repackaged Asset Securities" (BRAS), and "Latin American Securities Derivatives" (LSD). Scarecrow joked that clients would get "wood" about buying BREASTS and BRAS. Maybe he had a point, but they certainly didn't get any wood from CEDNs.

Several clients immediately rejected the deal, saying they wouldn't pay a 1 percent fee simply to obfuscate a rating. The insurance companies were also concerned, quite rightly, that although the National Association of Insurance Commissioners had rated Lehman's deal NAIC-1, the NAIC's top rating, they might downgrade the bonds if they realized that the bonds weren't a true AAA. The R rating worried everyone.

When the Queen heard about these responses, she was furious, though for an unexpected reason. She wasn't angry that clients had said they wouldn't buy the deal because they were concerned about illegitimate ratings; she was mad that we had implied we would do such a deal for a mere 1 percent fee. She yelled, "Why did you tell them only one percent? Tell them *two* percent!"

As we continued to fail with U.S. clients, I looked abroad. I had heard some interest in the AAA idea from Tokyo. The problem was how to turn the U.S. dollar-denominated Brady Bonds into derivatives denominated in Japanese yen. There were yen-denominated Brady Bonds, but they weren't available in large enough size to make a deal worthwhile. Using U.S. dollar bonds, it was very expensive to swap dollars into yen for the average Brady Bond maturity, twenty-five to thirty years, because you couldn't use Japanese government bonds, whose longest maturity was twenty years, to hedge the swaps. I estimated it would cost at least ten additional basis points to swap the payments from dollars to yen, and that amount might eliminate any profits from the deal. The trade was possible but complicated, and it would require at least one trip to Tokyo. I wasn't ready for that yet.

Meanwhile, our derivatives colleagues in Morgan Stanley's London office were busy trying to copy a deal of their own. Several London banks had closed profitable Italian derivatives trades, based on similar ratings agency tricks. There were reports that J. P. Morgan and Goldman, Sachs had each completed such deals. As we understood them, these deals were a common type of RAV, based on Italian government bonds. There were three steps to the trade. First, you put Italian bonds denominated in liras into a special company. Second, the company entered into a swap with a bank to pay liras and receive U.S. dollars. Third, the company issued bonds denominated in U.S. dollars. This three-step process had one very important result: The bonds were rated AAA. A clear theme was emerging. The ratings agencies seemed to be the key to the most profitable derivatives.

This trade was effective in Italy for the same reason PLUS Notes had been effective in Mexico: The country's local bonds had higher ratings than its foreign bonds. Italy's lira-denominated bonds were AAA; its U.S. dollar-denominated bonds were not. By putting the lira bonds into a special company and entering into a swap with a AAA counterparty, you could magically create AAA Italian bonds denominated in U.S. dollars. Presto. Just like PLUS Notes.

I knew there was a lot of variability in what types of bonds were rated AAA. Several banks, including Citicorp and J. P. Morgan, recently had set up so-called arbitrage vehicles to take advantage of this variability. Companies with names like Alpha Finance, Beta Finance, ARGO, and Gordian Knot made fortunes with a simple strategy of buying the cheapest AAA bonds and issuing their own more expensive AAA bonds to pay for them. This strategy was a cash machine – and a reasonably well-kept secret. You could convince S&P to rate your own bonds AAA because you could demonstrate that you were buying only AAA bonds. And yet, paradoxically, the bonds you bought were worth less than your own obligations. A little financial wizardry, combined with the screwy AAA ratings, could create a perpetual money maker.

Morgan Stanley faced two problems in copying the Italian transaction, once we obtained the required documentation. First, there was the usual problem of agreeing on an appropriate name. Many of the London DPG salesmen's special companies were incorporated in places such as Luxembourg or the Netherlands, which required that you submit a list of names for approval several days in advance of incorporation. After you submitted the list, typically within five business days, you would hear which names, if any, were available for use. For one deal, the salesmen had submitted thirty or so names, and the Netherlands had rejected all of them. A last-minute submission of names had included, in part as a joke, "Gopher," the name of a character from the television series *The Love Boat*. Of course, as luck had it, of all the names, only Gopher was available. When one Japanese buyer learned the deal was to be called Gopher and asked what it meant, he was horrified to discover that a gopher was a rodent. In Japan, rodents are bad omens, and the superstitious buyer wanted out of the deal. The salesmen had better luck with names in the Italian transaction. It required only about a dozen picks before "Eagle Pier" finally was approved. Eagle Pier, the pick of one of the senior managers in London, was the name of a Caribbean resort and didn't seem to offend anyone.

The second problem was S&P. Apparently no one had paid for an Italian lira government bond issue to be rated. Although Italy was one of the weaker economies in Europe, it was still likely to command a AAA rating in liras. For most countries, if their foreign currency rating was AA or better, which Italy's was, then their local rating would qualify as AAA. Again, the currency denomination mattered because it was easier for Italy to print liras to repay its lira debts than it was for Italy to generate hard currency to cover its U.S. dollar debts. S&P had accepted the rationale that if bonds are rated AAA in one currency, and the bank swapping them to another currency also is rated AAA, then the new bonds qualify for AAA treatment. That rationale made the Italian deal work. The only sticking point was that S&P wouldn't say the Italian lira bonds were AAA until somebody paid for a rating.

Our London colleagues needed someone to talk to S&P in the U.S. about Eagle Pier, so I called an S&P analyst to discuss Italy's ratings. He was very cagey, maintaining that he "could neither confirm nor deny that Italy is AAA in liras." He said he was not allowed to publicize his view of the local rating because no one had paid for Italy to be rated. If Morgan Stanley did a deal involving Italian government bonds, it wouldn't receive a AAA rating unless we paid for it. Rating a small derivatives deal was relatively inexpensive compared to rating an entire country's debt, and we certainly weren't going to pay for all of Italy to be rated AAA.

Fortunately, S&P was open to compromise. Instead of advertising this deal as involving Italian bonds, we would say the deal involved the bonds of one of seven European countries, six of which already were rated AAA. Of course, everyone knew that the actual bonds we were using were Italian bonds, but the uncertainty associated with having seven countries to choose from satisfied S&P. They could rate our bonds AAA without requiring us to pay Italy's fee because they didn't think anyone could cite Eagle Pier as evidence that Italy was rated AAA. If anyone tried, S&P could claim that the actual bonds for the deal might have been any of the other six countries, which did have paid-for AAA ratings. Eagle Pier was like a revolver whose chamber held only one bullet. As long as Eagle Pier maintained this Russian roulette structure and paid the required fee, S&P would rate it AAA, even though it knew that when Morgan Stanley pulled the trigger on this deal, it would fire the Italy bullet.

I couldn't believe how convoluted some of our RAVs had become. Did anyone know about these crazy trades? What would happen if the *Wall Street Journal* found out about them? I assumed the *Journal* didn't already know, or wouldn't we have read about it? I wanted to see what journalists really thought about our business. The *Journal* was about to hold a major conference on derivatives. Fortunately, I was able to secure an invitation.

Many of the highest-profile commentators on the recent derivatives disasters were there. Most of the leading investment banks were represented. The moderator was Douglas Sease, the *Journal*'s bureau chief for markets and finance; other *Journal* panelists included Barbara Donnelly Granito, Laura Jereski, Steve Lipin, and Jeffrey Taylor, staff reporters who wrote every day about various financial issues, including regulation, banks, hedge funds, high-tech finance – and derivatives. They were among the best-informed financial journalists in the world. Also there were several panelists from Wall Street: Fred Chapey, head of Derivatives Marketing at Chase Manhattan Bank; Patrick Thompson, president of the New York Mercantile Exchange; and Leslie Rahl, a principal of Capital Markets Risk Advisers, who was advising many victims and perpetrators of derivatives disasters. Surely, I thought, someone will at least mention the kinds of derivatives we have been selling. What questions would the journalists ask? Would "I don't know" be an acceptable answer from the bankers?

I was disappointed. The questions and answers were insipid, and there was no discussion of any derivatives even remotely related to our recent trades. The reporters obviously didn't know about them, and if the bankers knew, they certainly weren't talking. At one point the discussion turned generally to whether recent derivatives trades had been inappropriate for investors. Several stories had surfaced about investors agreeing to receive payments on exotic swaps, which involved, for example, an interest rate index, such as LIBOR, "cubed" – or multiplied by itself three times. Such trades obviously were pure speculation. Investors did not have LIBOR-cubed liabilities hedged with LIBOR-cubed swaps. Nevertheless, the industry representatives were unwilling to concede that such swaps were inappropriate bets for certain buyers. When asked what kind of a hedge a LIBOR-cubed swap possibly could be, Fred Chapey from Chase replied, only half jokingly, that the swap was a LIBOR-cubed hedge. That comment drew nervous laughter. A law professor on the panel concluded by saying that the only perfect hedge was in a Japanese garden. It seemed to me from the low level of debate at this conference that no one was likely to find out about our trades, ever. What would it take to get anyone's attention?

7

Don't Cry For
Me, Argentina

aria Eva Duarte de Perón, popularly known as Evita,
the wife of the late Argentinean political leader Juan
Domingo Peron, died her tragic death at thirty-three in
1952, exactly forty years before the Republic of Argentina issued
the ugliest bond in history. If Evita had lived to see this bond, the
mere sight of it not only would have offended her purported cultural sensibilities, it might well have killed her.

The enormous $5.5 billion bond issue was called Bonos de
Consolidación de Deudas Previsionales, but they were popularly
known as BOCONs. The Central Bank of Argentina issued the
BOCONs on September 1, 1992, as part of a legal requirement that
the Republic of Argentina consolidate its diffuse debts to provin-
cial governments, suppliers, retirees, pensioners, and litigants
against the government. The new bonds were issued in various series, one of which, called BOCON Pre4s, was by far the ugliest.

BOCON Pre4s were ugly for several reasons. First, they didn't
pay any interest, initially or for the first six years after their issuance. Not paying interest was great for the Central Bank of Argentina, but it wasn't so good for retirees and pensioners who
might have trouble getting by on zero dollars per month. Few in-

143

vestors were willing to hold bonds that didn't pay any interest unless they were issued by someone creditworthy, which Argentina was not. Second, the bonds' principal amount increased every month based on a complex average of several monthly interest rates. As a result, you never knew how many bonds you actually owned from month to month. You could start with $100 worth of Pre4s, but the next month you might have $100.43, then $100.79, and so on. Just keeping tabs on the amount of bonds you owned was a nightmare. Third, when you finally began receiving interest, your principal amount, after six years of going up, started going down. As you were repaid your principal in forty-eight monthly installments, your interest payments – which were based on the existing principal amount at any time – started going down, too, in equally unpredictable fashion. At least receiving zero for the first six years was predictable. After that you had no idea what your forty-eight payments might be. After six years you received 2.08 percent of your principal – whatever *that* was – every month, until the forty-eighth month, when you received 2.24 percent, and you received fluctuating monthly interest based on the complex formula and the remaining principal. How is that for convoluted? Evita would not have been happy.

It was almost impossible for the owners of BOCON Pre4s to determine what the bonds should be worth, and consequently investors hated them. As if these complications weren't enough, investors also had to worry about the very real possibility that after six years, Argentina would decide it had liked not paying any interest on the bonds. Most investors regarded default as a significant risk for the Pre4s, and the bonds received very low credit ratings. They had other unattractive qualities too: Taxes owed on bond payments, if such payments ever occurred, were uncertain, and the Central Bank could redeem the bonds anytime, without penalty. The Pre4s had one positive characteristic – they were denominated in U.S. dollars – but that didn't seem to matter much because the Argentine peso had recently been pegged one-to-one to the U.S. dollar.

The Pre4s were not my first choice when my bosses instructed me to look for a derivatives trade in Argentina. They were too unwieldy. Nevertheless, with the end of the year approaching, we were looking for a home run to ensure that we could claim responsibility for plenty of profits at bonus time. We still were looking for the derivatives group's "trade of the year." We already had tried Mexico, Brazil, and the Philippines. Now it was time for Argentina.

We started with the tried-and-true PLUS Notes idea, substituting Argentine bonds for Mexican bonds. We tried putting Argentine bonds called FRBs – which were much prettier than Pre4s – into a RAV and selling one of the RAV pieces to U.S. buyers. However, we were unable to obtain a favorable credit rating for the notes we would be selling, and that eliminated many large U.S. buyers. The aggressive PCS salesmen tried to find some wealthy individuals to buy, but they also failed.

Our next attempt was to offer derivatives that stripped apart the various risks associated with Argentina Brady Bonds, also much prettier than Pre4s. We tried to split the Brady Bonds into three pieces: short-term interest payments, long-term interest payments, and principal repayment. We offered different pieces of this trade to different investors, including the Republic of Argentina itself, to assist its continuing strategy of consolidating its debts. However, investors rejected the deal, and although we were able to arrange a meeting with Argentine government officials, the results were disastrous. Senior government officials didn't even bother to attend; junior officials arrived several hours late and rejected our proposal immediately. We were outraged. Can you imagine? The Republic of Argentina snubbing Morgan Stanley!

Our third idea was a more radical proposal to restructure the entire Argentine home mortgage system, in the same way the U.S. system had been restructured more than a decade earlier. The most pressing need seemed to be that Banco Hipotecario, the mortgage bank of Argentina, needed to raise about $400 million to finance the initial purchase of residential mortgages, which it eventually would try to pool together in the same way mortgages were pooled in the U.S. Many of Banco Hipotecario's mortgages were nonperforming, especially low-rate mortgages given as political favors, and Argentina's newly appointed Minister of Economy, Domingo Cavallo, had ordered Hipotecario to clean up its act. We hired an Argentine bank to help us submit a proposal, and spent weeks constructing a plan, but the Republic of Argentina rejected that proposal, as well. The response of one official was, "Too many cooks, not enough beef."

However, three strikes were not enough, and we continued to hunt for Argentine derivatives deals. We heard from a client that Goldman, Sachs had recently completed a large derivatives deal in Argentina. One of the DPG salesman quickly obtained a copy of the Goldman prospectus for the deal. It appeared that Goldman had taken some of the BOCONs, simplified them using derivatives, and sold the resulting mix to U.S. investors. They had made the purchase of BOCONs hassle free, and U.S. investors had purchased more than $100 million worth. By our calculations, Goldman had made several million dollars.

We began copying the Goldman deal shamelessly. The idea was simple enough, and Goldman's deal had some structural problems, which we began to correct. Goldman had used a series of BOCONs called Pre2s, which resembled Pre4s but were slightly more attractive. As far as we were concerned, the uglier the better. Pre4s were the ugliest of all the Argentine bonds, and consequently they also were the cheapest. That meant a simplified Pre4 trade would be even more attractive to investors than a simplified Pre2 trade. We chose Pre4s.

Essentially, our Pre4 trade was structured in three simple steps. First, we put the Pre4s into a trust vehicle, this time a Cayman Islands trust. Any payments on the Pre4s would be paid to the Cayman trust, until the maturity of the Pre4s in September 2002. Second, we set up an agreement between the trust vehicle and Morgan Stanley, in which Morgan Stanley would receive all of the Pre4 payments, whenever they were made, and would pay a flat 14.75 percent annual interest rate to the trust. Because the Pre4s weren't paying any interest as yet, Morgan Stanley was effectively lending 14.75 percent to the trust – at least at first. Of course, lending money to the Cayman trust was risky because Morgan Stanley would have to borrow the money to pay into it, and if Argentina defaulted on the Pre4s, Morgan Stanley might not be repaid. Finally, the trust would issue trust units backed by Morgan Stanley's agreement to make interest payments to the trust.

These trust units were simple, they paid a huge 14.75 percent interest rate, and they were backed, in part, by Morgan Stanley. For a prospective investor, these trust units were an enormous improvement over the Pre4s themselves: They paid interest immediately, their principal amount didn't fluctuate, and it was clear what their expected payments were, from the beginning. Compared to the Pre4s, the trust units were gorgeous.

Investors loved the deal, and we had no trouble selling it, despite our failure to invent a clever acronym. We settled on "Repackaged Argentina Domestic Securities Trust I." That title could be abbreviated to RADS, but we usually referred to the deal simply as "Pre4 Trust." Investors agreed to buy the trade despite its ho-hum name.

The Pre4 Trust fit the pattern of RAVs we had been selling throughout the past year. First we found bonds that were subject to some type of costly investment barrier or restriction in a country outside the U.S. For BIDS, the barrier was regulation; for PLUS Notes and FP Trust, the barrier was credit rating; for Pre4s, the barrier was pure ugliness. Then we found a way for investors outside the country to buy the bonds and bypass the barrier. That formula had generated deals with sizable fees.

Our trades also typically had one lead buyer, known as the lead order. For many of our RAVs, the lead order had been from an unsophisticated insurance company, often from the Midwest. The Pre4 Trust was no exception, and the lead order came from an insurance company in the heartland. Other Pre4 Trust buyers were more sophisticated and included Serfin, the still-hungry Mexican bank with the nuclear-waste logo, several large U.S. mutual funds, and even a few aggressive Private Client Services accounts. However, even the most sophisticated investors obviously did not understand the mechanics of the trade. It was incredibly difficult to calculate the value of exchanging the ugly payments for simple payments. We had built an elaborate computer model to make these calculations, but I don't believe any of the buyers were able to create anything similar. If they had, they likely would not have agreed to pay Morgan Stanley several million dollars more than we thought the trust was worth. The excess payments were our fees.

Unlike FP Trust, there were a surprisingly small number of disastrous sales calls for the Pre4 Trust. However, one of those calls was especially memorable. One of the more junior salesmen – a young, tall, blond guy – was pitching the deal to the director of private placements and credit at an insurance company and asked me to attend. I agreed, in part because I was eager to get a sense of how the younger salesmen thought about clients.

Our meeting went well. I explained the Pre4 Trust, and the director – a very attractive woman – seemed interested in the concept. She asked several detailed questions, and we discussed some other trades her company had recently purchased. The blond salesman stared intently at the woman throughout the meeting, barely speaking. After she left, he took me aside, told me that he had thought about the issue carefully, and he had made his judgment.

He said earnestly, "I would never, ever fuck her." I was quite surprised. I looked at the salesman and waited for him to laugh or even smile. But he didn't. He was serious. Although he had considered neither the specifics of the trade nor the director's questions, he had resolved one important issue during the meeting: He would never fuck this particular director. As a secondary matter, she didn't buy the Pre4 Trust, either.

A few investors had expressed concern about whether we would buy the trade back at a fair price. Many buyers didn't want to have to hold a trade for more than a few years and were worried that because the bonds were so unusual, they might not be able to find anyone other than Morgan Stanley to buy them. In such a predicament they feared Morgan Stanley would rip their faces off.

They were right to be afraid. One fund manager from San Francisco rejected the Pre4 Trust because he said it resembled a Swedish krona/Swiss franc PERLS he had purchased from Morgan Stanley. That PERLS had dropped in price from $100 to $75, virtually overnight. We assured the salesman that the Pre4 Trust was nothing like PERLS, but we couldn't guarantee that it wouldn't drop in price. The issue was a serious one. Morgan Stanley would commit to repurchase the bonds, but it wouldn't commit to do so at a fair price. We couldn't predict the financial markets, especially in Argentina.

Despite these protests, the bonds proved easy to sell. A dozen or so investors were satisfied with the terms of the trade and agreed to buy. All told, we sold $123 million of Pre4 Trust units.

A typical percentage profit for a complex derivatives trade was 1 or 2 percent. However, the Pre4 Trust was so complicated and difficult for investors to value properly that they agreed to pay much more for the bonds than they probably should have. The profits from the Pre4 Trust – approximately $4 million – exceeded those of any Morgan Stanley derivatives trade in 1994. The Pre4 Trust was our trade of the year, a clear home run, and my first "elephant." The derivatives group was euphoric.

However, the derivatives managers warned me not to celebrate. Although investors had given us orders committing to purchase the trust units, we didn't have their money yet. The Pre4 Trust was complicated, and it would take at least a week to negotiate the documentation, distribute final prospectuses, and close the trade. One of the unnerving aspects of my job was that even after a deal was sold, it wasn't finished. The Pre4 Trust could collapse at any time before it was closed and we received our money.

My job would be especially unnerving that week because it looked as if I would have to close the Pre4 Trust alone. Everyone else was leaving town. The Queen would be in Mexico, meeting with Mexican banks about other deals. The other members of the RAVs team would be on vacation. Marshal Salant said he was confident that I could get the job done.

As I worked with the lawyers in Argentina and the U.S. to close the trade, several other DPG salesmen tried to tell me a $4 million fee was no big deal. One salesman said he had made $8 million on one leveraged swap. Other salesmen said they had charged 5 or even 10 percent fees for derivatives trades. Even Bidyut Sen burst my bubble, telling me a 4 percent fee was "OK, but it's not that great. We've taken more than that out, ten, twenty or more points." I couldn't believe DPG had received a 20 percent fee on any trade, regardless of how stupid the buyer was. The financial markets were competitive, and a typical fee was much less than even 1 percent. I was proud of the Pre4 trade, and I thought derivatives trades with multimillion-dollar fees were rare. In fact, $4 million was the largest fee I had ever seen. I tried to ignore their comments.

The closing was progressing well. I had taken care of the Argentina side of the closing, which involved negotiating with Argentine lawyers and the Argentine bank that would act as custodian for the Pre4 bonds. Every bank and company in Argentina seemed to have "Stars and Stripes Forever" as their on-hold music, and I was grateful to turn to the U.S. side of the closing and listen to something else. Our attorneys were Cravath, Swaine & Moore, the aggressive old-line firm that the derivatives group preferred to Morgan Stanley's stately general purpose law firm, Davis, Polk & Wardwell.

There were two potential disasters on the Pre4 Trust deal. The first one involved the question of whether we should call the Pre4 Trust a "derivative." Based in part on conversations I had with a partner from Cravath, I decided we should amend the Pre4 Trust prospectus to state up front that the trust units we were selling were "derivatives" and carried the risks associated with an investment in derivatives. I thought that if Morgan Stanley was sued for the Pre4 Trust deal, it should be able to claim it did not mislead investors as to the riskiness of the deal and even went so far as to say that the trust units actually were "derivatives."

Although the term was becoming more popular at the time, in reality, this was a minor point. Everyone knew the Pre4 Trust was a derivative. Nevertheless, I thought a clear statement that the trust units were derivatives would bolster the firm's case somewhat in any future litigation. We finished editing some minutiae, added the term "derivative," and sent the prospectuses to be printed.

When the Queen of RAVs returned from Mexico, I handed her a freshly printed prospectus and told her we were right on schedule. Boxes of prospectuses were on their way to the various investors, and I had a large box of them ready to distribute to the salesmen tomorrow. A few minutes later, I heard a blood curdling scream. When the Queen saw the word "derivative" in the prospectus, she exploded. She began screaming at me, calling me every name she could think of.

"Goddammit, this says derivatives! These aren't *derivatives! Why does this say 'derivatives'? Who told you these were derivatives?"*

I tried to explain how the presence of the word might help us in any future lawsuit. She didn't care what it might help or what the partner from Cravath had said. She refused to let any of her deals be called a derivative, now that the term had such a negative connotation, and ordered me to halt distribution of any prospectuses with that filthy word in them. When I continued to disagree, the Queen tracked down Marshal Salant in St. Louis and convinced him that the evil word should be expunged. I argued for a few more minutes – we were still the Derivative Products Group, weren't we? There still was a *D* in DPG? Was she

151

actually denying that this unbelievably complex trade was a derivative? – but it was no use.

No, she said. "Just don't send it out. Hide the whole goddamn box." When a salesman stopped by and asked for a copy, she screamed, "*Nooooooo!*" and ripped it from his hands.

I convinced Federal Express to remove the prospectuses from their planes, just in time. I called the messengers in the various cities where the prospectuses were being delivered and instructed them to destroy any copies they received, in case Federal Express made a mistake. I needed to call the Cravath partner to tell him to excise the dirty word "derivative" from the prospectus and to reprint copies. He would have to conduct a global search for the *D* word in the sixty-page document to make sure it didn't appear anywhere.

I was mad and felt I had been right. If this trade wasn't a derivative, nothing was. I asked the Queen if she wanted to keep the old prospectuses as souvenirs. I shouldn't have taunted her. She yelled, "I don't give a fuck what you do with them! Burn them, wallpaper your apartment – whatever! Just get rid of them! Take them away from me!"

After the revised prospectuses were distributed and the closing documents were ready for signatures, all we needed was to wait for the closing day. By Friday, September 30, the details were done. The deal would close the following Monday, as planned. I stayed late Friday night, after everyone had left for the weekend, just to make sure I hadn't forgotten anything. I was alone on the deserted trading floor. Without the bedlam of angry traders and frantic salesmen, the place was spookily quiet. The phone rang. I was about to experience the second potential disaster on the Pre4 Trust deal.

It was the small insurance company from the Midwest, the lead buyer for the Pre4 Trust. Convincing them to buy the deal had been the key to bringing in other orders. As the lead order, they were the deal's linchpin. I wondered what they could possibly want at this late hour.

"Frank?"

"Yes?"

"We've decided not to go ahead with the Pre4 Trust deal."

Pause. "Pardon me?"

"We've decided that the deal isn't right for us. I hope this doesn't cause any inconvenience for you."

"Inconvenience? What are you talking about?" I tried not to panic. This was bad. I had been working on the Pre4 trade for more than a month, and now the lead order was threatening to decimate it. If they backed out now, it would be a catastrophe. The derivatives group would lose an enormous fee, their largest of the year, and I might lose my job. I looked up and down the rows of empty chairs. It was crucial that I persuade the investors to stay.

I responded as calmly as I could. "You can't do that. We're closing the Pre4 Trust on Monday, as planned. We've relied on you for this deal. We've been working with you for weeks. You can't back out now." I paused again, then added, "There's no one even here. It's after 7 o'clock on a Friday night, for God's sake."

"Well, I have one of our attorneys here, and she says there have been some changes in the prospectus, and we just aren't comfortable with the deal. So we won't be participating."

Changes in the prospectus? My mind was whirring. How could this be happening? The entire trust was cratering. If they pulled out, everyone else would question the deal, and it probably wouldn't close. Our largest fee of the year was in serious jeopardy. Four million dollars, now precisely the value of my ass, was on the line.

I explained to the lawyer that the prospectus had not changed in any material way. They didn't budge. I said the company was obligated to purchase the deal. They disagreed. Finally I told them to stay by the phone while I found one of my bosses to explain how serious a breach their backing out of this deal now would be. "Whatever you do, don't leave," I cautioned them. To be safe, I copied down their home numbers before I hung up the phone.

I looked everywhere on the trading floor. No one. It was now 7:30 P.M. I tried calling various managing directors at home, but no one answered. They were either commuting home or traveling for the weekend. The Queen was nowhere to be found. None of the traders was home, either. I left urgent messages with spouses. I tried calling the in-house Morgan Stanley lawyers, but they were gone, too. After leaving more than a dozen messages, I reached the partner from Cravath. Lawyers at Cravath were always at work.

I will not reveal the substance of our conversation other than to say that he used the phrases "What the fuck?" and "Shove it up their ass" more than a Cravath partner typically would. After I had briefed him, we called the insurance company.

The insurance company's attorney began by saying that she had several problems with the transaction. We politely asked her what those might be.

"First of all," she said, "how do we know the Pre4 bonds even exist?"

There was a long pause. That seemed like a pretty basic question, even for a novice lawyer. Should I laugh at her? Or should I scream? Her question was not only naive and irrelevant, it was absurd. Ontology? At this hour? Somehow I held back. However, I recognized that this phone call was crucial, and I waited patiently for the Cravath lawyer's response. It was perfect.

"As a matter of fact, they don't exist," he said. I could almost hear the steam emanating from the other attorney's ears. "The Pre4 bonds are held book entry with Citibank in Argentina on behalf of the trust. There are no physical bonds."

The other attorney was undaunted, and she tried again, with a different argument. She must have been told to find some way – *any* way – to get the company out of the deal. For almost an hour she raised numerous objections, each of which we batted down, until finally there was only one issue remaining. They wanted an amendment to the trust deed for the deal. They said if Morgan Stanley could agree to this amendment that night, they would stay in the deal. If not, they were out.

How could Morgan Stanley possibly agree to an amendment that night? Morgan Stanley was a company, and only an officer of the company could bind it to such an amendment. I couldn't possibly find an officer of the company at such an hour, could I? Then I remembered. Bidyut Sen had given me a power of attorney to bind Morgan Stanley with respect to the Pre4 Trust. I could agree to the amendment on Morgan Stanley's behalf, although that would mean assuming a hell of a lot of responsibility. I told everyone I would call them back and hung up.

I considered the amendment carefully. It couldn't really hurt us. In fact, I was surprised no one had asked for it earlier. Still, did I feel comfortable binding Morgan Stanley to the agreement on my own, without anyone else's approval? If I did, I could do it. I had the power, with my signature, to bind the entire investment bank, with 10,000 employees worldwide, to a new set of commitments for the Pre4 Trust. It might save the most profitable deal of the year. Or it might get me fired. Was this really happening? I certainly wasn't in Kansas anymore. What should I do?

I decided to do it. I made one last effort to reach my bosses, but no one was there. I called the company official and told him to fax me the proposed amendment. The lawyers agreed on language, and he faxed the amendment for my signature.

Just minutes before I was about to commit Morgan Stanley to these new obligations on my own, the Queen called from home. I quickly explained the situation, and she agreed to the amendment. Relieved, I thanked her. I then signed the amendment on behalf of Morgan Stanley faxed it back to the official, and received his signed confirmation a few minutes later, a little after 9 P.M. The deal was saved.

I was a nervous wreck, sweating and delirious. There was no one there to congratulate me. My bosses better give me some credit for this, I thought.

With the amendment signed, on Monday, October 3, the Pre4 Trust deal closed as planned. I happily wired Cravath their fee, which roughly equaled the salary of one of my friends who was

F. I. A. S. C. O.

an associate there. I also figured out a way to extract an extra $300,000 profit by restructuring the swap payments to reallocate profits from later years. With that addition, we made well over $4 million on that trade.

Numerous people congratulated me on the deal, including everyone on the RAVs team and Steve Benardete from the Gang of Four, who said the trade was a perfect example of DPG's "bread and butter transaction." Bidyut Sen asked me to prepare a memo explaining the deal in simple terms, which I did. The next day, when Peter Karches, the head of the trading floor, walked over to DPG and asked, "Who did this Pre4 trade?" Sen took credit. I was angry and wished I had been able to claim full credit for my efforts. However, I understood the firm's hierarchy. At least if anything went wrong with the deal, everyone would blame him, not me.

Sen seemed happier now. He and I previously had argued, in a congenial way, about whether financial markets were efficient, with me taking the more commonly espoused view that they were. Now he told me "If I ever hear you talk about efficient markets again, I will make you go stand in the corner." I laughed. He had a point. How could you make $4 million virtually risk free in so little time in an efficient market? On the other hand, it hadn't exactly been easy for me.

The Pre4 Trust assumed a high profile at Morgan Stanley. One of the controllers told me that John Mack had stopped the weekly meeting of the firm's internal board of directors to ask several questions about the Pre4 Trust, including how the trade had made so much money. Even Mack the Knife was impressed. I was proud.

Meanwhile, the Republic of Argentina, unaware of our Pre4 Trust deal, was trying to complete a five-year global bond issue. At first it had appeared that the republic would be able to borrow at a spread to the risk-free U.S. Treasury of between 2.5 and 2.75 percent. However, now that the global issue was competing with other deals, including our Pre4 Trust, demand for the republic's bonds had sagged. The spread rose to 3.5 percent. It appeared that our deal had played a role in increasing the republic's borrowing costs. As far as we were concerned, the Republic of Argentina deserved it. This was sweet revenge after the republic had snubbed us on our previous proposals.

Of course, another bank now could copy our Pre4 deal just as easily as we had copied Goldman's Pre2 deal. A few days later Banamex, the Mexican bank, having heard about the success of our Pre4 deal, expressed interest in buying another similar trade. We estimated the price of the trade and assumed they would snap it up. Instead, they called and said they had found another bank to replicate the transaction. They wouldn't tell us who it was, but we assumed Goldman, Sachs had stolen the business back.

Then my phone rang. It was a salesman I had worked with at First Boston. He had obtained a copy of our prospectus – the one without the dirty *D* word in it – and First Boston had simply copied it. The salesman was gloating. I heard someone screaming, "Ish, ish!" in the background, and suspected it was my former boss, who had a habit of yelling "ish, ish" to cover himself when one of his prevarications had gone too far, to indicate that a statement had been intended only as an approximation. The First Boston salesman laughed and told me he was "having a good year this month."

He also said there was a new manager in emerging markets at First Boston, and he wanted to interview me for a job. Apparently First Boston was impressed by the deals I was doing. Should I go full circle, back to First Boston? That was the common path on Wall Street. Several of my friends had multiplied their salaries many times by switching jobs, back and forth. Sure, why not? I agreed to meet with him.

In the first few weeks after the Pre4 Trust closed, we had a brief scare. By October 25 the computer model we had built to calculate prices began behaving strangely. It was telling us that the price of the Pre4 Trust had dropped significantly. Was that possible? The computer model was incredibly complicated, and we arranged for several different rocket scientists to try to calculate the value of the trade, but for some reason everyone was getting different answers. I wondered how the buyers could possibly understand this trade when *we* couldn't even figure out what it was worth.

When the prices of other Argentine bonds began dropping, several buyers called to see how much the Pre4 Trust was down. One of the more sophisticated emerging markets mutual fund managers apparently was uncomfortable with his purchase and decided to test us, saying he wanted to sell. That was alarming because now we weren't convinced that we were correct in assessing the value of the Pre4 Trust. To be safe, one of the derivatives traders offered to repurchase some of the bonds for $95 per $100 face amount. The traders said they couldn't lower the price too much or the buyers might discover how much money we had made on the deal. Apparently none of the buyers was aware that the bonds they had purchased for $100 really might be worth much less, when you accounted for Morgan Stanley's fees. On the other hand, as Argentina had experienced problems in recent weeks, the bonds had dropped several points, and $95 appeared to be a fair price.

On October 27, 1994, this manager sold back $8 million of the Pre4s Trust to Morgan Stanley for $95 per $100 face amount. The sale made our traders nervous, and they hoped the selling would end. Then, just as suddenly as he had sold, the same investor bought back $6 million of the bonds at $95.50. With those two trades, the derivatives trader had made a market for purchases and sales of the Pre4 Trust at around $95. What were the bonds actually worth? Even using the computer model, I no longer was sure. Why had the investor sold bonds, then immediately bought them back at a higher price? I had no idea. It may have been worth a half-point loss to them for the peace of mind that we would make a market in the bonds.

I never heard the traders relay an inaccurate price to an account, although there certainly was speculation that they had.

Fortunately, I played no role in trading the bonds, and I could avoid these delicate trading situations.

Although the traders were worried about their behavior, our computer model was generating such varying prices that just about any price the traders quoted within a large range was defensible. In any event, conversations within the derivatives group were not tape recorded, and it would be almost impossible to prove that the traders' prices had been inaccurate.

The same could not be said downtown at Bankers Trust, where unfortunately for BT traders were giving clearly inaccurate prices – and saying so in tape recorded conversations. As we finished dealing with the Pre4 Trust, the Securities and Exchange Commission was closely examining one of those taped conversations and negotiating with BT for a consent decree charging it with securities fraud in its dealings with Gibson Greetings. That taped conversation, from February 23, 1994, included the following statement by a BT managing director:

"I think that we should use this [market price movement] as an opportunity. We should just ... chip away at the differential a little more. I mean, we told him $8.2 million when the real number was 14. So now if the real number is 16, we'll tell them that it is 11. You know, just slowly chip away at that differential between what it really is and what we're telling him."

To translate this statement, the "differential" that the BT manager was discussing was the difference between the true value of a trade to Gibson (the "real number") and the value BT was representing for the trade. The differential of $5.8 million ($14 million minus $8.2 million) included BT's fee. For example, at first Gibson might think it owed only $8.2 million on the swap, when in reality Gibson owed $14 million. BT didn't want to tell Gibson about the "real" $14 million number right away because Gibson might question why it owed BT the extra $5.8 million. Instead, BT waited for a market price movement, and then it moved the two numbers closer together, thereby narrowing the differential, as the statement indicates, to $5 million (the "real" $16 million minus the $11 million BT would represent). Eventually, BT would close the gap between these two numbers, and Gibson would never realize that BT had extracted a $5.8 million fee.

That was merely one of many such conversations at BT and, I imagined, at most other investment banks. If a client couldn't figure out how much a complex derivatives trade was worth on a given day, the investment bank could misrepresent the up-front value of the trade, then revalue the trade over time until the bank had extracted a larger fee. I hoped Morgan Stanley's traders weren't doing this same thing.

As Thanksgiving approached, the markets quieted, and we spent long hours gabbing about various business issues. Bidyut Sen, immersed in one chess game, exclaimed, "I sacrificed a queen and jammed them, just what I want to do to the Argentina market." Everyone was laughing, and Sen started talking about how bad this year had been, especially compared to last year. The bad publicity about derivatives clearly had hurt our market. We discussed the big derivatives losses of the past year, and everyone hoped that the worst was over. With any luck, the next few months would be better. Sen's attention reverted to his chess game, which he won. He proclaimed, "My cup runneth over."

8

The Odd Couple

They were an admixture of old-fashioned and uncouth, a duo almost as unlikely as Neil Simon's odd couple. The seventy-year-old had been married to the same woman for forty years, in the same job for more than twenty, and in the same place – Orange County, California – forever. The fifty-four-year-old had recently divorced and remarried, switched jobs often and moved even more frequently, most recently to a million-dollar home in swanky Moraga, east of Oakland, California. Despite their obvious differences, they spoke on the phone virtually every day for many years. They first met in 1975 and had traded billions of dollars of securities with each other. The elder of the pair was the Orange Country treasurer, Robert Citron; the younger was a Merrill Lynch bond salesman, Mike Stamenson. Together they created what many officials described as the biggest financial fiasco in the United States: Orange County's $1.7 billion loss on derivatives.

Robert L. Citron fit the Republican stronghold of Orange County, which travel guides have described as "the most like the movies, the most like the stories, the most like the dream." For Citron, the 1980s and 1990s *were* like a dream. He became one of the nation's best-known municipal treasurers, and his investment strategies produced consistently high yields, approaching 9 percent during the early 1990s. Citron had a reputation as a proud but stubborn man, not unlike John Wayne, for whom Orange County's airport is named, or Richard Nixon, who was born in Orange County.

Like many of Orange County's 2.6 million residents, Citron lived in the past. He wore oversized turquoise Indian jewelry, garish neckties, polyester suits, pastel slacks, and white-patent leather shoes. He was an avid supporter of the University of Southern California, which he had attended in the 1940s. His car horn played the USC Trojan fight song, and his desk was adorned with a bronzed lump of horse manure from Traveler, USC's mascot. At treasurer's dinners Citron gathered colleagues around the piano to sing 1940s standards. He kept investment records on index cards, ledgers, and even a wall calendar. He ate lunch on the Formica tables of the Santa Ana Elks Club or Western Sizzlin'. His one nod to technology was dividing his lunch tabs to the penny on his wristwatch calculator. Citron refused to visit Wall Street and had been to New York only four times in his life. He was hard working and never took vacations, preferring to spend time with his wife in their modest ranch-style home in Santa Ana.

The secret to understanding Citron was that, as one former Merrill salesman put it, "he knows thirty percent of what he thinks he knows." For example, although Citron appeared to be a faithful USC alumnus, he had failed numerous courses there and never graduated. Citron often demonstrated his ignorance in public. In one television interview he was showing off for a reporter how he used a row of color-coded telephones, each connected to a different broker. While he was saying, "Now I'm talking to Merrill.... Now I'm talking to Solly [Salomon Brothers]," he inadvertently bought bonds he didn't want and had to call a broker to reverse the trade. Citron was known for rambling and incomprehensible oral presentations, so much so that the county's board of supervisors eventually forced him to put his thoughts in writing – although that didn't help much. An example from a September 26, 1994, report read, "We do not have the large inflationary wage increases, runaway building, both in homes, commercial, and those tall glass-office buildings... . Few, if any, tall office buildings are being built." Few, if any, Orange County employees understood Citron's concerns about tall buildings. At another point Citron seemed unable to grasp the concept of "buy low, sell high," and he flubbed by buying securities at the highest offered price.

For younger and savvier Michael Gus Stamenson, Citron was like a dream. Stamenson is short and aggressive and a skillful salesman. He is popular among county treasurers and has been the featured speaker at many gatherings. Citron quickly became Stamenson's best customer. In all, Orange County paid Merrill almost $100 million in fees, and several million went directly into Stamenson's pockets.

Stamenson's background was modest. His father was a Greek immigrant, and his mother was from Oklahoma. He grew up in a farm town called Livingston in the Central Valley, and after two years at San Joaquin Delta College in Stockton went to Cal State Fullerton, then the U.S. Marine Corps. Stamenson joined Merrill Lynch's Newport Beach office in late 1970. He later moved to San Francisco, where he became the top salesman.

Stamenson has a hot temper and a long history of altercations and conflict. He has been known to slam down phones and curse loudly. In other words, he is just like most people who work on a trading floor. One of his favorite lines, reportedly, is the eloquent "I don't give a rat's ass." Bernard Mikell, a senior vice president at Sutro & Company, a regional bond firm, has cited specific evidence of Stamenson's temper. According to Mikell, at a 1988 conference of municipal treasurers in San Mateo, he was supporting a proposal for municipal investment vehicles backed by auto loans that Merrill Lynch didn't sell. Stamenson deplored the proposal, and after debate continued for several minutes, he began shouting. When the conference finally ended, Stamenson found Mikell in a hallway, and said, "We're going to settle this right now." He then put his head down and charged, knocking Mikell across the hall and coming away with a bloody face.

In the 1980s Stamenson had been Merrill Lynch's point man selling bonds to the city of San Jose. According to a San Jose attorney, Merrill Lynch represented that certain investments the city later purchased were "absolutely safe" and that "you couldn't lose money." In 1984, after San Jose lost $60 million on those investments and fired its treasurer as part of the scandal, the city sued Merrill Lynch for fraud and professional malpractice. Merrill paid the city $750,000 to settle the lawsuit, just as it later would pay to settle a suit filed by West Virginia. In neither case was Stamenson disciplined.

Stamenson was known for his abrupt treatment of clients other than Citron. According to then San Francisco Chief Investment Officer Daniel Patrick Daly, one day Daly was having lunch at a restaurant when Stamenson burst in and urged him to dump an investment he had just made a few days earlier. Stamenson said the city could make a quick $17,000, and Daly agreed to do it. However, when Daly later discovered he had only earned $12,000, Stamenson tried to excuse the difference, saying he had "miscalculated." Daly said Merrill should make up the difference or the city would never do business with them again. Merrill never paid the extra money, and San Francisco never did business with Stamenson.

Nevertheless, Stamenson remained the top salesman in the San Francisco office, and, as a result, he was rich. A huge share of his commissions had come from Orange County. Merrill admitted it received $62.4 million from buying and selling financial products for Orange County in 1993 and 1994 alone, although the county insisted the number was much higher. Merrill also admitted Stamenson made $4.3 million during the same two years.

As Stamenson was accumulating his wealth, Robert Citron was

deteriorating badly. When interest rates began to increase in 1994, Citron began to lose money on the large bets he had made buying leveraged structured notes from Stamenson and others. Although the newspapers later would portray Orange County's bets as complex, they actually were quite simple, especially compared to the derivatives I had been selling.

This is what Citron did. He took Orange County's $7.4 billion investment pool, borrowed about $13 billion more from various securities firms, and bought short-maturity, highly-rated bonds whose returns were tied to changes in interest rates. These were the structured notes I knew all too well. Many were so-called inverse floaters, bonds that declined rapidly in value when interest rates increased. The coupon of an inverse floater typically was some high percentage rate, say 13 percent, minus a floating rate such as LIBOR. So long as LIBOR remained low, the inverse floaters were valuable. For example, if LIBOR stayed at 3 percent, the bonds would pay a 10 percent coupon (13 percent minus 3 percent). However, if LIBOR began to rise, the coupon would shrink. The more LIBOR rose, the worse the losses.

Another type of structured note, called a Trigger Note, paid a higher-than-normal coupon for just a few months, as long as interest rates were below a specified rate called the trigger rate on a specified date called the trigger date. However, if interest rates increased above the trigger rate, the Trigger Note extended in maturity to several years, leaving an investor stuck with a low coupon.

Although inverse floaters have been well publicized, Trigger Notes have not. Let me give you an example of one Trigger Note that Orange County bought. This note may seem wild, but it's actually one of the more conservative types of structured notes. (Although Citron bought most of his structured notes from Stamenson, he also bought several hundred million dollars worth from others, including plenty from Morgan Stanley. This note is one of them. Fortunately, I was not involved in the sale.)

On January 6, 1994, Morgan Stanley sold Orange County

$100 million of a structured note issued by the AAA-rated Federal Home Loan Bank of Boston, a bank whose bonds were backed implicitly by the U.S. Treasury. The bonds appeared to be very low risk.

The trigger date for the bonds was June 30, 1994, less than six months away. If three-month LIBOR was less than or equal to 4.25 percent on the trigger date, the bonds would mature. For Orange County, that meant interest rates had remained low, and Citron would then have to find some other investment, but for the first half of 1994, he would have earned an above-market coupon for several months. Not bad.

However, if three-month LIBOR was greater than 4.25 percent on the trigger date, the maturity of the bond would extend for another three years, but the coupon would remain at just 4 percent. Therefore, the risk with the bond was that if interest rates increased, even a little, the maturity would extend, and you would continue to receive a low coupon. This maturity extension was risky because it would happen just when you didn't want it to: when interest rates had increased. In other words, Citron would be stuck with a three-year bond that paid 4 percent for three years, even if interest rates increased by several percent. Depending on the amount of increase, the bond's returns could suffer, or if you sold the bond before maturity you could incur a substantial loss.

Evaluating Trigger Notes was difficult, especially given Citron's level of investment expertise. You couldn't just make a simple present-value calculation, because you didn't know what would happen to interest rates. Would you own a five-month bond with a high coupon or a three-and-a-half year bond with a low coupon? How could you tell? To calculate the value of the note, you needed a computer model to simulate different interest rate scenarios. Investment banks hired math and computer-science Ph.D.'s to design these systems. It was apparent that Citron, with his index cards and ledgers, couldn't properly value these bonds; consequently, the banks selling Citron these notes charged him big fees. Citron must have been a man of many faces, given the number of times his was cleanly ripped off. On the single Trigger Note I just described, Morgan Stanley made more than $200,000.

Throughout 1994 Orange County was warned repeatedly about the risks imbedded in the exotic structured notes it had bought. A March 1994 industry newsletter called Citron's investment strategy "a death spiral." Merrill Lynch claims it warned Citron at least eight times to reconsider his risky tactics, including one specific warning that the county would lose $270 million on certain investments each time interest rates increased 1 percent. Merrill said it began warning Citron about these risks in 1992, even offering to repurchase the derivatives it had sold to the county.

Bob Citron didn't heed any of these warnings and rebuffed his critics. When prestigious Goldman, Sachs criticized Citron's investment practices, he wrote Goldman a letter saying they didn't understand the type of investment strategies Orange County was using and suggesting that Goldman not seek business with Orange County. When asked how he knew that interest rates would not rise after 1993, Citron replied, "I am one of the largest investors in America. I know these things."

In April 1994, after interest rates had begun to rise and derivatives had begun to fall, the Securities and Exchange Commission in Los Angeles called Citron to ask him some questions about the county's investments. They held a three-hour meeting, during which Citron was extremely nervous and barely spoke. On the advice of outside attorneys, Orange County delayed the SEC's request for documents for a month. Citron was facing reelection and wanted to put off these questions until after the campaign.

The reelection campaign was stressful and much closer than anticipated. As interest rates continued to rise, Citron's opponent, John Moorlach, a Costa Mesa C.P.A., seized on the warnings about the level of risk in the county's investment portfolio, badgering Citron with questions about the county's risky investments in derivatives. In May 1994 Moorlach predicted a $1.2 billion Orange County loss (that proved to be a pretty good guess). Despite the nasty campaign, Citron was reelected in June.

However, the campaign left him drained, and he began behaving strangely. He arrived at work late and left early. He developed a pronounced nervous habit of whistling through his teeth. In a bizarre move, he began consulting psychics for investment advice and used both a psychic and an astrologer to predict changes in interest rates. His psychic adviser predicted Citron would have money worries beginning in November but that they would be over by the end of the month. That prediction would prove as wrong as Moorlach's had been right.

Citron had lost his grip on life. He fell asleep at his desk, stared absently into space, and missed appointments. A neuropsychologist found deficiencies in his ability to reason, process information, and discern relevant details. As Citron's lawyer argued prior to a presentencing hearing, Citron suffered from dementia and was a man of "limited intellectual capabilities." Orange County's attorney claimed Merrill had taken advantage of Citron and had used him as a "pigeon."

In early November 1994, assistant treasurer Matthew Raabe went to county officials to warn them of the crisis in the portfolio. The county finally hired an outside consultant to determine its level of risk. On November 8, 1994, county officials received what they term the "Angel of Death" call from the consultant, who described in graphic terms the worst-case scenario for the investment pool. By the time they absorbed this information, it was much too late. The county had lost more than a billion dollars.

I first learned of Orange County's losses when they were announced at Morgan Stanley at 3:45 P.M. on Thursday, December 1, 1994. The investing public wouldn't learn of them until 5 P.M., when Orange County held a press conference. Most of the world wouldn't learn that Orange County had lost more than a billion dollars until they read about it in the newspaper the next day.

The loss was less of a surprise at Morgan Stanley than elsewhere. My bosses obviously knew about the possibility of such a loss, and the salesmen who had sold structured notes to Orange County must have known a little bit about the county's financial circumstances, based on the bonds they had sold.

In fact, for over a month Morgan Stanley had been preparing for the impact of more derivatives losses, whether from Orange County or from other investors. The increase in interest rates had made additional losses inevitable. On October 25, 1994, when Orange County already had lost millions but still didn't know how many, the chief lawyers at Morgan Stanley called a huge derivatives compliance meeting. A half-dozen lawyers and several dozen members of the derivatives group crowded into a large conference room to hear the warnings. We had been comforted that Procter & Gamble and Gibson Greetings hadn't involved Morgan Stanley. However, we knew that there were literally hundreds of other similar situations that might.

Orange County was not the first public entity to lose a fortune on bets it had made with investment banks. Several years earlier West Virginia had lost almost $200 million and sued eight investment banks in an attempt to recover these losses. Only Morgan Stanley had refused to settle the case, and it went to trial – a rarity in disputes with investment banks.

The evidence had been damning for Morgan Stanley. It included one phone call during which a Morgan Stanley options executive had asked the state director of investments, a former secretary, if she needed to "walk through the steps" of a deal they had completed the previous week. She had responded, "Do I need help? Do bears go in the woods?" The case made both West Virginia and Morgan Stanley look terrible. The judge called the firm a bunch of blow-dried Harvard types. Of the $190 million West Virginia said it lost in 1986 and 1987, the verdict was against Morgan Stanley, for $48 million.

With that verdict as a backdrop, our compliance meeting was tense and heated. Everyone was nervous. Afterward we discussed how we were "sitting ducks" and agreed we should be very careful about what we sold – and to whom. I reiterated my view that structured notes were designed to let investors make bets that they were not permitted to make. Now, several people concurred. Many of the recent derivatives problems stemmed from structured notes, and I was grateful that I sold mostly Repackaged Asset Vehicles, not those dangerous notes. Bidyut Sen, who for months had been complaining that the derivatives group didn't sell enough structured notes, quipped, "The good news is that our market share sucks so much that we can't get into that much trouble."

The day after Orange County announced its losses, Friday, December 2, we discovered that in fact Morgan Stanley could get into a great deal of trouble. It appeared that Morgan Stanley had sold roughly $600 to $700 million of structured notes to Orange County, about 10 percent of their overall purchases. We weren't the leading culprit, but we certainly had been one of them. The notes we sold were substantially similar to those Merrill had been selling: essentially, they were bets that interest rates would not rise. It appeared that the sales had begun in 1992 and continued into 1994. Morgan Stanley had made a fortune selling these notes to Orange County. The $200,000 fee for the Trigger Note was typical. There were a few news reports about Morgan Stanley's role and chairman Dick Fisher appeared on television briefly to comment on Orange County's losses. Fortunately, the bulk of the publicity was focused on Mike Stamenson and Merrill.

But Morgan Stanley had another problem. It appeared that the firm had loaned about $1.6 billion to Orange County, and there was some risk that the firm would not be repaid. The county had borrowed about $13 billion in total from various investment banks by pledging the structured notes it had bought as collateral. These loans were called reverse repurchase agreements, or "reverse repos." The good news was that at least the derivatives group wasn't responsible for the loans. The repo desk at Morgan Stanley, not DPG, had made the loans – and the repo desk was in big trouble. They desperately needed our help now, especially to calculate the value of the collateral for the loans. There was one central question: Was there enough collateral to ensure that the firm would be repaid?

The derivatives managers quickly arranged a conference call with Orange County and numerous lawyers and consultants. Only managing directors from Morgan Stanley were on the call; I was not. When the managing directors finished this call, they began barking orders: Cancel lunch! Get me this data! Fax this! One director warned us that Orange County would be a fire drill for about a week because the officials at the county, and even their consultants, "didn't know shit."

The trading floor was in a frenzy. The fire drill included everyone in DPG, even Peter Karches, the head of fixed income, who was stopping by for updates every few minutes. Reporters began calling us, and we were instructed not to comment. Someone kept calling the Queen asking for structured note prospectuses, posing under various identities, including a student in a tax class at Harvard. Karches was busy demonstrating why he was regarded as the firm's future leader. He was in total control, by far the most logical, careful person involved in the drill. One salesman asked Karches if he should destroy any documents, and Karches calmly said no. Karches asked who had inside knowledge of the details of Orange County and assembled those people to discuss strategy. Again, fortunately, I was not involved.

On Monday, December 5, Robert Citron's face was plastered across the front business page of the *New York Times*. Bidyut Sen mocked Citron, saying, "Look at this guy's face. Can you believe it? He wears turquoise jewelry. Can you believe this guy would buy and repo structured notes?" No one could. The previous day, Orange County officials had arrived at Citron's door with a brief resignation letter, which Citron signed. According to reports, Citron was bumbling and refused to acknowledge the losses, even then. County officials were so concerned about Citron's mental state that they made sure a mental health counselor was on call for him.

Also on December 5, Orange County filed the largest municipal bankruptcy petition in history. Orange County's funds covered nearly two hundred schools, cities, and special districts. The losses amounted to almost $1,000 for every man, woman, and child in the county. The county's investments, including structured notes, had dropped 27 percent in value, and the county said it no longer could meet its obligations.

The bankruptcy filing made the ratings agencies look like fools. Just a few months before, in August 1994, Moody's Investors Service had given Orange County's debt a rating of Aa1, the highest rating of any California county. A cover memo to the rating letter stated, "Well done, Orange County." Now, on December 7, an embarrassed Moody's declared Orange County's bonds to be "junk" – and Moody's was regarded as the most sophisticated ratings agency. The other major agencies, including S&P, also had failed to anticipate the bankruptcy. Soon these agencies would face lawsuits related to their practice of rating derivatives.

On Tuesday, January 17, 1995, Robert Citron and Michael Stamenson delivered prepared statements in an all-day hearing before the California Senate Special Committee on Local Government Investments, which had subpoenaed them to testify. It was a pitiful display. Citron left his wild clothes at home, testifying in a dull gray suit and bifocals. He apologized and pleaded ignorance. He said, "In retrospect, I wish I had more education and training in complex government securities." Stuttering and subdued, appearing to be the victim, Citron tried to excuse his whole life: He didn't serve in the military because he had asthma; he didn't graduate from USC because of financial troubles; he was an inexperienced investor who had never even owned a share of stock. It was pathetic.

Stamenson also said he was sorry and cited the enormous personal pain the calamity had produced. He pretended naivete. He said Citron was a highly sophisticated investor and that he had "learned a lot" from him. Stamenson's story was as absurd as Citron's was sad. When Stamenson asserted that he had not acted as a financial adviser to the county, one Orange County Republican, Senator William A. Craven, couldn't take it anymore and called him a liar. Stamenson finally admitted that he had spoken to Citron often – Citron had claimed every day – but he refused to concede that he had been an adviser. At this point Craven exploded again, asking, "Well, what the hell *were* you talking about to this man every day? The weather?" Citron's lawyer, David W. Wiechert, was just as angry. He said, "For Merrill Lynch to distance themselves from this crisis would be akin to Exxon distancing themselves from the *Valdez*."

Stamenson's goal clearly was damage control, and he had remained safely on Merrill's payroll. Orange County was suing Merrill Lynch for $2 billion, and the firm obviously was concerned about what Stamenson might say. He was being a good company man. When one reporter found him in his office in Merrill's pink marble tower in the heart of San Francisco's financial district – fourteenth floor, 101 California Street, if anyone wants to check it out – Stamenson refused to speak and said, "You know what you can do, you can go trot yourself right out the door where you came in."

Virtually overnight, Citron went from being one of the most popular public figures in the history of Orange County to public enemy number one. Just after the bankruptcy was announced, one California taxpayer saw a photograph of Citron in a county office and threatened to return with a gun and shoot the photo down.

Citron wasn't just a pariah; he was a criminal. He was later found guilty of violating various state investment laws. The sentencing inquiry revealed that not only was Citron a college dropout, he had the math skills of a seventh grader. Psychologists put his ability to think and reason in the lowest 5 percent of the population, according to one standard test. A court psychologist told Citron's sentencing judge, "Bob Citron was like an empty bottle on the ocean being pushed along a wave."

Citron wrote a letter to the sentencing judge, begging for leniency. He said that after he resigned, he had contemplated suicide. He admitted he had bought something that, although it wasn't called a derivative, was one. Citron spoke of his wife of forty-one years, how it had been love at first sight and how they had been apart overnight only six times. He said that because of his age and physical problems, jail would be difficult to survive. Ultimately, he was sentenced to only one year, which he was permitted to serve through community service.

Back at Morgan Stanley, the firm's repo traders were still struggling to determine the firm's risks on the loans to Orange County. The repo desk hadn't been calculating daily price changes of the collateral, in part because they didn't know how to value the structured notes precisely. Instead, they had been "marking-to-market" the collateral only once a month. One trader, when warned that the value of the collateral was declining rapidly every day, said, "Oh, shit, I better look at that."

The repo desk is never the most sophisticated part of any investment bank. As a trainee at First Boston, I had spent some time on the repo desk and in a related area, short-term bond sales. Short-term bond salesmen sell very low risk, low margin, simple, short-maturity bonds. On a football team, the short-term salesman would be a third-string offensive lineman; in fact, many of the salesmen looked like, or actually had been, linemen. One guy I sat with was massive. His giant head was the size of a large computer monitor. The simplicity of his job gave him plenty of time to eat and to talk, and he was eager to do both. We discussed only two topics: professional football and McDonald's. He seemed impressed with the breadth of my knowledge of both areas, especially the American Football Conference and McDonald's menu. We discussed the menu in great detail, comparing and contrasting the various chicken items, celebrating the death of the McLean and McDLT, and expressing our shared rage at the McRib. We traded eating stories, although even my proudest accomplishment – eating four triple hamburgers from Wendy's, three pounds of meat, to win a $250 bet – paled beside the feats of his gargantuan gut and gullet. He seemed especially captivated by tales of my high-school job at McDonald's. In short, he was as close to Steinbeck's Lenny as any human being I have ever met, except that he made several hundred thousand dollars a year and had befriended me, not a mouse.

Unfortunately, Morgan Stanley's repo traders weren't much more sophisticated than Lenny, and now any mistakes could have disastrous consequences. In December 1994 Orange County officials had frozen the investment pool's assets. Any sale of collateral by Morgan Stanley or others would be highly controversial, possibly illegal. On December 8, 1994, I learned that the collateral backing Morgan Stanley's $1.6 billion repo loan to Orange County was approximately half high-quality U.S. government agency bonds and half structured notes. Morgan Stanley and other banks were coordinating the liquidation of the structured notes. If they could sell the notes in an orderly fashion, the banks might even make some money from the sales.

Normally a creditor can't sell loan collateral once the debtor has filed for bankruptcy; creditors have to go through the bankruptcy process after that point. However, Morgan Stanley and others had determined that they were entitled to sell the structured notes in spite of Orange County's bankruptcy filing because they said Chapter 9, the bankruptcy chapter for municipalities, contained an exception for repo loans. The managers decided to cut the firm's losses by selling the structured notes now rather than waiting for the bankruptcy process, even if that legal position later proved wrong.

With the blessing of Morgan Stanley's lawyers, a prearranged auction of the structured notes began at 1 P.M. The auction was held by speaker phone in conference room 2, just off the trading floor near the derivatives group. This was one of the most important auctions in the firm's history. Everyone was there, including President John Mack, fixed income chief Peter Karches who had just flown in from London, and Ken de Regt, who soon would be promoted to succeed Karches, and had flown in from Hong Kong. The derivatives traders had been calculating prices of these structured notes around the clock for two days, stopping only briefly to eat or go to the bathroom. One of them was grumbling about how the ratings agencies' employees should be thrown in jail for giving Orange County such a high rating. Rumors on the desk were that our potential losses were as high as $50 million.

The structured-note auction rattled the entire bond market. All the institutional trading markets moved down when the sales were announced. Scarecrow, never one to miss the opportunity for a laugh, announced during the auction that there was a story across the tape that Robert Citron had been seen driving around L.A. in a white Ford Bronco.

I didn't participate in the auction. Instead, I was assigned – along with several other employees – to help distribute an important package of documents to each bank participating in the sales. This job was too important for a messenger. I was assigned to deliver the documents to Goldman, Sachs. During the cab trip downtown, I held the package tightly, and although I was dying to open the carefully sealed package, I didn't.

After delivering the documents, I took a break to walk past the New York Stock Exchange building, located on Wall Street near Goldman. Years earlier, before I had joined First Boston, a friend of mine had arranged for me to walk the floor of the stock exchange. It had been a thrilling experience, with the shouting and blinking lights and ringing phones. Years ago I had thought the stock exchange was the center of the financial world. How wrong I had been. That building, indeed the entire NYSE, had become almost irrelevant to the modern practice of an investment bank. Instead, the most important activity occurred behind closed doors, in secret meetings, often outside of the United States.

When I returned, the repo desk was claiming it had lost only a very small amount of money, although it later turned out the desk had lost several hundred thousand dollars because an employee had entered some data incorrectly into the computer system. Our group had actually *made* money selling the structured notes. Everyone was relieved.

Everyone, that is, except Orange County and its lawyers. At 1:54 P.M. on December 8, Morgan Stanley and the other banks completed their sales of structured notes. At 2:36 P.M., Orange County announced it would sue every broker who had participated in the liquidation. Although the county ultimately sued Nomura Securities, one of the brokers who had participated in the auction, I never heard anything about a suit against Morgan Stanley.

Orange County was the highest-profile county in southern California to confront a financial disaster, but it wasn't the only one. In September 1994 the derivatives group learned that San Diego County had restructured a $700 million derivatives portfolio to allow them to postpone disclosing losses. Our group had submitted a similar restructuring proposal to San Diego County, but it decided to use a different investment bank. The derivatives they owned were called CERLS – Coupon Exchange Rate-Linked Securities – and were related to PERLS, except that the formula applied to the bonds' coupon, not the principal (hence the *C* in place of the *P*). At the time Morgan Stanley submitted its proposal, I had mentioned the idea that San Diego officials might be trying to extend the recognition of losses beyond the next election, and I even had called the San Diego County Elections Board to find out when the next election was. Sure enough, the restructured notes would mature, and the losses would be recognized, just after the next election. It was enough to make you a conspiracy theorist.

Other public entities from the bellwether state of California also used derivatives. Morgan Stanley sold structured notes to Sonoma County, San Diego County, San Bernadino County, and

Orange County. The $74 billion California Public Employees Retirement System, known as CALPERS, used hundreds of millions of dollars' worth of derivatives. Other states facing derivatives losses included Florida, Louisiana, Ohio, Wisconsin, and Wyoming – and of course West Virginia. Even the Cleveland public authority building the Rock and Roll Hall of Fame had purchased derivatives to hedge $38 million of floating rate bonds they had sold.

The $32 billion State of Wisconsin Investment Board was one of the most aggressive purchasers of derivatives, led by fund manager Skip Gibson, a very popular guy among Wall Street derivatives salesmen. Wisconsin had even bought PERLS. In August 1994, after one of Wisconsin's PERLS trades had gone sour, Morgan Stanley restructured the trade to extend its maturity several years and perhaps – like the San Diego County trade – to hide and postpone losses. Whatever the purpose of this deal, my group clearly had ripped Wisconsin's face off. For a relatively small $35 million trade, we had charged almost $1 million in fees. Wisconsin didn't seem to mind, however, and continued its risky investments. Even in the heat of the Orange County fire drill, Wisconsin expressed interest in buying some exotic zero-coupon yen call notes. A few months later Wisconsin officials would finally discover many of the losses from these exotic trades, and manager Skip Gibson would be out of a job.

The managers of these funds seemed willing to chance buying risky derivatives, even if it meant they might be fired. These managers were like contestants playing *Let's Make a Deal,* choosing either what was behind door number one or door number two. Behind one door was a modest, above-market return; behind the other, a financial time bomb.

Imagine you are managing one of these funds, with John and Mary Doe's pensions or investments or even tax payments to invest safely. If you make John and Mary a return of 6 percent instead of 5.5 percent, they will be very happy with you. Your bosses will be very happy with you. You will be a star. That's what happens when you choose door number one. For a fund manager an extra one-half-percent return is pure gold. A couple of extra basis points alone would put you in the upper echelon of managers. And if the investment appears to be a low-risk, highly-rated note, it was the proverbial no-brainer, even if a bank charged a huge fee. You couldn't afford *not* to buy such derivatives.

Now imagine the look on the Does' faces when they learn they have been ripped off. How will they react when they discover that instead of short-term low-risk bonds, you have purchased "Yield Enhanced Floating Rate Notes," derivatives whose interest payments vary widely based on changes in the three-month London Interbank Offered Rate, known as LIBOR? Will they be over-joyed about the extra one-half percent? Maybe. Will they be happy about their sudden exposure to the volatility of three-month LIBOR? Will they check the three-month LIBOR rate, set daily at 11:00 A.M. London time, based on an average of U.S. dollar interest rates quoted by different banks, and published by the British Bankers Association on the Telerate date service (page 3750, for anyone who's interested)? Probably not. What if you pick the wrong door?

Despite these concerns, are you, as a fund manager, willing to take these risks? Absolutely. Because most likely you *will* pick the right door, the Does will never know the difference, your bosses will think you're a genius, and you'll receive a big, fat bonus check. On the off chance you pick the wrong door and three-month LIBOR rises dramatically, your fund might collapse, the county might lose a fortune, the Does might sue. But even if you're fired, you'll be able to find a new, better job. There's plenty of demand for aggressive fund managers.

Many of the notes Orange County and others bought were even more exotic than Yield Enhanced Floating Rate Notes, and more than a few involved complex bets outside the United States. Wisconsin bet on Japanese yen, Canadian dollars, and Italian liras, to name a few. Many governmental entities bought PERLS, which could depend on just about any country's foreign exchange.

I was interested to discover that county governments, state investment boards, and municipal investment funds loved the Brits. "Sterling Inverse Floaters" – inverse floating rate bonds based on British interest rates – were especially popular during the early 1990s, and these governmental entites bought sterling deals as if they were pints of Guinness offered for ten pence each. In all of 1992 there had been about a billion dollars equivalent of new sterling issues. In 1993 there were $813 million of new issues in *one week*.

I found one trade, called a Three-Year Currency Protected Sterling Inverse Floater, especially interesting. Because this note was an "inverse floating rate" note, the payments on the note moved in the opposite direction as the interest rate referenced in a formula listed on the term sheet. Therefore, as interest rates increased, the payments on the note decreased.

However, the referenced rate for this note wasn't merely any old LIBOR rate. In this case the referenced rate was called the Two-year Constant Maturity Sterling Swap Rate. The two-year swap rate is the fixed interest rate offered on an interest rate swap if you agreed to pay a floating rate of LIBOR flat. In this case, the rates were denominated in British currency, sterling. So every six months you would determine this rate, and the coupon you received would be a fixed rate less a multiple of the two-year swap rate. Basically, by buying this note, you were betting that British interest rates would decline. Except, as with the other notes, instead of placing this bet directly, you would be betting indirectly in the most unbelievably convoluted, complex manner possible.

The beauty of this structured note was that it effectively hid the derivatives trade from public view. If you were a fund manager and you bought the sterling structured note, you wouldn't have to tell your boss or a regulatory agency, "Hey guys, look what I just bought – a Three-Year Currency Protected Sterling Inverse Floater." The packaging hid all that. The note, too, looked innocuous, this time like a three-year bond issued by the AAA-rated Federal Home Loan Mortgage Corporation, popularly known as Freddie Mac. A buyer was like an underage kid who pays the local bum to buy booze for him, then pours the booze in a Coke can so his parents won't notice. Except, in this case the local bum, an investment bank, was receiving more than a few dollars for the effort.

Freddie Mac, headquartered in swanky McLean, Virginia, was the perfect safety package. Freddie Mac is a U.S. government agency that guarantees residential mortgages and since early 1993 has issued complex derivatives, too. The agency simply uses the derivatives the investment bank creates to borrow at a slightly lower cost. The bank structures the note issuance and parcels out the risk; Freddie Mac provides the credit guarantee. So never mind that the coupon payment is 16.050 percent minus two times the Two-Year Pound Sterling Swap Rate, payable semi-annually for three years in U.S. dollars. It's Freddie Mac, for God's sake. It's AAA and implicitly backed by the U.S. Treasury. *Anyone* can buy this.

Imagine your local investment board buying this trade. Can you picture them at their monthly meeting – after they've approved the new zoning plan and heard complaints about the new neighborhood watch program – switching on their computer trading screens and waiting anxiously to check the Two-Year Offered Side Sterling Swap Rate published by the International Financing Review, on Telerate page 42279, two days before their coupon payment?

When I discovered these trades, I entered the twilight zone of investment banking, where the ranks of investors who lost money on intricate, enigmatic inverse floating rate derivatives included not only now-infamous Orange County, California, but Escambia County and St. Petersburg in Florida, Sandusky County and various municipalities in Ohio, Odessa Junior College in Texas, and even the Baptist Missionary Association of America.

Why might unsophisticated state and local governments want to bet that British two-year swap rates would decline? It's hundreds of miles from most of these buyers to the Mississippi River, thousands to the Thames. Why might the leaders of a community college, or a city council on this side of the Atlantic think British swap rates would decline?

Well, for one thing the bank's researchers said they would. And guess which derivatives trade those unbiased researchers were recommending that you should buy to take advantage of anticipated lower rates? Research suggested inflation was declining in Britain and that such a decline would lead to lower interest rates. At the same time, the sterling yield curve was very steep, which meant the "magnified" forward curve also was even higher, and steeper, predicting that rates would increase. This seemed to be a perfect opportunity to bet against the forward curve. Could you afford not to?

The researchers at an investment bank had an amazing capacity for generating predictions that contradicted those of the forward curve. And every time they did, the bank's derivatives group would create a derivatives trade supported by the research. Or maybe it was the other way around.

Adding international flavor to the U.S. derivatives losses was the fact that many issuers of the structured notes U.S. public entities bought were foreign, including such European banks as Rabobank, Nordic Investment Bank, Svenska Handelsbanken, Deutsche Bank, and Abbey National. The derivatives problems of public entities extended well beyond U.S. borders. A British court had recently ruled that the London borough of Hammersmith and Fulham, which had lost a huge amount of money on various swaps, was entitled to void those swaps. The rationale was that the borough didn't need to repay because as a public entity, it hadn't been entitled to enter into such derivatives trades. They were therefore null and void. The ruling prompted hundreds of lawsuits in British courts, most of which were settled. Litigants in the U.S. have closely watched these British cases, especially now as the numerous Orange County lawsuits progress.

The involvement of European issuers seemed fitting. The first active derivatives markets had opened in Europe in 1688, when traders on the Amsterdam Stock Exchange began writing derivatives contracts. Now, after years of increasing derivatives business in the U.S., much of the business was shifting abroad. Derivatives were returning home.

The globalization of the financial markets was unavoidable and not limited to derivatives. Even Morgan Stanley had recently discussed merging with a European bank to take advantage of the shift in business toward London and Europe. One proposed merger, with S. G. Warburg, collapsed in part because of debate about what the successor firm's name would be. Scarecrow suggested that the new bank be called Mor-War; its new slogan could be "Look British, think Yiddish." That was just a joke. Any real global expansion by Morgan Stanley couldn't jeopardize its hallowed name.

9

The Tequila
Effect

Even with its aggressive new global approach, Morgan Stanley always planned for the worst. The firm's senior officers prepared for every major financial catastrophe. What if the stock market crashed? What if several large institutions went bust? What if Mexico ... ? The specific mechanism the firm used to protect itself from financial calamity was well known in the investment community and had been publicized in an article in *Institutional Investor* magazine several years before. It was called the blue book.

Of course, Morgan Stanley didn't use just any blue book. Unlike the blue-covered notebooks you may have filled with answers to essay examinations in school, these blue books were filled with detailed descriptions of the consequences for the firm of various worst-case scenarios in the financial markets. Morgan Stanley held periodic meetings in which a brain trust of industry veterans met to review staff reports in these blue books about the consequences of different risk positions. The officers didn't necessarily like the meetings. They grumbled about constantly writing these stupid blue books and compared them to term papers. However, everyone agreed that the benefits of such a meticulous approach outweighed the costs. The firm typically didn't make big mistakes. In the six years after going public, Morgan Stanley, by averting major disasters, had achieved the highest return on equity of any public U.S. securities firm, an average of 25 percent. The blue books were evidence that despite the firm's move into progressively riskier businesses, at least some of Morgan Stanley's old, white-shoe conservative demeanor remained. And it worked.

As we approached the end of 1994, the party was continuing in Mexico, but the blue-book scenario was ominous. One of the firm's emerging markets traders was taking up to $2 million of risk per basis point change in interest rates, a huge exposure, and we were continuing to sell "creative" derivatives trades related to Mexico. There were signs that some managers at Morgan Stanley were beginning to worry that Mexico might overheat. Many experts believed a meltdown in one Latin American country would spread to all of the others. We called this potential for spreading losses the "tequila effect," after the domino effect of decades earlier. My bosses believed such a theory might hold but doubted any such losses were imminent.

I was confident that my markets would keep emerging and decided to take a much-needed vacation. I returned on December 1st, just in time for the inauguration of Ernesto Zedillo, Mexico's new president. Zedillo hadn't been the front-runner; the front-runner had been shot and killed during the campaign. Yet even the assassination of the leading presidential candidate had not shaken confidence in Mexico's markets. Zedillo had replaced him and won the election easily. After the assassination Morgan Stanley had circulated a terse memorandum, which declared, "The assassination in Mexico had a negative impact on the market, as was expected." The markets quickly recovered. Bidyut Sen quipped, "Everytime I want to do a deal in Mexico, someone gets shot." That wasn't far from the truth. Nevertheless, the mood in Mexico was upbeat.

DPG suffered some anxiety in early December, when one

buyer of the Argentina Pre4 Trust said it wanted to buy some more. Two months earlier we had told the same buyer that the price was around $95. Since then the price of the bonds had declined. While we were trying to calculate the new value of the bonds, one derivatives trader stopped by for an update. The trader was nervous about whether we were offering to buy the bonds at a fair price. He was still concerned that if we lowered the price too much, the investors might realize how much money Morgan Stanley had made on the trade. The trader worriedly questioned me, "How are we doing on Orange County?"

I stopped working and stared at him. "Orange County?" I asked. "What are you talking about?"

He laughed and quickly corrected himself. "Some Freudian slip, huh. I mean, how are we doing on Pre4s?"

I told him, and we joked about how lucky the firm had been to avoid any disasters this year. Another manager joined us, complaining about how the firm's lawyers were holding him back from doing deals that might be regarded as illegal. He joked about the prospect of jail and imagined what his daughter would say when she saw him wearing prison stripes: "Mommy, look at daddy's new outfit. Does he have a new job?" Such prospects seemed remote.

Despite the Orange County disaster, throughout early December the mood in the derivatives group was festive. We felt the typical year-end combination of tension and joviality. We discussed our upcoming bonuses, speculated about colleagues' personal lives, traded gossip about bosses, and did very little business. The Christmas party was coming up, and it was an appropriate time for reflection. On the afternoon of the party, the markets were slow, and several salesmen gathered to reminisce. We talked about the questionable legitimacy of some of the group's derivatives sales, and one guy said, "You have to be a criminal to be good at this business." Nearly everyone agreed. Many of the salesmen were considering leaving DPG. One was considering returning to India to join his family's business. Several others were entertaining offers from other firms. A few were considering moves to other divisions within Morgan Stanley. No one was that excited about continuing to sell derivatives. Scarecrow, always full of good ideas, suggested we should rename DPG the Deviant Products Group, to attract some attention.

We joked about the firm's other less-profitable divisions and the firm's worst salesmen. Inept salesmen suffer through extreme pressure at the end of the year. A story at Morgan Stanley about one highly-strung sales manager perfectly captures the mood at year-end when a salesman has failed to perform his job.

As the story goes, the manager was trying to explain a relatively simple deal to one of the salesmen, but the guy just didn't get it. The salesman wasn't very bright, and he hadn't sold many bonds that year. The manager got angrier and angrier. He tried one last time to explain the deal, but it was no use. Finally the manager asked the central question.

"Why can't you do this job?"

No response.

"Listen, how stupid are you? This is an easy job. Anyone can do it. You call your accounts, and you sell them bonds. They like bonds. Why can't you just do that?"

Again, no answer. At this point, the manager completely blew his stack.

"Goddammit, anyone can do this job! A twelve-year-old could do this job! In fact, a fucking *dog* could do this job!" As the manager stared at the salesman, he suddenly got a brilliant idea. He yelled, "Somebody get me a dog! *Get me a dog!*"

No one moved. The manager continued to scream.

"I mean it! Get rid of this salesman! I want a dog to replace him! Somebody get me a dog! I want a dog! Right now! Get me a fucking dog!" A crowd gathered as the sales manager continued to yell.

A few sales assistants scurried away to see if, on such short notice, they could find a dog in midtown Manhattan. The salesman sat silently, humiliated, as his boss, not exactly full of the holiday spirit, continued to shout, *"Get me a fucking dog!"*

This story since has filtered throughout Wall Street, and it's not uncommon to hear a senior salesman or trader express disappointment with a more junior employee by asking someone to replace the employee with a dog.

I didn't think dogs could replace any of us.

I continued joking with the salesmen as we left the trading floor and walked across town to trendy Maxim's, on Madison Avenue, the site of this year's holiday party.

It was a sumptuous scene. Two red-carpeted staircases wound up to an enormous mirrored bar. The huge dining hall nearby was filled with elegant tables. The drinks were flowing. I stood at the bar and had a few scotches with Scarecrow until I spotted Peter Karches, the head of the trading floor and probably the man next in line to lead Morgan Stanley if John Mack ever retires. I had spoken to Karches briefly at work but only a few times. I was a little tipsy, so I decided to approach him. I said hello, shook his hand, and told him I was in the derivatives group. He said he recognized me, and we discussed some of the higher-profile derivatives trades of the year. He talked about how difficult it would be to make money in derivatives the following year. When I asked him not to fire me, he laughed. We joked about the negative publicity surrounding derivatives, Orange County, and Bankers Trust. We seemed to be old friends. I wished I could work for him instead of the Queen or Scarecrow.

The party was fine and nonviolent, a rarity for investment banking gatherings. One of my past colleagues had been thrown out of a firm gathering, and later asked to resign, after getting into a fist fight with the head government bond trader. I had witnessed plenty of salesmen in drunken brawls, including one whose head was smashed with a broken beer bottle. This party was tame by comparison. There were slide shows and skits and dancing and plenty of alcohol. But no fighting.

Back at work, the tension level increased a little when it appeared for several hours one afternoon that Banco Serfin, the Mexican bank with the nuclear-waste logo, had failed to repay $65 million it owed Morgan Stanley on a foreign-exchange transaction. Fortunately it turned out to be a false alarm. There had been a delay in the Fed Wire service, and the money hit the derivatives group's account later in the day.

Although this near miss didn't hurt the group financially, it caused some concern about Mexico, Mexican banks, and especially about MEXUS, the PLUS Notes deal I had worked on in June. MEXUS was only a six month deal, and it would mature soon, on Tuesday, December 20. Banco Serfin owned the junior note from MEXUS, and the value of that note depended in large part on the closing price of the peso the previous Friday. There had been some bad news related to a rebel uprising in Chiapas, and the Mexican markets were a little jittery, but fortunately the peso closed on Friday well within the "peso band" that the Mexican Central Bank used to try to manage the currency. The MEXUS deal looked as if it would pay off without a problem.

Still, we were concerned about Mexico. The Central Bank's foreign reserves were diminishing rapidly, and Mexico's trade deficit was up to around $17 billion. The Mexican peso, by far the biggest risk for Mexican bond buyers, was under significant downward pressure. In addition to MEXUS, another PLUS Notes deal was due to mature on January 15. Many large investors, including Morgan Stanley, were pulling out of the country. In recent weeks, U.S. dollars had been flying out of Mexico, sometimes literally in suitcases. The next few weeks promised to be tense.

There were other potential problems. Although PLUS Notes had been too risky for some investors and nearly perfect for investment managers, they weren't nearly risky enough for the Mexican banks. They craved risk, and PLUS Notes had merely whetted their appetites. From their perspective, PLUS Notes were really sales, not purchases. By 1994 the Mexican banks

F. I. A. S. C. O.

were hungry to buy, not to sell, and they wanted to buy something with much more upside than PLUS Notes. They wanted to gamble. They wanted, they demanded, "leverage" – the ability to borrow to take on greater risk. As the charismatic Gerardo Vargas from Banamex was fond of proclaiming in inflected English as he cast off his dark sunglasses, "I *love* leverage."

We had decided to gratify the Mexican banks with a hearty meal of hugely leveraged derivatives called Total Return Swaps. I had done one of these Total Return Swap trades with my former boss at First Boston, just before I quit, and Morgan Stanley had done many more of them thoughout 1994. Total Return Swaps are just like buying securities on margin except that you can borrow more than 50 percent of the total investment.

The first time I learned about Total Return Swaps, I was at a bar with a derivatives trader, trying to convince him to explain something called an Equity Swap. I had heard that numerous wealthy individuals were using Equity Swaps to avoid payment of taxes. It turns out that an Equity Swap is one type of Total Return Swap, although I didn't know that at the time.

I knew a "swap" was simply an agreement to exchange payments during some period of time. I thought there were many good reasons for entering into swaps. For example, the most basic type of swap, an interest rate swap, might have prevented the Savings and Loan crisis: suppose it's sometime during the 1980s and an S&L has loaned money at a fixed rate of interest to people who are buying houses. Because these borrowers are paying a fixed rate of interest to the S&L, the S&L has fixed-rate assets. However, the S&L must pay its depositors a rate that "floats" – changes – on a daily basis. Because the S&L pays a floating rate to its depositors, it has floating rate liabilities. When an S&L has fixed-rate assets and floating-rate liabilities, it has a problem. If short-term interest rates increase, its floating-rate liabilities will increase, but its fixed-rate assets won't. In such a predicament the S&L, like many S&Ls in the 1980s, might go broke.

190

One solution to this quandary is the interest rate swap. The S&L finds an investment bank, and the parties agree to a "notional amount" (say, $10 million) and a maturity (say, five years). Then the S&L pays the investment bank a fixed interest rate (that is, a fixed percentage of the notional amount), until maturity, and the investment bank pays the S&L a floating interest rate. Now the S&L has matched the rates on its assets and its liabilities. When the S&L receives fixed-rate payments from its borrowers, it pays fixed-rate swap payments to the investment bank; when it receives floating-rate swap payments from the investment bank, it pays its floating-rate deposits. I thought this sounded like a pretty good reason for using swaps. It certainly would have been a good reason for S&Ls to use swaps in the 1980s.

However, as I discovered, swaps are the Dr. Jekyll and Mr. Hyde of the financial markets and can be used for some not-so-good reasons, too. Equity Swaps are based on the same concepts as interest rate swaps, but they're used for vastly different purposes. An Equity Swap is a contract, usually between an individual and a bank, where the individual agrees to pay the return over time on some stock to the bank, and the bank agrees to pay the individual cash, often up front. An Equity Swap is not a security, and until recently Equity Swaps were entirely unregulated and didn't need to be reported to anyone, including the Internal Revenue Service.

For example, a wealthy individual – call him Mr. Bar – who wanted to avoid a requirement that he not sell a stock could *effectively* sell the stock by entering into an Equity Swap. The investment bank would pay Mr. Bar cash, and over time he would pay the bank the total return – dividends plus price appreciation – on the stock. Mr. Bar would get cash, just as if he had sold the stock, even though technically he hadn't sold it.

Anyone who wanted to sell an appreciated stock without recognizing a capital gain, and paying capital gains tax, could use an Equity Swap. An Equity Swap was not deemed a sale because the individual still owned the underlying stock. Consequently, an individual could liquidate the gain on a stock *without paying any tax*. There no longer was any need for wealthy shareholders to lobby politicians to repeal the capital gains tax; for a fee, investment banks offered a top-secret individualized do-it-yourself capital gains tax repeal. In recent years the capital gains taxes collected from wealthy individuals in the U.S. have been close to zero, in large part because of Equity Swaps.

As for the investment bank, it faces *no* market risk from the Equity Swap because it can hedge its exposure to the stock payments from the investor by "selling short" – that is, selling stock it doesn't own. If the price of the stock declines, the bank will receive a lower payment from the investor, but it will owe a correspondingly lower payment on its short sale. For investment banks, the Equity Swap is a virtually risk-free cash cow.

More than one of these Equity Swaps has since been publicized, and regulators have struggled to figure out how to stop them. For example, on March 29, 1994, A. Lorne Weil, the well-known chairman and chief executive of the Autotote Corporation, a provider of lottery and gambling equipment, completed a highly publicized Equity Swap with Bankers Trust. Weil effectively sold his Autotote shares without paying capital gains taxes and without giving up his corporate voting power. BT agreed to pay Weil $13.4 million for 500,000 Autotote shares plus floating interest on the $13.4 million. Weil, in turn, agreed to pay BT all quarterly dividends from the shares. After five years, Weil would receive additional payments if the stock price decreased and make additional payments if the stock price increased. Economically, Weil no longer had a real position in the stock, even though technically he still owned it.

I remember seeing the article about this trade. I couldn't believe the trades were so common. These Equity Swaps were a pure, unadulterated tax scam. I asked one salesman if the banks made a lot of money offering Equity Swaps. He groaned, rolled his eyes, mumbled, "Jesus Christ, are you kidding me? *Points!*" A "point" was 1 percent of the transaction's "notional amount," which typically was set as the current value of the stock. "*Points!*" meant that banks were making a fortune in fees. For example, suppose Mr. Bar owned $100 million of stock and would owe $10 million in taxes if he sold it. For a $100 million Equity Swap, an investment bank could make more than $1 million in fees, risk-free and for very little work. Mr. Bar would still save several million dollars in taxes, the derivatives salesman would earn a huge commission, and everyone would be happy. Everyone, that is, except the United States Treasury Department. Oh, yes, and the taxpayers.

Equity Swaps were one reason why U.S. corporations paid essentially zero capital gains taxes. They had been around for a few years, and it didn't take long for Wall Street to take the idea of the Equity Swap and expand it to other markets, including Mexico. One of Morgan Stanley's more popular versions of this swap was the Total Return Swap I mentioned earlier. This is how it works.

Suppose a Mexican bank wants to do a Total Return Swap with DPG. The Mexican bank and DPG simply sign a contract providing that (1) the Mexican bank will pay interest to DPG and (2) DPG will pay the "total return" on some preselected securities to the Mexican bank. For most Mexican banks, the preselected securities were Mexican bonds, usually short-term peso-denominated Mexican government bonds called Cetes. We often referred to such contracts as Cetes Swaps or, even more commonly, Peso Swaps. For example, a Mexican bank might agree to pay DPG interest of 8 percent on $100 million for six months, in exchange for DPG's agreement to pay the bank the return on $100 million of Cetes for six months. If the peso didn't depreciate against the U.S. dollar, the Cetes might return 16 percent. Those terms were typical of a Peso Swap. From the Mexican banks' perspective, the Peso Swap was a leveraged investment in Mexico. The bank was borrowing money from Morgan Stanley and receiving the return on a Mexican bond.

Why were the Mexican banks so keen to buy Peso Swaps? For one thing, they were optimistic about Mexico. They wanted to place huge bets on relatively high local interest rates because they believed that the Mexican peso would remain strong and Mexican bonds would perform well. If the Cetes paid in full at maturity, and the peso didn't depreciate, the Mexican banks would receive a return on the Cetes of, say, 16 percent but would have to pay Morgan Stanley only their borrowing rate – say, 8 percent. If the 16 percent in pesos hadn't depreciated, relative to the 8 percent in U.S. dollars, the banks would make a spread of 8 percent. Given the large amount of Peso Swaps, this 8 percent spread amounted to a fortune.

More importantly, Peso Swaps allowed Mexican banks to increase the size of such bets without any negative consequences or publicity. Ideally, the banks wanted to borrow as much as they could and buy as many Mexican bonds as they could. Peso Swaps were basically the same as borrowing U.S. dollars and buying Mexican bonds, but the banks faced credit limits and regulatory constraints in Mexico if they borrowed directly.

When a bank borrowed money and bought a bond, those positions appeared on the bank's balance sheet, which had a cost. The borrowing was a liability, and the bond was an asset. International banking regulations require that banks maintain certain minimum capital levels based on their balance sheet assets and liabilities. If those assets and liabilities increase, the bank needs more capital to guard against a loss. These regulations were designed to prevent bank failures by ensuring that banks always have sufficient capital to cover any losses, especially in the event of a market collapse.

By 1994, based on Mexican banking regulations, the banks' balance sheets were "full." They had binged on leveraged Mexican peso bets, and the high capital requirements and strict banking regulations were preventing them from borrowing or buying any more. Peso Swaps let Mexican banks increase their bets while avoiding these costs and regulations. Banks loved swaps because, unlike loans or other forms of borrowing, swaps would not appear on the banks' balance sheets, and therefore were not subject to capital requirements or other regulation. In other words, from a balance sheet perspective, Peso Swaps were free.

Mexico wasn't the only country that had liberal, favorable, rules for swaps. The International Swaps Dealers Association, which represents 150 swaps dealers worldwide, had been lobbying to exempt swaps from regulation for several years, saying, "It is worth emphasizing that swap activity has not been marked by fraud or other illegal conduct or coercive practices." In October 1992 Congress gave the power to exempt swaps from regulation to the Commodity Futures Trading Commission, the CFTC. Swaps dealers lobbied hard during the Bush administration for the CFTC to exercise this power, and finally, just before Bill Clinton was sworn in as President in January 1993, the CFTC, led by Chairwoman Wendy Gramm – Republican Presidential candidate Phil Gramm's wife – approved the exemption. This approval was declared a "farewell gift" from Republicans to swaps traders.

Peso Swaps were a clandestine way for Mexican banks to borrow money in U.S. dollars and buy Mexican government bonds. The Mexican banking regulators would likely have caught any banks that tried actually borrowing and buying more bonds. That practice was transparent. In contrast, there was little risk that Mexican authorities would discover a privately negotiated contract that the bank wasn't required to disclose.

The Mexican bank fiesta had no bounds, and the profitable peso party in Mexico quickly became obscene – and as long as the currency didn't collapse, the Mexican regulators would never know. However, by secretly consuming such huge amounts of Peso Swaps, Mexican banks were acquiring a serious fiscal eating disorder. They should have been following a healthy diet, given the post-NAFTA economic changes in their country. Instead, they had gorged themselves on PLUS Notes and now were devouring Peso Swaps. When a bank eats that much and doesn't appear to gain any weight, something is wrong.

Morgan Stanley had a much healthier approach to these trades. In a Peso Swap, we took the opposite side of the Mexican banks' bets. Our side of the bet was just as complex and risky as the Mexican banks' side. We agreed to receive U.S. dollars and pay Mexican pesos, each at a specified rate. If we did nothing to hedge our position, we would make money if any of three things happened: U.S. interest rates decreased, Mexican interest rates increased, or the Mexican peso depreciated versus the U.S. dollar.

However, Morgan Stanley had no interest in such exposure, being "long" dollars and "short" pesos (you're "long" something you buy; "short" something you sell), and so the firm wanted to hedge some of these risks by passing them on to another investor. We didn't want our profits to depend on fluctuations in various U.S. and Mexican rates. We just wanted to collect our fee.

We eliminated much of the risk by hedging, simply buying and holding Cetes, the same Mexican government bonds that were the benchmark for the Peso Swap payments. Once we bought Cetes, we were covered, regardless of what happened to the various rates. If the Cetes increased in value, our payments to the Mexican bank on the Peso Swap would increase by precisely the same amount, and vice versa. And while the Mexican bank was paying us a high U.S. dollar interest rate, with a typical "spread" over U.S. Treasury rates of about 200 basis points, or 2 percent, we could borrow at a much lower spread, around 25 basis points. By purchasing the Cetes, we became an intermediary, earning the difference in borrowing spreads. That difference could mean enormous fees, depending on the amount of Peso Swaps we did.

Unfortunately, owning Cetes posed additional problems. Although Morgan Stanley's borrowing costs were cheaper than a Mexican bank's, the firm didn't like to use its borrowing capacity for such activities. Morgan Stanley's balance sheet was too precious to hold Cetes, even for a few months. Fortunately, we were able to "lay off" our Cetes position by lending the bonds to another bank whose balance sheet was relatively less precious, until the maturity of the Peso Swap. This trade, which became quite common, was referred to as "renting the balance sheet" of another bank. The other bank, commonly Wells Fargo, would "buy" the Mexican bonds from us, we would agree to "repurchase" them in a few months, and we would pay Wells Fargo a fee for using its balance sheet during this period. Even with the fee we paid to lay off the Cetes, there still was plenty of juice in the Peso Swaps, and investment banks commonly made 1 percent fees on such deals. On a billion dollars' worth of Peso Swaps, a 1 percent fee for a year was $10 million.

The Cetes posed yet another problem for Morgan Stanley: What if Mexico defaulted on its debt? In the event of default, we were screwed. (In my bosses' words, we were completely fucked.) Why? Although we wouldn't have to pay the Mexican banks anything because our obligations on the Peso Swap would be extinguished if Mexico defaulted, we wouldn't receive anything from the Mexican banks, either – and we still would owe the money we had borrowed to buy Cetes to hedge our risks on the Peso Swaps. How large was our obligation? As large as our Peso Swaps. However, most emerging markets salesmen assumed that neither Mexico nor the Mexican banks would default.

The Mexican banks said they were prepared to "swap 'til they dropped," and they did not disappoint. DPG ultimately sold dozens of Peso Swaps, more than a *billion* dollars' worth. I built a computer model to track the risks of the various swaps and the firm's exposure to different Mexican banks. I was stunned by the amount of risk the firm was taking. Basically, Morgan Stanley had decided to lend more than $1 billion to Mexican banks, almost overnight. That amount was roughly equivalent to a major commercial bank's exposure to Mexico prior to the Latin American debt crisis of the 1980s. Yet few people, even at Morgan Stanley, were aware of the size of these risks.

Morgan Stanley had loaned tens of millions of dollars to a single bank, Banco Serfin (the nuclear-waste logo bank), one of the riskiest banks in Mexico. Our exposure on the Serfin swaps alone should have raised some eyebrows among Morgan Stanley's management. The blue-book scenario was frightening. If Mexico defaulted and we remained obligated on our full Peso Swap positions, the firm would be ruined.

Derivatives had allowed these changes to be both sudden and secret. In the span of a few weeks, Morgan Stanley had loaned more to Mexican banks than many commercial banks had loaned in years. This was the "hot money" politicians and regulators often warned of. Such funds flowed very quickly into a country – but they could flow out just as quickly. If Morgan Stanley sensed any impending crisis in Mexico, it would withdraw the money in a flash. These transactions would be almost impossible to track. Whereas commercial bank loans had been subject to both Mexican and U.S. regulation, Peso Swaps were subject to neither. Again, the Mexican banks weren't required to record any of these transactions on their books because Peso Swaps were classified as "off-balance sheet." Morgan Stanley didn't disclose the swaps because they weren't securities and were exempt from certain U.S. regulations, thanks to the Republicans' last-minute gift from January 1993. With derivatives, financial institutions could completely reconfigure their investment positions, with speed and little effort. In a very short period, the fundamentals of the Mexican financial system had totally changed.

I was very worried about the implications of these changes. My computer spreadsheet described the risks associated with changes in certain variables in Mexico, and the analysis didn't look promising. Mexico's foreign currency reserves continued to diminish, and the Central Bank was struggling to maintain the value of the peso. To keep the peso from falling, Mexico had to spend the precious U.S. dollars it had accumulated to purchase pesos. Supporting the peso was becoming an expensive proposition.

If disaster struck, it would strike with lightning speed. In such an emergency, the Mexican banks would not have the support of any established regulatory structure. Either the banks or the Mexican government itself might default. What faith did I have in the Mexican bankruptcy courts? None.

Many of our derivatives deals, including PLUS Notes, were tied to the value of the peso, and if the peso collapsed, our investors would lose a fortune. They would likely sue us. At this point, any adverse publicity about derivatives could be deadly. However, when I expressed these concerns to my colleagues, I found I was in a distinct minority.

As I saw it, the problem stemmed from the fact that the Mexican peso was what is called a managed currency. The Central Bank of Mexico established a band of prices within which the peso could trade. This band set the lowest and highest possible price at which investors could buy and sell pesos. If you wanted to buy or sell pesos, and no one in the market would sell them at a reasonable price, you always could fall back on the Central Bank's published prices.

The "top" of the Central Bank's band acted as a cap on the price of the peso. The peso wouldn't rise above the top of the band in part because the Central Bank had committed to sell pesos and buy dollars at that top price. However, the top of the band typically was irrelevant because most of the pressure on the peso was downward. There were always plenty of people willing to sell pesos and buy dollars. The thinner part of the market was people willing to sell dollars and buy pesos. Especially in late 1994, investors in Mexico were more likely to be "pulling out," by exchanging their pesos for dollars rather than vice versa.

Conversely, the "bottom" of the band acted as a floor for the price of the peso because the Central Bank had committed to buy pesos and sell dollars at that bottom price. Or at least that was what everyone seemed to believe. When there was significant downward pressure on the peso, the Central Bank would satisfy sellers of pesos by using its foreign exchange reserves to buy pesos and sell dollars. Participants in the Mexican markets seemed to think the bottom of the band was sacred and that the Central Bank would protect the peso, regardless of the cost.

In recent years the Central Bank had kept the top of the band firm but permitted the bottom of the band to inch downward every day, to allow the peso to devalue slowly. A slight devaluation should have been expected in Mexico – indeed, it was necessary – because Mexican interest rates were higher than U.S. interest rates. Generally, between two countries, the country with the higher interest rate could expect its currency to decline in value. In the long run, this basic rule of economics almost always proved right.

But Mexico didn't seem to know about the long run yet. The expected decline in the peso had not occurred. Instead, the peso had remained near the top of the band for a long time. This stability had led to the Mexican banks' aggressive betting. If the peso remained near the top of the band, the Mexican banks could collect easy profits by continuing to borrow in U.S. dollars and buy Mexican peso bonds. Of course, such a strategy would only work in the short run. The peso couldn't remain at the top of the band forever. At some point in the long run the basic rules of economics would cause the peso to decline.

The question was, in the long run would these banks be dead or alive? Despite my painful experience believing in the long run, I still argued that we should take heed of these fundamental economic rules. Eventually, I insisted, economic theory would win out, and the peso would collapse. I was so convinced of my position that after a heated argument about the peso with one colleague, I bet him $10 that the peso would crash through the band within one year. On the trading floor a $100 bet, or even a $10,000 bet, was meaningless. Bets of that size were merely about money. However, when you bet $10, it meant something. My $10 bet against the peso wasn't just about money; it was about pride.

Meanwhile, in December 1994 Morgan Stanley and the Mexican banks were continuing to tally their profits. The peso was well within the band. But one problem remained for Morgan Stanley: What if Mexico, instead of defaulting on its peso debts, decided to repay its bonds in pesos and prevented bondholders from converting them into U.S. dollars? As I mentioned before, it was much easier for Mexico to print pesos than to generate U.S. dollars.

We referred to the risk of being stuck with pesos as "convertibility risk." The risk was real. The Mexican government had suspended convertibility of its currency before, by prohibiting foreign exchange transactions. If it did so now, Morgan Stanley would end up owning a hell of a lot of Mexican pesos instead of U.S. dollars. How could we get rid of this risk?

Our method of transferring convertibility risk to other parties was both creative and comic. We simply created a new bond that looked normal in every way except that if Mexico suspended convertibility of the peso, the bond would pay in Mexican pesos, not U.S. dollars. Such a bond, if we could sell it, would effectively transfer all of our convertibility risk to the owner of the bond.

Who would buy such a bond? You might think it would have to be someone who wouldn't mind owning a lot of pesos. We considered such possibilities. A sophisticated hedge fund? A Mexican company? An emerging markets mutual fund? No, none of these. Think of the least sophisticated, sleepiest investor you can. That's right. Morgan Stanley sold its Mexican peso convertibility risk to a small midwestern insurance company.

The derivatives group needed to recruit one of the firm's most aggressive salesmen to sell these bonds. For reasons I never have understood, many of the most aggressive salesmen worked in the San Francisco offices of investment banks, even though their clients weren't necessarily in San Francisco. Mike Stamenson of Orange County fame was a typical San Francisco employee. Perhaps if you had to be at work every day at 4 A.M., you naturally became aggressive. Whatever the reasons, this Morgan Stanley salesman was the right choice. He immediately called one of his clients, a small midwestern insurance company. You can imagine the sales pitch. It went something like this:

"Hey, guys, how are things in D_? Not bad? Well, I've got a

one-year bond for you here. It's issued by a highly rated bank – take your pick, Republic Bank of New York or Deutsche Bank. It pays an extra fifty basis points, half a percent, more than the London interbank rate. That's fifty, count 'em fifty, basis points, all basically for free. It's a no-brainer. What's the catch? There is no catch. Oh, by the way, if the government of Mexico restricts foreign currency transactions, you might end up with Mexican pesos instead of U.S. dollars. What do you think?"

"Did you say something about Mexico?"

"Yeah, Mexico. What do you think?"

"Was that Mexican pesos?"

"Yeah. How many bonds do you want?"

"Well, if I'm getting an extra fifty basis points, I guess I'll take $40 million, to start."

And so the small midwestern insurance company bought Morgan Stanley's new high-tech peso convertibility notes.

Try to imagine the potential consequences of this purchase: A poor midwestern grandmother, suddenly widowed, notifies her late husband's insurance company of his death. She receives some good news and some bad news. The good news is that she will receive the insurance proceeds very soon. The bad news is that she will have to retire to Acapulco to be able to spend the money. I couldn't conceive of a less appropriate pairing of investor and investment. These bonds would mature in one year. The insurance company could only pray that I lost my bet, and Mexico made it to 1995 without a disaster. Once again, derivatives had allowed a bet to be placed and then hidden. The insurance company appeared to be buying a simple, highly rated bank note. The potential for repayment in Mexican pesos was mentioned only in the fine print. And absent a financial catastrophe, these risks would be hidden forever from the policyholders.

It seemed as if these investors in Mexico were being set up for a big fall. There certainly were warning signs. Mexico's foreign currency reserves were tumbling. The Central Bank of Mexico had to expend its precious foreign currency reserves to keep the peso trading at current levels when foreign investors began withdrawing pesos in significant quantities. At the same time, political tensions within the country were increasing. There were rumors of violent uprisings on an almost daily basis.

Amazingly, despite these warnings, Morgan Stanley still was bullish on Mexico, at least publicly. The firm's Mexico analyst, Chip Brown, continued to say good things. Barton Biggs, the emerging markets guru at Morgan Stanley Asset Management, had been issuing positive reports about emerging markets. The most optimistic voice at Morgan Stanley was Robert J. Pelosky Jr., another research analyst, who wrote in a December report about how a recent wilderness vacation had convinced him that Mexico was "compelling" and "his favorite market." Pelosky predicted that the peso would remain within its current trading band.

I wasn't sure whether these comments were insincere or just naive. Surely *someone* at Morgan Stanley was guarding against a Mexican meltdown. The esteemed Professor Rudi Dornbusch of the Massachusetts Institute of Technology accused many of these analysts of talking about how attractive Mexico was while their firms "used the back door." I knew some people at Morgan Stanley were ignoring the firm's Mexico analysts and lightening their exposure to Mexico instead. Regardless of whether the analysts' comments were well intentioned or not, they soon would be eating their words.

On Tuesday, December 20, 1994, the Mexican peso crashed. The Central Bank of Mexico stunned the financial world by approving an immediate 12.7 percent devaluation in the peso. Without the Central Bank's support, the peso plunged through its trading band, dropping from 3.46 pesos to the dollar to 3.92 pesos to the dollar in two minutes. The Mexican stock market collapsed along with the currency, and Mexican interest rates spiked upward. After the peso fell, it fell some more, and then some more – about 40 percent in a few days.

We called our clients at the various Mexican banks, but many of them couldn't even speak. One was sobbing uncontrollably. The peso's drop had pushed the fattened Mexican banks over the edge, and they now fell to pieces like Humpty Dumpty. Anyone who still thought of the banks as piñatas waiting to be broken was disappointed to find nothing inside. Accounting for the currency decline, the Mexican banks' balance sheets were empty. That meant Morgan Stanley might be crying, too, if any of the banks defaulted. Although the derivatives group had decreased some of its Peso Swap positions, we were owed tens of millions of dollars on the remaining swaps. It wasn't clear if we would be repaid.

My first thought was the all-important ten-dollar bet I had made with a colleague. I had predicted the peso would crash through the band, and now I had the ten dollars to prove it.

The next day, the peso dropped below four pesos to the dollar down toward five pesos to the dollar. The Central Bank of Mexico hosted a conference call in which they told investors everything would be okay. No one believed them. Mexican and U.S. government officials appeared on television to reassure investors. Their pleas were ignored, too, and the peso went into a free fall. At one point the collateral for our various Peso Swaps had declined so much that we had several hundred million dollars' worth of naked exposure to Mexican banks. That got the attention of senior management. Members of the Gang of Four, along with Peter Karches and Ken de Regt, were nervously pacing the trading floor again. The worst-case scenario had occurred.

Fortunately, the MEXUS bonds had been repaid on December 20, just hours before the peso crashed, narrowly avoiding tens of millions of dollars of losses. My deal was saved, literally at the last minute. Other investors weren't so lucky. Scarecrow, always a conspiracy theorist, suggested that Serfin, and perhaps other Mexican banks, had been in cahoots with the Mexican government in timing the peso devaluation. Was it merely a coincidence that Mexico had devalued the peso just after Serfin's MEXUS notes matured? There *were* $100 million of those notes outstanding, and Serfin would have suffered all of the first losses from the peso's decline. Moreover, it appeared that Serfin would lose a fortune on Peso Swaps, from the double whammy increase in value of U.S. dollars owed and decrease in value of pesos owing.

Scarecrow said Serfin was politically connected and desperately needed to recover the full amount on its MEXUS trades because of its dire financial condition. How far-fetched was this idea? Serfin was the third largest bank in Mexico, and its managers *were* well connected. However, there was no direct evidence of a conspiracy. Serfin did cause a few raised eyebrows when it reported a financial *gain* from the fourth quarter of 1994, due to foreign currency transactions. Either Serfin's accounting standards were absurdly lax (and the bank really had lost money), or Serfin's political connections had allowed it to sell before the peso collapsed. I thought the former seemed more likely. Despite its "gain," Serfin was clearly feeling pain. The bank announced it was cutting its staff in New York by one third.

The investing community was surprised to learn that numerous companies and mutual funds had been placing large bets on Mexico. For example, Citicorp, once barely capable of introducing a Mexican Diner's Club credit card, now admitted that 40 percent of its $3.2 billion in 1994 earnings was from emerging markets operations. Chemical Bank announced a $70 million loss from Mexican peso trades it claimed were "unauthorized." Fidelity's flagship mutual fund, the "Asset Manager" – one of the largest individual mutual funds in the world – had invested 20 percent of its assets in Latin American debt. In 1994 alone, sixty new emerging markets funds had been created. Perhaps you owned shares of one. The *Wall Street Journal* reported that Morgan Stanley had been among the largest sellers of Mexican derivatives to these funds. That wasn't exactly great marketing publicity, and we prepared for the worst. A managing director of one hedge fund told the press that there was "blood on the street."

The ratings agencies scrambled to downgrade every Mexican bond they could find. Standard & Poor's downgraded numerous issues, including the PLUS Notes due to be repaid on January 15. In an abrupt about-face, Morgan Stanley's analysts also changed their tune about Mexico as they declared an "economic emergency." Barton Biggs, in telling the *Wall Street Journal* about how emerging markets had been one of the hottest jobs in investment banking, moaned, "A lot of smart young guys who took Spanish in prep school got hired for $400,000 as Latin American analysts." At least I knew he couldn't have been talking about me. I had never taken Spanish.

The spillover from Mexico into other Latin American countries – the "tequila effect" we had feared – was quick and pronounced. Argentina's stock market fell 8 percent; Brazil's dropped 6 percent. The rout spread to every emerging markets country that had issued Brady Bonds, including Argentina, Brazil, Nigeria, and Poland. Other countries, including China, also were hit. Investors were baffled as to why a currency devaluation in Mexico might cause completely unrelated markets halfway around the world to crash. One explanation was that when the owners of emerging markets mutual funds began selling, the fund managers had to sell something to repay them, so they sold the investments that were dropping the least. This downward pressure spread tens of thousands of miles. Like Morgan Stanley, the tequila effect had gone global.

The Argentine Pre4 Trust was among the victims. It lost $50 million in a few weeks. Investors were furious, and called constantly for explanations and up-to-the-minute prices. Traders no longer had to worry about whether a fair price was $90 or $95. Suddenly, $60 seemed pretty good. One trader said we should prepare to be sued.

The Pre4 Trust wasn't even close to the worst-performing derivative. During the weeks after the collapse, as we swapped war stories, I learned about many derivatives trades that had dropped by more than 50 percent. One of the buyers of the Pre4 Trust, a fund manager from Morgan Stanley's own asset management group, said the Pre4 Trust was only his second worst performing investment. Another bank had sold him a Mexican peso structured note that had dropped from $100 to $27 in one day. I heard about several other derivatives that had dropped from $100 to zero. By comparison, the Pre4 Trust didn't look so bad, and FP Trust was unscathed.

As we entered 1995, the new year promised new hope and, more importantly, a $50 billion-plus bailout package for Mexico. Investors weren't convinced that the bailout package would help, and the peso continued to fall, toward six pesos to the dollar, roughly half its value two weeks before. The Mexican bankers were despondent. When I wished Blades from Banamex happy New Year, he responded, "No, not happy New Year; just better New Year. That's all we can hope for." Banamex hosted a conference call for investors to discuss their troubles. The bank said it had a 508 million peso foreign exchange loss in 1994, more than $100 million based on the average peso rates for the year. The bank said it wasn't required to admit any of these losses publicly because many of them were "off-balance sheet." That included the Peso Swaps we had sold them. However, Banamex management was disclosing the loss, not necessarily because they were upstanding citizens, but in part for tax reasons. Serfin was in even worse shape. They were under serious pressure to raise cash and needed to sell their positions in deals we had sold them, including BIDS and the Pre4 Trust.

Morgan Stanley was only slightly better off. One Morgan Stanley trader predicted the firm would lose at least $30 million in total from the devaluation. (Worrying that the losses would hurt his bonus, due in February, he moaned, "Why couldn't Mexico wait one more month?") Our remaining PLUS Notes deal was in serious danger. We had to execute a very large foreign exchange transaction to convert pesos into U.S. dollars. The peso dropped another quarter point while we were selling, but we managed to exchange the full amount into dollars and pay off our investors.

There were a few happy endings. The Brazilian deal, BIDS,

repaid even more than we had expected it would because of discrepancies related to the complex inflation indices. The small midwestern insurance company that had bought peso convertibility notes received U.S. dollars, not pesos because Mexico did not suspend convertibility. But those trades were the exceptions.

Salesmen commonly said that they were "a big buyer" of a particular transaction at a certain price. For example, they might say, "I'm a big buyer of MEXUS at $99." As the Latin American markets continued to crash, the Pre4 Trust was among the worst-hit victims. The DPG trader who was giving out Pre4 Trust prices was about to snap. When one client called for a price, he said, "Use fifty, sixty, I don't give a shit. We're all fucked anyway." By mid-January, DPG was offering to buy the Pre4 Trust at $42, and offering to sell at $50. An eight point bid-offer spread was unheard of. Could it get any worse? One of the salesmen said he was a big buyer of the Pre4 Trust at zero.

Salesmen and traders, like most people confronting a crisis, try to use humor to ease their predicament. I had learned that much Wall Street humor revolves around lines from the movie *Caddyshack*. For example, in the movie, when Bill Murray is caddying for a priest who's having the best round of his life, and a torrential downpour begins, Murray says, "I don't think the heavy stuff's gonna come down for some time yet." That line was repeated constantly during the weeks following the peso crash.

(By the way, if you are planning to succeed on Wall Street, you must be able to quote from this movie with great facility. Intimate knowledge of *Caddyshack* is more important than any finance-related skill. The movie permeates every aspect of investment banking. Often a flip reference to "cinch bugs" or "manganese" is just what it takes to get a deal closed. Occasionally, the best way to pacify a hot-headed opponent is to slip him a $20 bill, and whisper, "Keep it fair." And when the shit is really hitting the fan, everyone appreciates the above Bill Murray comment. When a Manhattan bar named Caddyshack opened – playing a tape of the movie on several televisions over and over – investment bankers burrowed into the place like inebriated gophers.)

On January 19, Morgan Stanley announced that its fourth-quarter net income would be significantly less than expected. The West Virginia Supreme Court heard arguments in Morgan Stanley's case that same day, and worries mounted that other lawsuits might appear soon. Morgan Stanley's chairman, Dick Fisher, told a Bloomberg News reporter that hiring so many people in the past year had cost the firm dearly, about 4 percent from its annual return on equity. Suddenly, everyone was at risk of being fired.

At the end of January, Peter Karches, the head of Fixed Income, was scheduled to gave his annual "State of the Trading Floor" speech to all of fixed income. I loved hearing speeches by Wall Street executives, which almost always were blunt and hilarious. I hoped Karches would find a way to generate some badly needed laughs in the current market environment.

Karches addressed the recent problems at Morgan Stanley head on, but there wasn't anything funny about it. He said 1994 had been a lousy year, but we all knew this was a cyclical business. He said we had "made our beds" and should expect compensation to be down significantly when bonuses were paid in a few weeks. He tried to comfort us about our job security, but all he could say was that there would be "no mass layoffs." What did that mean?

Later that day Marshal Salant gave a "State of DPG" speech, and it was even bleaker. Salant emphasized that the firm was tightening its belt and that DPG was instituting an austerity plan to reduce its noncompensation expenses, especially for lower-level employees. He accused the associates of abusing the reimbursement system and said we had regarded DPG's $25 dinner expense cap as a goal, not a limit. Going forward, the DPG managers would check our meal and cab expenses carefully.

DPG also was planning a major employee restructuring. Several employees would be leaving, and others would be moving to new positions within the group. Scarecrow was seen interviewing for an asset management job outside of DPG, and I assumed he was on his way out. Marshal Salant told me that DPG management was considering moving me to a new position. They didn't believe DPG could generate much revenue in 1995 by trying to sell exotic emerging markets derivatives. Salant said, "We're not in the turbocharged widget business any more. We know no one buys that shit now." He thought I should move into a more direct role, selling simple derivatives rather than creating complex ones. He said my reviews at the firm had been very positive, and I should view an opportunity to move as a promotion – but I wasn't so sure.

Several people were thinking about leaving the firm for the "buy side." Morgan Stanley and other investment banks were called the "sell side" because we sold bonds to investors. Mutual funds, hedge funds, and other asset managers were called the "buy side" because they bought bonds from us. One salesman explained the difference to me, as follows:

"Do you know what the difference is between the buy side and the sell side?"

"No, what?"

"The buy side says fuck you and then hangs up. The sell side hangs up and then says fuck you."

On the buy side, hedge funds were especially hot, and there were more than six thousand of them. The term "hedge fund" clearly was a misnomer because hedge funds typically didn't hedge. Instead, hedge funds were overseen by risk-seeking, offshore investment managers who placed some of the biggest bets in the bond market. Most hedge funds were unregulated and avoided the reach of U.S. securities laws because they were structured as private investment partnerships limited to ninety-nine investors and located outside the U.S. Immunity from U.S. securities laws fed the funds' aggression, and they often leveraged up to twenty times the amount of capital originally contributed by investors.

As my friends continued to express interest in moving to hedge funds, I couldn't help laughing at the difference between hedge-fund employees and the salesmen at investment banks who covered them. I remembered a morning I spent long ago with one guy from First Boston, known as the firm drunk. He was a tough, swaggering salesman, and he covered some of the firm's most aggressive hedge-fund clients. The salesman was already drunk at 7:30 A.M. when I arrived. He had been to Atlantic City the previous night (and that morning) and was bragging not only about the money he had won, but about the number and diversity of cheese steaks he had eaten.

I remember our conversation especially well because it was the closest I ever came to vomiting on the trading floor. He described each of the cheese steaks he had eaten in great detail. One was greasy with peppers, another was sopping with provolone and soggy grilled onions. I have an iron stomach, and I love Atlantic City cheese steaks, but still I was beginning to feel queasy. He asked if I had eaten at DiFranco's on the Boardwalk. In fact, I had. He was glad to hear it. How about the White House restaurant? Yes, their cheese steaks were excellent, too.

Then he asked about another restaurant, which I hadn't heard of. He asked if I wanted to try a cheese steak from that place. I thought he might have been suggesting a return daytrip to Atlantic City. Normally, such a trip would have been fun, but after his vivid descriptions of fatty meat and cheese, I felt too sick to go. Besides, the sun had just risen. I shook my head no. He stubbornly insisted that I try one and began rummaging around his desk, shuffling some papers off to one side and then the other.

At first I thought he might be looking for a coupon or advertisement, but then to my horror I realized he was not. Sure enough, he shuffled some more, and under a stack of papers there it was: a hunk of squishy, decaying cheese steak with all the trimmings, a little mildewed but identifiable nonetheless. I don't need to tell you which one of us ate it.

I wasn't sure if the aggressive nature of hedge funds had made this salesman deteriorate or if hedge funds had selected him because of his debauched state. In any event, it was clear that given the choice, you would rather become George Soros than this guy.

As part of the planned shake-up in the derivatives group, we began reviewing our client lists. When people moved, they started calling on different investors. Our lists were outdated and included numerous investors who had "blown up" using derivatives in the past year. Robert Citron from Orange County was on the list. Several fund managers who had left their firms were on the list. Marshal Salant said that he hadn't found anyone dead on the list, but it was always a possibility. Scarecrow said O. J. Simpson was on the list. All those names were removed.

We discovered that for years, DPG had been mistakenly sending faxes to McDonnell Douglas instead of to McDonald's, apparently because a secretary had thought "McDonald's" must have been a misprint and DPG couldn't possibly be trying to sell derivatives to McDonald's. She was wrong.

A few weeks before bonus time, the prebonus process began dominating my colleagues' lives. All conversations were about bonuses. I wasn't particularly concerned about that year's bonus because I was in the small group of people DPG had recently hired from other firms, and the firm committed to pay lateral employees a certain amount for their first year. However, the other associates were clearly worried about their pay.

The day before bonus day I couldn't stand the talk about bonuses anymore. I played hooky and went to the Westminster Dog Show at Madison Square Garden. One associate left me a phone message at home that Bidyut Sen had asked everyone to bring their checkbooks tomorrow because not only would our bonuses be zero, but we would have to repay a portion of the salaries we already had been paid. I hoped it was a joke.

Bonus day morning was busy. One of my colleagues gave me a T-shirt imprinted with my revision of Morgan Stanley's six-decades-old credo. The shirt said FIRST CLASS BUSINESS IN A SECOND CLASS WAY. I tried to hide it from my bosses, who wouldn't have appreciated the humor. Headhunters called repeatedly throughout the morning to see whether we "were happy" with our bonuses. I ignored the calls.

One by one, the managers called various DPG employees into a room and told them their "number." When Scarecrow emerged, he was shell-shocked and could barely speak. He said it had been the worst year ever for Wall Street.

He left early that day, for Springfield, Massachusetts, to attend a military helmet convention. He would try to find solace in adding to his collection of more than two hundred of these items.

Another salesman said he was considering setting up a distressed-real-estate fund to buy expensive houses in Greenwich, Connecticut. He said after the meager bonus payments, block after block of homes would be for sale.

One normally quiet DPG trader who claimed he was responsible for $50 million in profits and had been grossly underpaid, stormed from the bonus room, immediately ordered his assistant to call every cruise line in the world, and announced that he would be gone for the next several weeks. He was a mystery to everyone in the group. He appeared to be a meek, geeky guy with thick glasses and an unassuming personality, but he took hundreds of millions of dollars' worth of risk at a time and often was seen late at night meeting attractive six-foot-tall blond women on the trading floor. I suspected I would never see him again.

Another salesman, who previously had been close to Bidyut Sen (they even had taken a yoga class together), could be heard screaming at the top of his lungs, *"Dudes, that number is completely unacceptable! I am not leaving this room until you pay me at least $500,000!"*

Men always fared better than women at these meetings, though. One female employee was told, "There are two kinds of women in this business: bitches and pushovers. And you're falling into the latter category."

During my bonus meeting, Marshal Salant inadvertently read me another associate's number. He quickly realized his mistake and read me my number, which was in line with what I had been promised. Salant begged me not to tell the other associate I knew how much he had been paid. I agreed.

The news was even worse over at First Boston. Several members of my training class there had quit or been fired. One was now a teacher in the Bronx; another was looking for a job. Several had been divorced. I heard that one veteran salesman had received no bonus at all. The head Brady Bond trader from First Boston called me to say he now was an ex-head Brady Bond trader. That clinched my decision not to go back to First Boston. I told him I was sorry. He wondered if Morgan Stanley might have an opening. I didn't hold grudges, and I liked the guy, so I happily passed his name along. I had never imagined that in less than two years he would go from ordering me to retrieve his McDonald's lunch to begging me for a job.

My colleagues were angry. Our group had no excuse for not paying large bonuses to everyone. We had made about *$400 million* during the previous year. Yet several managers claimed their pay had been cut significantly, by as much as 50 percent. One salesman, who had recently turned down another bank's guaranteed two-year pay package of $1.6 million, said he had made the dumbest decision of his life. Even the midlevel managers' bonuses were down some 30 percent. The responses to the headhunters echoed throughout DPG's trading floor, "No, I'm *not* fucking happy."

Meanwhile, the Mexican market continued to drop. On February 16 the peso weakened to a rate of 6.1 pesos per dollar. The yield on another Mexican derivatives deal we had sold was up from its original level of less than 10 percent to around 71 percent. As I mentioned before, when the yield on a bond goes up, its price goes down. In this case, the price went way down. The bottom was still not in sight.

The U.S. had agreed to lend $20 billion to Mexico to help it support the peso and repay other debts. By doing so, the Clinton administration saved Wall Street a fortune and secured many of my group's risky positions. However, the administration had a difficult time explaining why the Mexico bailout was such a good deal for the rest of the U.S., outside of Wall Street, and Treasury Secretary Robert Rubin struggled to explain why interest rates of 50 percent and higher would be good for Mexico.

Along with just about everyone else in my group, I began looking for another job. I had planned to stay at Morgan Stanley, but I didn't want to be moved to a low-profile job. If emerging markets derivatives were dying, I wanted to try to find the next hot area. I spoke to the firm's junk bond desk about a potential opening. One junk salesman who heard I was interested in a job, warned me that the desk had lost around $80 million the previous year trading emerging markets bonds. I asked others about this loss, and the consensus rumor appeared closer to $50 million. Still, it raised questions.

If I wasn't going to the junk bond desk, what was I going to do? Ironically, even though I still did not speak Spanish and knew very little about Latin America, I had become an emerging-markets derivatives expert. Perhaps I could find something different and convince everyone I was an expert in that area, too.

As morale continued to dip, I became the group's resident skeptic and cynic, questioning our collective urge to work on Morgan Stanley's trading floor. The place really was disgusting and unpleasant and rapacious. On the other hand, despite the poor year, we still had been paid a fortune. Was it worth it? Were we *that* greedy? These were the pressing questions of our time. Until recently the answers clearly had been yes, yes, yes. Now I wasn't so sure.

I asked the other salesmen if they shared my mixed feelings and was surprised to discover that most did. However, they insisted that the money was worth it, maintaining that the love of money was not the root of any evil at all. Out of curiosity, I asked everyone what other jobs they would be willing to take instead of their current job at Morgan Stanley if the pay remained the same. The answers were extraordinary.

215

For the same pay, I asked, would you rather work a summer construction job on the Long Island Railroad or at Morgan Stanley? Everyone agreed, without question, construction on the LIRR. Would you rather work at McDonald's or at Morgan Stanley? For the same pay, McDonald's, without any doubt. Mowing lawns or Morgan Stanley? Definitely lawns. Shoveling manure or Morgan Stanley? Manure sounded pretty good to everyone. Prostitution? Sign us up. Ditch digging? Sure. Sewer repair? No problem.

The only job the salesmen wouldn't switch to, even if the pay remained the same, was practicing corporate law in New York. I had worked two summers at New York law firms, and I couldn't help agreeing. However, I regretted asking the questions. A sense of perspective was not exactly morale boosting. I wondered if I *could* make a million dollars shoveling manure.

On February 24, the rest of the RAVs team left town on vacation. I stayed at the firm to consider my options. Perhaps the spring would bring a better opportunity.

10
MX

The most titillating kind of spring fever is "derivatives spring fever," especially if you live in Tokyo. The needs and desires of American teenage boys who yearn for spring break are nothing compared to those of Japanese bond salesmen who lust for lucrative derivatives deals. Fortunately, as a rule every year, when cherry blossom season nears, the Japanese derivatives business blooms, and salesmen and clients fall in love.

At first 1995 looked like it might be an exception. The winter had been calm, almost celibate, for many Tokyo salesmen. During January and February, they had tried to woo clients with derivatives rap – soft but persuasive talk about attractive new trade ideas – but received only mild interest. The Japanese fiscal year ended on March 31, and clients usually caught derivatives fever some time in February as they scrambled to generate last-minute profits to make up for losses incurred during the year. Some investors simply placed big bets, hoping that if they bet right, they would erase the losses. Others used accounting gimmicks to push losses from the previous year into the following one, to hide the previous year's poor performance. Year after year one thing had become certain: Japanese investors would display astonishingly bad judgment in making loans and investments, and they invariably would have losses to hide.

But so far that year, Japanese investors seemed to be doing pretty well, and we hadn't heard of any major investment disasters. Real estate losses, including Rockefeller Center, were in the distant past; entertainment industry losses, including Sony's failed investment in Universal Studios, were in the near future. Through February 1995, the Japanese actually had made money. It was shocking but true. For once they seemed to have nothing to hide, and they politely ignored the derivatives salesmen's advances.

Until Monday, February 27. On that day, the news first hit that Barings P.L.C., the venerable British bank of the queen of England and the Louisiana Purchase, had collapsed. Poof. After 233 years of service to prominent British companies, wealthy individuals, and royalty, more years than any other bank in London, it was gone. It may seem odd at first, but it was the collapse of Barings that finally piqued the interest of Japanese derivatives buyers. I'll get to this connection in a moment.

First, though, why did Barings collapse? You may recall the story of the Barings bankruptcy. Within days, a twenty-eight-year-old derivatives trader in Singapore named Nicholas ("Nick") William Leeson piled up such enormous losses that Barings simply couldn't repay. Leeson skipped town, and by the time Barings discovered the losses, it was too late.

Leeson was an unlikely bank killer. He began his career in the back office, the most risk-averse part of any bank, where he processed trading records. By 1995 Leeson had moved up to the Barings futures trading desk in Singapore, where he was following a low-risk "arbitrage" strategy of trading Japanese stocks: Instead of betting that stocks would go up or down, Leeson bought and sold futures contracts on Japanese stocks to take advantage of price discrepancies among different stock exchanges.

Remember, a future is an exchange-traded obligation to buy or sell something at a set time and price. The futures Leeson bought and sold included Nikkei-225 futures contracts, the obligation to buy the top 225 Japanese stocks at a certain future time and price. Leeson had discovered that these futures contracts were traded on exchanges in both Singapore and Osaka, Japan. If the Singapore contract was cheaper than the Osaka contract, he could buy in Singapore, simultaneously sell in Osaka, and lock in a riskless arbitrage profit. Buy low, sell high. The strategy made sense, and if the buys and sells were simultaneous, the strategy involved little or no risk. In fact, Leeson's conservative trading had generated solid, low-risk profits, and Barings had recently recognized Leeson for his steady performance.

Then around January 26, 1995, Leeson abandoned his conservative strategy and began gambling. Instead of simply matching buys and sells, he began betting on whether the Japanese market would go up or down. To place these bets, Leeson was required to post a fraction of the total size of the bet as a down payment, called margin. Margin requirements were slim, and a trader speculating on Japanese stocks could, for example, make a 100 million yen bet with only a few million yen of margin.

Leeson's bets were straightforward. First, he bet that the Japanese stock market would go up. Almost immediately after Leeson placed this bet, Japanese stocks went down. As he increased the size of this bet, stocks went down even more. Leeson increased this bet repeatedly, until he had bet a total of $7 billion that stocks would go up. Second, Leeson bet that Japanese interest rates would go up or, equivalently, that Japanese bond prices would go down. (Remember, interest rates and bond prices move in opposite directions.) Again Leeson began to lose money almost immediately. He increased this bet, too, and it continued to move against him. Leeson ultimately bet $22 billion that bonds would go down.

Leeson's increased trading activity lasted only a few weeks. By late February he had run out of margin for these bets and was forced to quit trading. Although Leeson may have wanted to continue, in many ways it was fortunate that his losses were capped.

At Morgan Stanley we sarcastically referred to the notion of "downside limited to the size of your initial investment." In this case, Leeson's downside was limited to the amount of Barings' total capital; Leeson couldn't lose more money than Barings had. For Leeson and for Barings, the concept of a limited downside wasn't just a joke. Although Leeson's trading performance for February 1995 couldn't exactly be called stellar, it could have been much, much worse. Of the almost $30 billion he had wagered, he lost only about $1 billion.

On Friday, February 24, as I was considering my future at Morgan Stanley, Barings executives were calculating the results of Leeson's bets, realizing to their horror that the losses, then thought to be at least $750 million, exceeded the bank's net worth. Barings family members were not known as the most sophisticated members of the British banking community, just the oldest. But even they knew this situation was bad. They called the Bank of England immediately.

Bank of England governor Eddie George returned early from a ski vacation to deal with the Barings crisis, calling an all-day meeting at the Bank of England's headquarters on Threadneedle Street in central London. On Sunday morning, Britain's most senior bankers were seen filing through an unmarked entrance on Threadneedle. The bank had taken extensive security measures, and the bankers passed through both an iron door and an airlock. This meeting was serious.

It lasted late into the night as the Bank of England struggled to save Barings. The key was convincing someone to assume Leeson's obligations on the billions of dollars of futures contracts he had bought and sold.

These contracts, and their underlying obligations, were extremely risky. Imagine if you – betting that the price of Corvettes would decline – had committed to sell one million Corvettes for $40,000 each. If the price instead increased to $41,000, you would suffer losses of roughly $1 billion, the same amount Nick Leeson lost. That was bad enough, but what if the price kept increasing? It might prove difficult to close out such obligations, at any price.

No single bank appeared willing to take a risk of this magnitude, although many had considered it. Reportedly, even Morgan Stanley had been contacted at some point about buying Barings but said it wasn't interested. The Bank of England labored to convince several bankers to assume the obligations as a group, but there wasn't enough time to negotiate the terms of a multiparty deal. Ultimately, it was up to the Bank of England itself to save Barings, and eventually it declined. Leeson's derivatives bets were so large and uncertain that the risk of assuming them simply could not be quantified. As one official put it, "The Bank of England cannot put itself in the position of signing a blank check." When the meeting ended without a deal, the mood was bleak. Observers described the day as "the blackest day in the history of British banking" and as "the stuff novels are made of." Barings was pronounced dead later that night.

Meanwhile, where in the world was Nick Leeson? There were signs of hasty departure at his Singapore condo. Newspapers were piled at the doorstep, and shirts were drying on the balcony. Not even Nick's family knew where he and his wife, Lisa, had gone. One rumor was that they had fled to Kuala Lumpur, Malaysia. Another placed them on a yacht somewhere in the Pacific Ocean.

The authorities in Singapore were mad as hell. Their country was known for its cleanliness and safety. Now, Leeson's misdeeds had dirtied Singapore's entire financial system. What would investors think about Singapore now? The authorities were not only humiliated by Leeson's losses, they were fuming about his escape, promising that when he was found, his punishment would be harsh. In Singapore, you ignore the rule of law at your peril. Even chewing gum is illegal there, to ensure that the undersides of tables and chairs are unsullied. When Leeson eventually was discovered in Europe, he was extradited to Singapore, where he was accused of financial fraud. His conviction was a formality, and he was sentenced to serve six years in a Singapore prison.

I felt sorry for poor Nicky, as he was known, and could relate to his troubles. I remembered from my interview at Bankers Trust what it was like to lose a billion dollars and from my card counting trip to Las Vegas what it was like to lose bet after bet when you were convinced the odds were in your favor. Nicky was the son of a plasterer and had moved into the derivatives business the hard way, from a modest background and without family connections. He was my age. Some of my colleagues said he even looked like me. In fact, one of my friends from Kansas had seen the headline BANK RUINED BY TWENTY-EIGHT-YEAR-OLD TRADER and a photo and called me in panic, wondering if I was a fugitive. Poor Nicky Leeson. Not even his book was doing well.

Do you remember where you were or what you were doing, when Barings collapsed? If you were a derivatives salesman, you undoubtedly do. For us, it was more than the high drama of the Barings bankruptcy and the global manhunt for Leeson. It was even more than the spectacle of George Soros gloating, after he had wagered against Leeson's bet that the Japanese stock market would decline and made several hundred million dollars doing so. The connection between Barings and derivatives spring fever may not be obvious to you, but for us derivatives salesmen, the collapse of Barings left an indelible imprint on our memories and led to one overwhelming conclusion: It would be an excellent year for Tokyo's derivatives business, after all.

For those of you who weren't selling derivatives when Barings collapsed and may not immediately see the connection to Japanese derivatives profits, let me outline my thoughts and emotions on Monday, February 27, when I learned the news. I felt and thought: (1) a brief, insincere tear for the death of the queen's bank, (2) a scheme for what I might be able to sell to Barings in bankruptcy, (3) concern about whether someone at Morgan Stanley had been involved in Leeson's trading, (4) fear that even if Morgan Stanley had not been involved in the trading, it had loaned money to Barings and would suffer losses when Barings defaulted, and (5) bliss when I discovered who actually had loaned money to Barings.

Who were the unlucky lenders who now faced hundreds of millions of dollars of losses from bad loans to Barings? The Japanese, of course. This was the connection to derivatives spring fever.

Barings was an odd Cupid to match derivatives salesmen and Japanese investors, but the collapse of Barings set in motion an inevitable chain reaction. When Leeson's trades were unwound, they were so large that they caused the Tokyo Stock Exchange to collapse again, to a fourteen-month low. This decline generated huge losses in March, just before fiscal year-end, for many Japanese companies who held Japanese stocks. More importantly, Japanese institutions, especially banks, faced losses of several hundred million dollars on the loans they had made to Barings. Now that Barings was bankrupt, these institutions could not expect to be repaid. These defaulted loans, plus the stock market collapse, were the losses the derivatives salesmen had been waiting for.

The double whammy hit the Japanese institutions like a gallon of sake, and now they were desperate to buy derivatives, either to make up their losses very quickly or hide them. Only derivatives could magically turn a bad year into a good one. In an about-face, Japanese buyers suddenly found derivatives salesmen incredibly attractive. This abrupt change was the most compelling evidence I had seen of the world's interconnectedness. Just as a butterfly flapping its wings can cause a monsoon thousands of miles away, the collapse of a venerable British bank can generate financial aftershocks in Tokyo. The Barings bankruptcy, far away on another continent, was breeding a series of brief, stormy romances as Japanese buyers, confronting limited options, finally succumbed.

The difficult question for Morgan Stanley was how to consummate this new-found love ... and fast. Japanese institutions needed a financial instrument that would generate profits of hundreds of millions of dollars in a few weeks. My bosses often told me, "We love desperate clients, we get excited about them. We've made a lot of money off desperate people." These Japanese buyers were desperate people. And we had just the right trade for them, the crown jewel of the derivatives group, the most profitable trade in the history of Morgan Stanley.

I remember very clearly when I first learned about this special trade. I had been working in New York on the FP Trust deal with the Queen, and I had asked her an open-ended question about the Tokyo derivatives business. During the previous months, she had been reluctant to discuss the more clandestine Tokyo activity with me in any detail, but now she must have thought I was ready. Slowly, she unveiled to me a few of the tricks of this trade (although I didn't learn any details until much later, after I had left the firm). Sure enough, it could generate instantaneous, false profits. It could be used to hide just about any investment loss.

As she deciphered this peculiar loss-hiding trade, my eyes grew wide. I had seen some shady transactions thus far in my career, and I had been openly critical of some of our deals. In fact, I had told several of my bosses that I thought many of the trades they were selling were outright deceptive. PERLS, PLUS Notes, and FP Trust hadn't exactly been squeaky clean. But compared to what I was hearing now, the U.S. deals were virtuous. At least Morgan Stanley and its clients weren't doing anything illegal with them, as far as I knew. Now I was learning that in Tokyo, Morgan Stanley's Japanese clients seemed to be sailing close to the wind.

I know that is a serious allegation. And in Morgan Stanley's defense, the firm can credibly point its finger at the Japanese and say, "It's their fault." I later learned that DPG was careful to obtain a letter from each client stating that the trade was not a sham and Morgan Stanley had not done anything illegal. One of the ten commandments of the derivatives business was "Cover thy ass," and Morgan Stanley followed this commandment religiously, especially when it came to derivatives. Nevertheless, these deals involved concealment by the Japanese investors, and if Morgan Stanley ever ends up in court on these deals, disclaimer letters notwithstanding, it may find its ass badly exposed.

According to the Queen, the dubious trading began in early 1992, just after several Japanese clients had experienced significant losses. They were worried about the upcoming fiscal year-end and asked Morgan Stanley how they might be able to generate some quick profits to hide the losses. The Japanese companies wanted to know if there was a way they magically could turn a bad year into a good year, using derivatives and perhaps some creative bookkeeping. Japanese accounting standards were lax, and the Japanese banks and trust companies knew that if they somehow could create a transaction that showed an artificial profit, they probably would be able to hide the offsetting loss for years, perhaps for decades.

I doubted Morgan Stanley was the only bank receiving such inquiries. There were rumors that numerous U.S. banks already were doing deals to generate false profits for Japanese investors, and I suspect many of those rumors were true. I knew of one U.S. bank that tried to structure a transaction to compete with one of Morgan Stanley's, but that transaction had failed.

The Japanese securities firms were well ahead of the U.S. firms, engaging in financial fraud for years with great success. Nearly every Japanese securities firm has admitted to paying improper compensation to Japanese clients to make up for their trading losses, and the Japanese securities business has been absurdly crooked. Several firms have even admitted to dealings with organized crime, and at least one is still under investigation for links to the Japanese mob. In the U.S. fraudulent financial activities are subject to liability, sometimes criminal. In Japan they have been routine and, until very recently, without penalty.

However, the largest Japanese investors, regardless of their desperation, no longer seemed willing to use Japanese securities firms to commit financial deceit, in part because it was more likely that Japanese authorities would catch them if a Japanese securities firm were involved. The investors needed credibility and a safe haven for these deals, and they sought out U.S. banks to replace their shady Japanese counterparts.

An even more compelling reason for Japanese investors to seek out U.S. banks for these deals was secrecy. The investors needed to be able to trust whoever was helping them generate a false "profit" to keep the trade from the regulators. Although the Japanese Ministry of Finance, called the MOF, could raid a Tokyo securities firm at any time, it had no jurisdiction over U.S. banks. The MOF had a tough time policing financial misdeeds, regardless of how well known they were in the markets. Not all U.S. banks could be trusted, and only a few with Tokyo branches could be trusted with any degree of confidence. In the Tokyo banking community, if you needed to execute a complex scheme *and* you didn't want to get caught, there was only one place to go: Morgan Stanley.

Many of my colleagues at Morgan Stanley were nervous about the firm's role in assisting Japanese investors in such transactions. Nonetheless, by comparison to Japanese securities firms, U.S. investment banks, including Morgan Stanley, were saints. Whereas the link between organized crime and Japanese securities firms is well known, such a link has never been established for any top-tier U.S. investment bank. I certainly have never heard of any Morgan Stanley employee dealing with the Tokyo mob.

U.S. investment banks were not only safer, they were also much more sophisticated and creative. It took a bank of Morgan Stanley's caliber to create and implement the basic trade idea that Japanese investors have been using for many years, in various permutations, to generate false profits.

The idea behind this special trade, presented in its most primitive form, is this: Suppose you pay $100 for a pot of gold. Half of the pot is real gold, worth $90, and the other half is fool's gold, worth only $10. If tomorrow the two halves still are worth $90 and $10, and you sell the real gold for $90, can you claim a profit? The answer must be no, right? If the real gold cost $90, and you sold it for $90, the profit should be zero. Right?

Wrong. At least if you're in Tokyo. Suppose you buy the pot of gold and claim that each half cost "on average" $50. Tomorrow you sell the real gold for $90. Presto, you have booked a $40 profit. How? The real gold didn't cost you $90; it cost you $50 – "on average" – and you sold it the next day for $90, a gain of $40. Of course, you didn't really make a profit, but by Tokyo accounting standards, it was close enough, and such trading was quite common.

Obviously, if you recognized a $40 profit on the real gold, then eventually even under Tokyo rules you would be required to recognize a $40 loss on the fool's gold. The key word is "eventually." If you could avoid telling anyone that the fool's gold was actually only worth $10 when you were claiming it still was worth its "average" cost of $50, you might not have to recognize that loss for a long time. In Japan that long time could be your entire career. In fact, if you could retain the fool's gold for long enough – say, until you retired from the company – who cared? At that point the loss would become somebody else's problem.

I was amazed by this idea. It was financial alchemy at its best. The only problem with the pot of gold example is that it's too easy to distinguish fool's gold from real gold. The accounting and regulatory authorities, even in Japan, were sophisticated enough to catch an investor using this simple trick because they would be able to discover that the two halves were really worth $90 and $10, respectively, not $50 each "on average." In other words, even they could tell what was fool's gold.

Consequently, an investor needed to construct a more complicated way of doing the same deal, using "halves" so complex that the accountants and regulators couldn't easily discover their actual worth. For this higher level of sophistication, Japanese buyers turned to Morgan Stanley, and to derivatives.

As with many derivatives deals, Morgan Stanley employees

debate who gets credit for the complex idea that allowed Japanese institutions to recognize billions of dollars of false profits. I certainly don't claim any credit for it, nor do I want credit. The idea predated my arrival at the firm, anyway, so it can't be blamed on me. Whoever invented the trade, one thing is clear: They gave it a horrible acronym.

I have mentioned Morgan Stanley's obsession with acronyms, especially for derivatives. This trade's acronym – AMIT – was an unmitigated disaster as acronyms go. AMIT originally stood for American Mortgage Investment Trust. Morgan Stanley called the first AMIT they sold the First American Mortgage Investment Trust, or FAMIT. That acronym worked OK. Similarly, the Second American Mortgage Investment Trust was called SAMIT, and the third, TAMIT. Even those three names would have worked out fine if the firm had stopped there. However, the transaction idea became quite popular, and after three deals, the acronym collapsed (the fourth AMIT would be FAMIT again). From a profitability perspective, the AMIT was Morgan Stanley's best transaction ever. From an acronym perspective, it was a catastrophe. The fourth and fifth deals would have to be called FAMIT, the same as the first. That duplication couldn't happen, so the derivatives gurus had to skip the numbering order. But the sixth and seventh deals would each have to be called SAMIT, which would duplicate the second AMIT. The eighth deal didn't work either. No one knew how to pronounce EAMIT, and it looked ridiculous, anyway. Ultimately, the acronym rocket scientists surrendered, and although Morgan Stanley completed several of these transactions, the firm was forced either to clip the name of the deals to just AMIT preceded by the number of the transaction, or to use an entirely different code name instead.

Not many people at Morgan Stanley, even in DPG, know about the AMITs. The firm completed its first AMIT on February 14, 1992. That $100 million trade generated profits of almost $2 million, with minimal work. Numerous clients wanted similarly quick and easy profits, and by the end of the year the group had closed the fourteenth AMIT, although admittedly a few numbers had been skipped.

The next year was even better. In less than a month, just before the 1993 fiscal year-end, the firm closed several hundred million dollars more of AMITs, including five transactions – the twenty-first through the twenty-sixth – all on one day, March 11, 1993. Another AMIT, codenamed the Santos Securities Trust – after the Santos Brazilian soccer team that Pelé played for (the Japanese were avid soccer fans) – closed on July 15, 1993. Santos was a $241 million trade with a $4 million fee.

In 1994 demand for AMITs lagged somewhat. Instead of AMITs the derivatives group sold its Japanese clients emerging markets derivatives trades, including PLUS Notes. However, by late February 1995, after Barings collapsed, it was AMIT time again.

It's also time to give you the inside scoop on the AMIT – which DPG salesmen often called Shamit or Scamit – described in the same way it was relayed to me. It's no different in principle from combining real gold and fool's gold. But I should say at the outset that these things are not easy to understand – one reason the AMIT succeeded was that its complexity masked its true nature. I certainly didn't understand this trade the first time I heard about it in general terms, and I didn't truly comprehend any of the AMIT trades until I learned all of their details, long after I left the firm. Hang in there. This trade is worth understanding. Whoever said one of the greatest cons in the history of investment banking would be easy?

Let's start with the biggest and baddest AMIT of them all. This trade was not only the mother of all AMITs, it was the mother of all derivatives. It arguably was the most profitable single trade in Wall Street history. And it certainly was the most profitable trade in Morgan Stanley's six decades.

I am not exaggerating here. The first time I heard the story of the big, bad AMIT, I couldn't believe it. For the time spent, this deal was the easiest money anyone in the securities business, perhaps anyone in the world, has ever made. This AMIT, like many others, deserved a special code name. It was referred to simply as MX. The trade embodied Morgan Stanley's new militant approach, and the parallels to Ronald Reagan's favorite toy, the infamous MX missile, were plain.

MX was to be a massive trade, not unlike the ninety-two-foot Peacekeeper missile, formerly known as the big dumb booster. The derivatives version of the MX was big – more than a half billion dollars – although it certainly wan't dumb. Morgan Stanley's MX was designed for a quick, precision strike. The trade would originate in New York, travel several thousand miles to Tokyo, and lodge itself in the balance sheet of a major Japanese institution. Once the trade had been tested, the preparation for launching would require only a few hours of actual work. Properly executed, the MX trade would not expose Morgan Stanley to any unwarranted risk. Just a few days and it would be over.

Morgan Stanley imposed strict quality controls on the new MX trade. By comparison, in the mid-1980s, when the U.S. fired seventeen MX missiles (without nuclear warheads) 6,000 miles from California into a lagoon in Kwajalein – a remote atoll in the west Pacific – the missiles fell within a 300-yard diameter circle. That wasn't bad. But the rocket scientists at Morgan Stanley couldn't afford even that slim margin of error. Initial test results were positive, but the derivatives gurus at Morgan Stanley continued to tweak and fine-tune this turbo-powered trade. It had to work perfectly.

Only a handful of people at Morgan Stanley were aware of this new derivative, and they had been sworn to secrecy. MX was a joint effort by DPG and the mortgage trading desk, but few people in either area knew about the trade. Thousands of other employees at the firm who worked near these people were unaware that a weapon of mass destruction was being designed nearby. At least one salesman working on the trade was told he would be fired immediately if he disclosed its terms to anyone, even another Morgan Stanley employee. They couldn't be too cautious.

The MX trade was structured as a typical AMIT. Believe it or not, the recipe for an AMIT trade begins at home, with home mortgages. In fact, some of the billions of dollars actually paid to Japanese investors through Morgan Stanley's various AMIT trades, including MX, may originally have been from a check you wrote to make your mortgage payment.

AMIT trades use mortgage derivatives, which split up the pieces of mortgage interest and principal payments. The ability to split mortgage payments into pieces was the spark that generated the idea for the AMIT trades. Remember, the goal of the AMIT trade is to create two "pieces" that appear to be the same size but actually aren't. In the example I described earlier, the real gold was worth $90, the fool's gold was worth $10, and each half was worth $50 "on average." In that example, the $90 of real gold would be called the "premium" piece, and the $10 of fool's gold would be called the "discount" piece. The AMIT trade requires both a premium and a discount piece.

For the MX trade, as well as for many AMIT trades, the more valuable premium piece, the one worth $90 in my example, is called an IOette. The less valuable discount piece, the one worth $10 in my example, is called a zero coupon bond, also known as a Zero or a Strip. The Zero is the same type of bond that Joseph Jett allegedly lost $350 million on at Kidder, Peabody, that the Strips traders at First Boston supposedly made $50 million trading one year, and that we used in FP Trust. The zero coupon bond is simple. It's just a single payment, made by the U.S. government, at some specified future date. That's it.

In contrast, the IOette is much more complicated. An IOette is a type of collateralized mortgage obligation, or CMO. CMOs may sound complex, but they actually are very simple. When you make your home mortgage payment, your check typically is passed through to a federal agency, such as Fannie Mae, that, as part of its day-to-day business, receives mortgage payments from various homeowners and collects them in mortgage pools. These pools form the basis for various mortgage securities, including mortgage derivatives such as CMOs, and your mortgage payments may be pooled through these securities and passed throughout the world. CMOs are simply different kinds of strips of home mortgages. They come in various shapes and sizes, of which the IOette is one of the most unusual.

The most common way to strip apart mortgages is by interest and principal: the "interest only" pieces (IOs) have a claim on only the home owners' payments of interest, and the "principal only" pieces (POs) have a claim on only payments of principal. IOs and POs are the two most basic types of CMOs, and every monthly mortgage payment you make is part interest and part principal, that can be thought of as part IO and part PO. There are many more complex CMO derivatives, with exotic names like PACs, TACs, inverse floaters, and Z bonds.

The special difficulty with all mortgages, including CMOs, is deciding what portion of the mortgage pool's principal will be prepaid by a given date. If interest rates decline by several percent, you might decide to refinance your current mortgage by prepaying the principal, then taking out a new mortgage at a lower rate. However, if every home owner in a pool prepaid their mortgages, certain CMO owners would be devastated. For example, an owner of IOs wouldn't receive any more interest payments once the mortgages in a pool were prepaid, so his IOs would become worthless.

Predicting prepayments of mortgages isn't easy, and every investment bank has multimillion dollar computer models for valuing CMO derivatives. Yet, even when modeled correctly, some of the most volatile CMOs can become worthless almost instantly. Victims of CMOs have ranged from tiny municipalities, who experimented with the exotic bonds, to the most sophisticated CMO funds, including a $600 million mortgage fund managed by Askin Capital Management. Askin based the value of its CMOs on what its computer model said they were worth, not on what the market said they were worth. Unfortunately its computer model was slightly inaccurate. With volatile CMOs, even a small error can be fatal, and for Askin it was. Incredibly, one day the fund was worth $600 million; the next day – *poof!* – it suddenly was worth nothing at all.

What makes CMOs especially dangerous is that although they're extremely risky, they can appear quite safe. One deceiving and dangerous aspect of CMOs is their credit rating: AAA. Because payments on most CMOs are guaranteed by an agency of the federal government, the companies who rate the bonds' credit quality, Standard and Poor's and Moody's, assign most CMOs their highest credit rating. But this AAA rating is misleading. Although an agency of the federal government is unlikely to default on its guarantee, default is only one of the risks associated with CMOs. Investors in CMOs can and do lose money for other reasons, including the risk of prepayment of principal. These additional risks are not captured by the AAA rating. Just ask Askin Capital Management.

Because mortgage payments are so unpredictable, even the most sophisticated investment banks that actively trade mortgages have suffered significant losses; in 1987, Merrill Lynch lost $377 million when a trader made several large losing mortgage trades. To some extent, mortgage derivatives are a zero-sum game. The different mortgage strips must add up to one whole mortgage, and if the price of that mortgage remains constant, there will necessarily be both winners and losers.

IOettes are among the most volatile CMOs and have caused massive unexpected losses throughout Wall Street. An IOette is a special hybrid derivative, a blend of mostly IOs with a tiny sliver of POs. When we set up a new trust we can mix and match these interest and principal payments as we wish. If we mix the IOs and POs according to a special formula, we can create IOettes. Typically, an investment bank creates IOettes from a pool of mortgages. Morgan Stanley, or any investment bank, simply calls a federal mortgage association – usually either the Federal

National Mortgage Association, popularly known as Fannie Mae, or the Federal Home Loan Mortgage Corporation, known as Freddie Mac – and says it wants the association to issue a new mortgage derivative. In fact, *you* might be able to create a new IOette if you really wanted to – and you had enough money.

For example, suppose we call Fannie Mae and tell them we want to create some IOettes. For a fee, Fannie Mae sets up a special trust for us and transfers a mortgage pool to the trust. We simply need to tell Fannie Mae which underlying pool of mortgages we would like to use and how we would like to split the pool into pieces. When homeowners in the specified pool pay their interest and principal payments to Fannie Mae, that money is paid to our trust. The trustee then splits the payments into pieces, according to our instructions, and pays the money out to the owners of the various pieces.

Morgan Stanley had discovered that creating these magical IOettes was the key to the AMIT transactions, including MX. Remember, an IO – interest only – receives only the interest payments paid by homeowners, but none of the principal. The IOette consists primarily of IOs, but it's slightly different from "normal" IOs because it receives a modicum of principal from the tiny sliver of POs. However, most of the value of the IOette comes from the IO component. Because the IOette uses only a tiny amount of PO, when we make an IOette, we are left with an extra amount of PO, which we – or someone else – will need to hold separately.

Because the IOette consists of only a very small amount of PO, it has two strange but important properties. The first is that an IOette has a huge coupon. A bond's coupon usually is stated as a percentage of the bond's face amount. A typical bond's coupon might be 8 percent – for example, $8 of annual interest for every $100 of principal. Normally, the coupon is only a fraction of the bond's principal.

However, an IOette with a $100 principal amount might receive annual interest payments of $1,000 or more for up to thirty years. Because the IOette has only a sliver of principal, the bond's interest payments are enormous by comparison to the PO face amount, which serves as the IOette face amount. As a result, the IOette can have a coupon of several *thousand* percent. Theoretically there is no limit to the size of an IOette coupon, although I was told not to set the coupon too high because the computers at the Federal Reserve Bank, where the trades were settled, might run out of decimals.

The second strange property is that an IOette has a huge price relative to its face amount. If an IOette with a $100 face amount paid interest of $1,000 a year for thirty years, you would receive $30,000 of interest in total. You might receive interest for a much shorter period of time if the underlying mortgages were prepaid. However, regardless of prepayments, the value of an IOette almost always exceeds the value of its face amount, usually by a large margin. An IOette with a $100 face amount might be worth ten or more times that amount. Its price really is arbitrary, based on the face amount of POs chosen for the IOette, but it is a price nonetheless.

These two properties make the IOette an excellent candidate for the more valuable, $90 piece in the earlier example. Again, because the price of an IOette exceeds its face amount, it is called a premium instrument. It is pure gold. In fact, some underlying mortgage collateral is referred to as Gold collateral.

As I mentioned before, for the AMIT trade to work, we need both a premium and a discount piece. The zero coupon strip, or Zero, qualifies as the discount piece, because it's worth much less than its face amount. Again, a Zero is a bond that makes only a single payment at a fixed future date, say thirty years from today. The Zero is by far the simplest discount instrument. They are similar to POs, which also are discount instruments, except that Zeros involve U.S. government bonds instead of mortgages. As I noted earlier, the U.S. government set up a program, called Strips, that allows certain brokers to split the interest and principal payments on U.S. government bonds. As a result, instead of buying a U.S. government bond that pays interest twice a year, you can buy a Zero, which represents the right to receive from the U.S. government a single payment of $1,000 on a date up to thirty years from today. This right is called zero coupon because it involves only one payment, with no interim coupons.

The right to receive $1,000 in the future is always worth less than $1,000 today. Remember present value? Specifically, the value of such a right depends on when the money is to be received – the longer the maturity, the less the Zero is worth. For example, the right to receive $1,000 ten years from now is worth about $500 today. The right to receive $1,000 thirty years from now is worth about $150 today. Because a thirty-year zero coupon strip with a $1,000 principal amount is worth only about $150, it is called a discount instrument. It's like fool's gold because it's actually worth less than the face amount makes it look like it might be worth.

Unlike IOettes, Zeros are easy to buy and already exist in a wide range of maturities. You can find prices of various Zeros quoted in the *Wall Street Journal* every day. Zeros are traded daily in large volumes. At Morgan Stanley, if I wanted to buy some Zeros, I would simply pick up the phone and tell a trader the maturity and size. He would quote me a price, and I would either buy them or not at that price.

The idea of the AMIT trade was that the investor would be buying both pieces – IOettes and Zeros – in equal face amounts. (The extra POs left over from creating the IOettes would be put to the side.) For example, the investor might buy $10 million face amount of each. Remember, a bond with a $10 million face amount doesn't necessarily cost $10 million. In this case, the cost of $10 million face amount of Zeros might be only about $2 million, whereas the cost of $10 million face amount of IOettes might be *$200* million. After Morgan Stanley added its fee, say $3 million, the total cost of the package might be about $205 million. That package is an AMIT.

However, for the AMIT trade to work properly, the investor

couldn't actually buy the two pieces directly. Instead, Morgan Stanley would arrange to create a separate trust to purchase both the IOettes and the Zeros, and then the investor would purchase interests in that trust. Sticking to the above numbers, the newly created trust might have 200,000 trust units, representing $20 million face amount of underlying bonds: one unit for each $1,000 face amount of Zeros ($10 million total) and one unit for each $1,000 face amount of IOettes (also $10 million total).

Obviously the individual trust units would have different intrinsic values. A trust unit associated with an IOette would be worth $2,000, whereas a trust unit associated with a Zero would be worth only $20. On average, the trust units would be worth about $1,000 each, although one half of the units would be worth much more than the other half because a given face amount of IOette (real gold) was worth much more than an equivalent face amount of Zeros (fool's gold).

The investor would purchase all 200,000 trust units for $205 million, an average cost of slightly more than $1,000 per unit. Then the investor would be ready for Morgan Stanley to work its magic.

A few days later, after the investor had purchased the trust units, it would notify Morgan Stanley that, as planned, it wished to sell 100,000 trust units, half of its initial investment. The proffered rationale for the sale might be that the trust units had been a great investment and the investor was cashing out for half. Was this rationale plausible? Not really. In all likelihood the value of the underlying IOettes and Zeros would not have changed much in just a few days. Consequently, you would expect half the trust to have a current value of about $100 million, roughly the same as its initial cost of about $100 million. Therefore, the investor's gain would be zero. Right?

Wrong again. This is when Morgan Stanley waved its magic derivatives wand. The trust is structured so that if the investor wishes to sell any trust units, the trustee is instructed to liquidate the more valuable IOettes first, before selling the Zeros. Suppose the investor wants to liquidate half of the trust, or 100,000 units, for which the investor paid about $100 million. To liquidate them, the trustee sells $10 million face amount of IOettes but doesn't sell any Zeros. Those IOettes are worth much more than the average purchase price of the trust units. If the IOettes' price hasn't changed, they still are worth their original purchase price, about *$200* million. The trustee receives $200 million for the sale of the IOettes and pays the investor that amount.

Let me sum up the two steps again. First, the investor bought 100,000 trust units for $100 million. Second, a few days later, the investor sold 100,000 trust units for $200 million. With two simple steps, the investor realized a quick profit of $100 million. Pretty neat, huh?

Of course, the investor still owned the other 100,000 units, which it also had bought for about $100 million. Those remaining units now were worth only about $2 million, the value of the $10 million face amount of Zeros remaining in the trust. When those Zeros finally paid off, thirty years from now, the investor would recognize a $90-plus million loss. However, that loss would become someone else's problem.

The Japanese investors loved the AMIT trades, but they were absolutely terrified of being caught. They gladly paid Morgan Stanley millions of dollars in fees to generate the immediate hundred million in profits, although they nitpicked the details of the AMIT trades. The expected profit had to match the actual realized gain exactly, so nothing looked suspicious to the regulators, and the investors instituted elaborate procedures and conventions for calculating profits, including truncating certain numbers to four decimal places. DPG spent an inordinate amount of time adjusting the accrued interest or some other trust unit variable to account for a two- or three-cent discrepancy on a $100 million-plus transaction, simply because the Japanese insisted that the numbers must be accurate, to the penny. In several instances there was an error of a few dollars, and DPG had to spend innumerable hours correcting the error, not to mention the fee to wire the smidgen of additional money. The investors believed the devil was in the details, and that if they dotted their i's and crossed their t's, the AMIT trades somehow would appear to be legitimate. However, there are no i's or t's in "fraud."

The most common AMIT buyers were large Japanese leasing and trading companies, who often preferred to remain anonymous. I never could uncover the identity of the MX buyer. The MX trade ticket didn't list the name of the buyer, and the name had been expunged from the DPG databases, if it was ever there. The code name MX came from Tokyo, possibly from the client itself, but that didn't provide a clue, either. My colleagues who worked on the transaction hadn't been given the client's name, presumably to preserve the client's anonymity. Several of my colleagues told me they believed the MX buyer was a "quasi-governmental" Japanese entity. There was some speculation that it had been either the Long Term Credit Bank of Japan (LTCB) or the Industrial Bank of Japan (IBJ). But the buyer's identity remains a mystery.

Whoever the MX buyer was, by early 1993 it had caught derivatives spring fever in a bad way. It needed to generate a quick gain of several hundred million dollars, and as with most AMIT buyers, it wanted the gain to be realized before March 31. Morgan Stanley was eager to meet this client's needs, and it did. The MX trade closed on February 10, 1993, with plenty of time to spare before fiscal year-end.

The MX trade used IOettes and Zeros in the same way I described earlier. The underlying mortgage pool for the IOettes was typical of most AMIT trades, consisting of Fannie Mae 7.5 percent mortgages. The Zeros – Treasury coupon strips with a maturity date of May 15, 2017 – were even more common. The Zeros this client used, and probably still owns, are listed every day in the financial pages of most newspapers. Take a look for yourself.

MX actually was structured as two AMIT trades, labeled the 15th AMIT and 16th AMIT. The total size was the most shocking

F. I. A. S. C. O.

statistic: $571.48 million. No Morgan Stanley derivatives trade, even a well-publicized legitimate trade, had been completed in such size. MX's half billion dollar face amount earned it the title of "mother of all derivatives trades." Of that $571 million, the investor immediately realized a huge gain, roughly $400 million. As with the other AMIT trades, the remaining trust units were held at a matching loss. However, the investor wouldn't have to realize that loss for another twenty years – that is, unless the Japanese authorities discover the identity of the MX buyer.

For generating such an enormous gain, Morgan Stanley would be paid handsomely. Based on the size of fees for other AMIT trades, a reasonable fee for MX would have been $5 to $10 million. On occasion, DPG had received fees of several percentage points, especially for smaller deals. A 4 percent fee – the fee paid for the Pre4 Trust – was rare but not unheard of. Some PERLS trades had earned 4 percent or even more. For the half-billion-dollar MX trade, a 4 percent fee would have been enormous – $23 million, roughly the same as Morgan Stanley's entire fee for the RJR Nabisco deal, then the largest transaction in the history of Wall Street.

How much would you guess Morgan Stanley was able to earn on the MX trade – $5 million, $10 million, $20 million? Go on. Just take a guess.

The key to Morgan Stanley's fee for the MX trade was the agreement that the MX buyer would compensate Morgan Stanley for any losses the bank might experience during the short time the trust owned the IOettes. Remember, the trust was buying IOettes and Zeros. But someone had to keep the POs – which were leftover from creating the IOettes – until the two could be recombined and sold back to Fannie Mae as a complete mortgage security. Because the POs and IOettes were a matched set, it was much easier, and cheaper, to return them to Fannie Mae than to sell them separately in the marketplace. However, Fannie Mae would take only the matched set because it needed both the POs and the IOettes to reconstitute the original mortgage.

240

Morgan Stanley agreed to own the extra POs until the two could be recombined, but the firm didn't want to take the risk that the POs would decline in price. POs were volatile, and this risk was substantial. So Morgan Stanley negotiated a one-sided agreement: Morgan Stanley would be entitled to keep any gain on the POs, but it would be reimbursed for any losses. Then Morgan Stanley would sell the POs and IOettes, together, to Fannie Mae.

Normally Morgan Stanley would hold the POs for only a few days, so the profits and losses, even on the volatile POs, would likely be small. The AMIT buyers typically regarded this agreement as unimportant, a mere detail. Nevertheless, Jon Kindred, the manager in Tokyo who was responsible for many of the AMIT trades, always remembered to secure the buyer's agreement. And this transaction was no exception.

As I mentioned, the closing date for the MX deal was February 10, 1993. On that date, Morgan Stanley would receive the Japanese investor's money, set up the trust, and issue the trust units to the investor. The back-office personnel at Morgan Stanley were in charge of the details required for settlement; they typically called early in the day to say that the deal had settled and to tell the DPG salesmen their precise fee, to the dollar. Everyone always waited nervously for that call because profits were never certain, and money was not actually delivered, until settlement was complete. The DPG salesmen were especially nervous about the MX trade. Not only was MX the largest AMIT by far, at a half billion dollars, but also the fee would be DPG's largest ever.

The back office did not call DPG that morning. In the late morning a DPG salesman left a message for one back-office person who was working on the MX trade. By 1 P.M. that person had not returned the call. DPG still had not gotten word that the MX trade had settled, and now the salesman began to worry. Finally the person from the back office called to say that they were waiting to hear from Fannie Mae that the trade had settled. A few minutes later, Texas Commerce Bank, the trustee for the MX trade, also called. They, too, were getting nervous. They said Fed Wire, the Federal Reserve Bank system used to settle these trades, would be going out of service in an hour or so. For a normal trade, it didn't matter very much whether settlement was delayed one day because any problems related to settlement usually could be corrected the next day. However, the MX trade was different. The Japanese investor had authorized formation of the trust only on a specific date, and if the trade failed to settle today, Morgan Stanley's profits would be at risk. There was no tomorrow.

Morgan Stanley called to find out what the problem was. Apparently, the settlement instructions in Fannie Mae's computer hadn't exactly matched the settlement instructions Morgan Stanley's back office had sent, so someone at Fannie Mae changed the instructions at the last minute. Now the settlement instructions were wrong, and if they weren't changed back to the correct instructions soon, a horrible chain of events would be set in motion. First, the mortgage trust would not be created. In Wall Street parlance, the trade would "fail." Without the mortgage trust, the IOettes would not be created. Without the IOettes, there would be no premium security to deliver to the Japanese trust. Without a premium security in the Japanese trust, there would be no trust units to sell to the investor. And without the trust units, there would be no pot of gold.

One DPG salesman had been responsible for settling the MX trade. Now it was collapsing right before his eyes. He desperately needed help. He began searching for Marshal Salant, the DPG managing director who was overseeing MX. He found Salant meeting with a client in a window office, just off the trading floor. Through the glass, the salesman could see that Salant's left arm was fully extended as Salant carefully sketched a diagram for the client. At first Salant ignored the salesman flailing his arms outside the door. Managing directors almost never pay attention to lower-level employees, especially when they're in a meeting. Finally the salesman flung open the door and announced, "Marshal, we have a problem with the MX transaction."

Salant sprang to his feet in record time and ran, like the marathoner he had been in his prime, to the DPG trading desk. The salesman briefed Salant. At this point there was no new mortgage issue, no collateral for the trust, and, potentially, no millions in profits. Fed Wire was going down in an hour. They had to work fast.

The salesman had notified the mortgage traders of the problem, and they sprinted to the mortgage desk, which by now was a beehive, buzzing with panic. The mortgage traders urgently needed the MX trade. Their desk was a weak link on the trading floor, and a few of them soon might be replaced by dogs. MX was their big chance to improve their fate. The mortgage desk would split the profits equally with DPG, but only if the trade settled.

Salant, normally calm and mild tempered, knew his ass was on the line. He did the only rational thing a managing director at Morgan Stanley could do in such a crisis. He began screaming.

"This is a serious fucking problem! I mean it! This is a serious fucking problem!"

The more junior DPG salesman tried to remain cool. "I understand this is a serious fucking problem," he replied. "Don't take from the fact that I'm calm now that I don't know this is a serious fucking problem. I know. This is a serious fucking problem."

They stared at each other for a moment. Salant yelled, "This is a serious fucking problem!"

Now the mortgage traders joined in the yelling. When one of the normally staid, conservative mortgage traders realized what was happening, he stood up and screamed, *"If this trade doesn't settle, heads are going to roll!"*

Even after several more cries of "Heads are going to roll!" and "This is a serious fucking problem!" the junior DPG salesman had remained calm. Fed Wire was scheduled to go down at 3 P.M, now less than an hour away. They needed to prioritize. Their first job was to try to convince the Federal Reserve to keep Fed Wire open until past 3:00. The traders and salesmen began begging their contacts at the Fed to keep Fed Wire open. They instructed the trustee to do the same.

Next, they called Fannie Mae and explained that Fannie Mae had made a mistake. Morgan Stanley was prepared to have Morgan Stanley's chairman, Dick Fisher, call Fannie Mae if they posed even the slightest resistance. However, Fannie Mae admitted their mistake and promised to correct the instructions immediately. The trustee called and said they had convinced someone at the Fed to keep the Fed Wire open for at least another hour.

The traders calmed a little. The salesman sat by the phone and willed it to ring. No one said a word.

At around 4:30 P.M. the phone rang. It was Morgan Stanley's back office. They had just received notice that the MX trade had settled. Everyone could breathe again. They cheered. Morgan Stanley's teamwork had saved the day. Despite heavy enemy fire, the soldiers of DPG had persevered.

In the midst of the rejoicing, one salesman suggested it would be a good idea to keep this close call to themselves. Everyone agreed. No one else at the firm needed to know they almost had blown a multimillion-dollar fee.

When the Japanese salesmen arrived at work in Tokyo a few hours later, they had no idea there had been a panic. Asked how the trade had gone, the DPG salesmen in New York said there had been a few glitches but no big deal. The client arrived at work to find that it owned the trust units, as it had expected.

However, for the salesmen and traders, the roller coaster ride of the MX trade was just beginning. Now it was time for the fun part.

Although the buyer of the MX trade had purchased the trust units as scheduled, instead of liquidating a portion of the units a few days later, the buyer decided to hold on to all of the units for *several weeks* before liquidating any of them. At this time the trust still owned both the IOettes and the Zeros.

Meanwhile, Morgan Stanley still owned several hundred millions of dollars' worth of leftover POs that had yet to be recombined with the IOettes. The mortgage desk was somewhat comforted by the buyer's agreement to cover any losses on the POs, but suddenly that agreement seemed much more important, now that it appeared the desk would be holding the POs for more than just a few days. Assuming the trust buyer honored its contractual commitments, the traders were in an enviable position. If the POs went up, the desk would keep any profits. If the POs went down, then the client should cover the desk's losses. In either case, when the trust finally sold the IOettes, Morgan Stanley planned to recombine them with the POs and sell them back to Fannie Mae.

The POs would go up when the bond market went up. Because POs represented principal payments, they tended to appreciate rapidly when interest rates declined and bond prices increased. This is because POs were sold at a discount, and if interest rates declined and people refinanced their mortgages, you would receive the full principal repayment immediately instead of years later, giving you a profit over the discounted purchase price of the PO. To give an extreme example, if you paid $15 for a PO with $100 face value and twenty years of payments remaining, and the market rallied so much that the PO was fully prepaid, you would receive $100 immediately instead of having to wait twenty years. This potential for large, immediate profit given a drop in interest rates was called convexity, and, as you may recall from an earlier discussion, convexity is good.

During the few weeks Morgan Stanley owned these POs, the bond market rallied – in the words of one salesman who witnessed the events – "like a motherfucker." The POs literally went through the roof. The client apparently hadn't understood just how volatile these POs could be when it decided to delay liquidation of the trust units. They went up and up and up. By the time the client finally decided to liquidate some of its trust units, to realize its roughly $400 million gain, Morgan Stanley had a little gain of its own, on the POs it had been holding.

Morgan Stanley's management was stunned, this time in a

good way. However, they now faced a difficult dilemma. The amount of money the firm stood to make from the MX transaction – including both fees and the gain on the POs – was now about *$75 million*. How's that for convexity? Of course, that fee was outrageously high, and it almost certainly would cause the client to gag if it were ever discovered. But would it be discovered? Several managing directors met to discuss whether they should consider giving any of the additional profits to the MX buyer.

The agreement with the buyer clearly allowed Morgan Stanley to keep all the profits. However, if Morgan Stanley kept all the profits and didn't at least inform the client of the amount, the firm arguably would be violating the client's trust. On the other hand, if the managers told the client about the additional profits, they would have to explain how they had made the additional tens of millions of dollars. The client obviously had not understood the potential value of the agreement it had made on the POs and might feel that Morgan Stanley had betrayed its trust even more early on by failing to mention the massive upside potential of the POs.

Moreover, even if the managers agreed to share some of the PO profits, how would they decide how much? They would then have to explain how they had decided what portion of the total gain the client was entitled to receive. That explanation would be tricky. It was a difficult business ethics question, and – as I mentioned earlier – sales-and-trading managers tend to think business ethics is an oxymoron.

What did the managers do? They made the most ethical choice they could, under the circumstances: They kept it all. The decision was easy. The client seemed happy with its $400 million gain. Why did it need another $30 million or so? Besides, the client would never know.

Ultimately, Morgan Stanley's total profit from the MX trade was $74.6 million, split equally between DPG and the mortgage desk. For other trades DPG and the mortgage traders had battled viciously to allocate compensation between the two groups, but for the MX trade there was plenty to go around. DPG listed its share of the profits from the MX trade at $37.32 million.

The DPG managers kept this fee as quiet as they could. In fact, they never "officially" communicated the size of the fee to anyone in DPG. The standard procedure for any DPG deal was to write a TPV – transaction present value – ticket, which listed the total profits from the trade and the allocation of profits among different groups at the firm. A managing director typically told an associate the total profits and allocation in clear terms, instructing the associate to write the TPV ticket. For the MX deal, the orders for the TPV Ticket were different, but just as clear: Leave it blank. Those employees who knew about the MX trade were not supposed to discuss how much money the firm had made on the transaction. Even mentioning the amount of the fee was considered grounds for immediate dismissal.

The total amount of work involved in MX was paltry, perhaps two weeks in aggregate. Most of the work was done by a handful of people during less than a week. A great deal was done in a hour, during the settlement panic. Yet the firm had pocketed $75 million.

One of the lower-level DPG employees who knew about the MX trade calculated its effect on Morgan Stanley's quarterly earnings, which soon would be announced. The effect was significant. It turned out that the firm had outperformed analysts' expectations that quarter by almost exactly the amount of profits on the MX trade. Analysts may have had good inside information about Morgan Stanley's business, but none of them had expected the firm to make $75 million on a single trade that quarter. Several DPG employees had a good laugh about that one.

The AMIT proved to be the most efficient means anyone has been able to devise for generating false income for Japanese investors. The AMIT's success didn't go unnoticed among Morgan Stanley's top management. On March 24, 1993, Bob Scott, then a senior director in investment banking at Morgan Stanley, sent a letter to several DPG employees in New York and Tokyo who had worked on the MX trade. Scott acknowledged the stress they had been under, given the market's volatility. He wrote, "Obviously, the excitement regarding this transaction continued in March as the Treasury market rallied." He also expressed sincere congratulations. Although the MX trade was not disclosed to many lower-level employees, Morgan Stanley's most senior management certainly knew about it. Scott wrote, "The final result, of course, was one of the most profitable transactions ever for the firm." He wasn't exaggerating.

11

Sayonara

I was intrigued by the MX trade and the unbelievable amount of dysfunctional financial behavior in Tokyo. Japan seemed to be a haven for anyone selling derivatives. By contrast, New York's business was stalled, and my job working on emerging markets deals had become boring and slow. From New York, I began assisting with a few trades that had originated in Tokyo. The Tokyo office recently had closed several elephant deals, each with million-dollar fees, and I thought they were well positioned for the next year.

The Tokyo office was run by Jon Kindred, an active, aggressive manager whose round face was almost always flushed red with excitement from new derivatives deals. Kindred sought profits like a pit bull, and once he had clients interested in a deal, he rarely let them get away. His employees were aggressive marketers, and they were now generating more revenue per person than the New York salesmen.

Spring was moving time at Morgan Stanley, and I wondered about moving to Tokyo. Every year after bonuses are paid, the managers moved personnel around based on how they perceived employees' relative strengths and weaknesses. I knew the ritual.

You could tell whether you were headed up or down by what your bosses asked you to do. If your future was bright, you would be promoted within the New York office or perhaps moved to London or Tokyo. If your future was bleak, you would be sent down to the Brooklyn office to work in record keeping. If your future was uncertain, you would stay put. I was concerned that Salant had asked me to move from emerging markets derivatives. I thought this was a bad sign. I hoped management would at least let me stay put, until I could negotiate a better deal.

After bonuses were paid, management began calling several employees in to discuss proposed moves. These conversations always started with "[Salesman's name], we've decided to make some changes for the upcoming year." That statement was deliberately ambiguous. It could mean either that you were being promoted or that you should pack your bags. The managers tried to gauge your reaction to the statement as you waited to hear what those changes would be. This waiting instilled great fear in some salesmen. If you displayed fear, the changes might become even worse. After a minute of silence, one of the managers would ask what you thought about a particular area, usually the one where they were planning to move you. You never wanted to hear, "So, what do you think about munis?" If they asked, "So, what do you think of our Brooklyn office?" your career was over.

Thus far my entire Wall Street career had been in emerging markets, and with the recent fallout from the Mexican currency debacle, I was concerned about the future of my current path. I had considered several options, including moving to a new division within the firm, but I hadn't discussed any of these plans with management yet. I hoped they might give me some time before moving me, up or down. That way I would have greater control and could negotiate my own move. Perhaps they would let me stay put. Perhaps they wouldn't even call me in.

No such luck. Marshal Salant called me into his office, and when I arrived, two other managers were waiting there. One of them shut the door, motioned for me to sit, and began the ritual.

"Frank, we've decided to make some changes for the upcoming year." I had learned by now not to speak in such circumstances, to avoid revealing even a hint of my reaction. I showed no fear. I stared silently and waited for them to make the first move. During the pause, I mentally retraced my brief career, wondering what, if anything, I might have done wrong. I thought I had been progressing nicely, and all of my formal reviews had indicated that clients and employees alike thought I was an able salesman. I tried to prepare for the shock of the word "Brooklyn" or maybe even worse. If I heard "munis," I was running for the door.

When one manager asked, "So, Frank, what do think of our *Tokyo* office?" I was both surprised and relieved. The question confirmed that management had confidence in me. If you are any good at an investment bank, they quickly move you to where the money is. In 1995, for DPG, the money was in Tokyo. Apparently my bosses thought I would be able to persuade our Japanese clients to buy high-margin derivatives.

I reflected briefly on the question. For some reason I have a knack for getting people to hire me for jobs I am utterly unqualified for. Just as First Boston had asked me to sell emerging markets derivatives to U.S. investors, now Morgan Stanley was asking me to sell even more exotic derivatives to the Japanese. I didn't speak a word of Japanese, I had never met or even spoken to a Japanese client, and I had no knowledge of the Japanese financial or regulatory systems. *Oh, well,* I thought, *here I go again.* I suppressed the urge to protest that I was unqualified or to tell them I had wondered about moving to Tokyo. I would be happy to visit – for a month, maybe. I confidently answered, "I'll tell you what I think of Tokyo. That's where the money is."

They gave me a day to think about the offer. They said I would be in Tokyo only temporarily, to assist the DPG sales force there. It was somehow reassuring to think that Tokyo needed me. The job they were asking me to do was exciting and, in many ways, easy. Our Tokyo office was swamped with feverish clients, many of whom – now that they had caught spring derivatives fever –

had begun opening their balance sheets like fragrant cherry blossoms. Management wanted to be sure there were enough men in Tokyo ready and able to pick our clients clean. The Tokyo DPG sales force included several experienced pickers, but apparently they needed some additional seasonal workers.

Tokyo was interesting to me for another reason, too. It was the last piece of the Morgan Stanley derivatives puzzle. By now I understood derivatives pretty well, I felt comfortable with the corporate culture of New York, and I knew plenty of people in London. But Tokyo was still a mystery.

I had never been to Tokyo or even within five thousand miles of Japan. It was ironic, but although I had sold derivatives from countries all over the world – Argentina, Brazil, Mexico, the Philippines – I had never once traveled to any of these countries or to anywhere outside the U.S. on business. Even as a kid I had never been outside the country for more than a few days, unless you counted a week-long high-school band trip to Germany where I played several high-pitched clarinet solos to drunken Octoberfest celebrants. I wasn't even sure I could pick out Tokyo, or possibly even Japan, on a map. My knowledge of Japan was limited to Speed Racer cartoons, Godzilla movies, and some ninja research I had helped a college friend complete. And yet here I was, about to start selling derivatives there. I was ready for some surprises. The next morning I said I would be happy to go.

I was comforted by the fact that I would not exactly be roughing it. When Morgan Stanley sends you to Tokyo, they send you in style. I began hearing about the lavish expenses showered on Americans in Tokyo. Some expatriate employees there had housing allowances of more than ten million yen ($100,000) per year. One trader received a $10,000 per month rent stipend. Moving to Japan was sounding as if it might not be such a bad idea.

My first glimpse of just how expensive my trip would be was my first-class plane fare – $7,500. When I asked one of the DPG secretaries if there were any guidelines for my meal and entertainment expenses, she laughed. One of my colleagues said I would need one million yen – about $10,000 – per week. That seemed a little excessive. I was used to traveling cheap, and was certain I could scrape by on a few hundred thousand yen per week. I was booked for three weeks in a suite on the top floor of the Imperial Hotel, one of the most expensive hotels in the world, where I would have one of the most expensive views in the world, directly overlooking the Imperial Palace, the house of the emperor of Japan.

Although I was getting excited about this trip, my family and relatives did not share my enthusiasm. My parents were concerned. Japan was a strange country, far, far away from my Kansas roots. I insisted that Tokyo was one of the safest cities in the world. I wouldn't be in any danger. My attempts to comfort them were unsuccessful. They were absolutely convinced something bad would happen.

Everyone at work seemed especially interested in wishing me good-bye. I got the feeling I might not see them for a long time. My flight had been booked with an open return, and my three-week hotel reservation was extendable. One of my colleagues told me he had heard I was being transferred permanently to Tokyo. My flight was scheduled for Monday, March 20, and he encouraged me to enjoy my last weekend in New York. Scarecrow told me to check out the Samurai Sword Museum there, but hinted that I shouldn't rush because I would have plenty of time. I knew of several salesmen who had been sent to Tokyo, never to return. I tried to keep an open mind as I packed my bags.

When I finally climbed into my plush, free-standing first class island seat, my worries slipped away. I inhaled several mounds of caviar and belted down half a dozen vodkas and a steak. I was content. I reclined the seat and opened an eight-hundred-page novel. The flight was nonstop. I had fourteen hours to relax, eat, drink, and read. My family had been wrong. What bad could possibly happen?

What I didn't know in my relaxed state was that at almost exactly the same time, during Tokyo's rush hour, several crazed members of a Japanese religious sect, including one forty-year-old man wearing sunglasses and a surgical face mask, were planting containers of deadly sarin nerve gas – a military toxin developed by Nazi scientists – on subway cars throughout Tokyo. Almost immediately, cars on three crowded subway lines filled with toxic fumes that killed a dozen people and injured more than five thousand. Men in business suits were sprawled unconscious on the platform at Kamiyacho station, near the American Embassy. Thousands of commuters panicked while trying to flee other stations downtown. The fumes caused vomiting, nasal bleeding, respiratory difficulty, coma, and death. Victims were rushed to more than eighty Tokyo hospitals and clinics. After the subways had closed and the commuters found fresh air, more than 2,500 police officers fanned out across Tokyo and quickly found and raided the religious sect that had been linked to the deadly gas attack.

Meanwhile, on my luxury flight I was quite oblivious to this news and, after a few hours, quite drunk. Little did I know that as I asked the flight attendant to open another bottle of port, I was flying toward a city that had just experienced one of the most devastating terrorist attacks in recent memory. Little did I know that all of my Kansas relatives were panicking like Tokyo commuters. Fortunately, from thirty-five thousand feet, I could not hear the refrains of "I knew he never should had moved out to the East Coast." Soon I would have to admit they were right to have been worried. If I had left on an earlier flight, I might have been sniffing sarin gas instead of expensive red wine.

By the time I arrived in Tokyo and took the bullet train, the Narida Express, from the airport to Tokyo Station, there was no evidence of any attack. Hours had passed since then, and at first I saw no hint of trouble. I did notice that nearly every person I saw downtown was wearing a blue surgical mask. This seemed a little odd. No one in New York had mentioned that they wore surgical masks in Tokyo. Was it a fashion statement? Were they afraid of germs? I supposed I would have to buy one. Apart from the masks, and the fact that Japanese cab drivers politely opened the passenger door with a little swing lever, life in Tokyo didn't seem strange at all.

The only Japanese words I knew were "Tae Koh Koo" – the Japanese name for the venerated Imperial Hotel – and when I said this to the cab driver, he seemed to know what to do. The Imperial Hotel is known as the grande dame of Tokyo's hotels, and the Japanese worship the hotel almost as much as the Imperial Palace. It has two parts – a seventeen-story steel and glass building overlooking Hibiya Park and a thirty-one-story annex, one of the tallest structures surrounding the Imperial Palace – more than a thousand rooms, fifteen restaurants, assorted shops and lounges, and every year it draws the world's statesmen, celebrities, and royalty, as well as thousands of Japanese couples who flock there to get married. I walked past one wedding reception on the way to my room.

The Imperial Hotel has a celebrated history. It has survived several disasters, notably the great Kanto earthquake of September 1, 1923, that devastated Tokyo the day after construction of the original hotel was completed. I had heard glowing stories about the genius of Frank Lloyd Wright's original design – he considered the Imperial Hotel his masterpiece – and about how structurally sound the original Imperial had been. Allegedly, it was one of the only buildings in Central Tokyo to survive the great earthquake. After World War II the hotel fell into disrepair, and the original structure was torn down in the late 1960s to make way for this larger, more modern creation. The swanky lobby and bars were crowded with high-powered guests and higher-powered business talk. The hotel was so exclusive, it had recently turned away pop stars Madonna and Michael Jackson to spare its guests from their groupies.

I was tired and happy to have some peace and quiet. The view from my suite on the top floor of the Imperial Tower annex was even more impressive than I had expected. My room faced directly north, and I could see the expansive Imperial Palace grounds to the northwest. The palace is at Tokyo's center, on prime real estate, yet no roads cut through the expanse, no sub-way lines pass underneath, and no planes fly overhead. Even from my catbird perch, I couldn't see the palace buildings, which are covered by woods. To the northeast were the flashing neon lights of Ginza, Tokyo's premier shopping district. Straight ahead was Ote Center – and Morgan Stanley's offices. I took one last peek at the panorama, then collapsed into bed.

I woke early to go for a jog around the palace. The concierge offered a complimentary jogging outfit and shoes, but they didn't have my size thirteens. Outside, I immediately spotted more blue surgical masks. They were everywhere. This was really strange.

When I returned to my hotel room, someone had slipped a copy of the international fax version of the *New York Times* under my door. Finally I read about the deadly attack. I was more than a little afraid. Why hadn't I heard about this before? Of course, it's difficult to keep track of news when you're traveling, but this was ridiculous. My family had been right. I was convinced I would never see the U.S. again. I needed to call them to say I was alive. At least the news had made one decision easier: I would walk to work instead of taking the subway. On my way out of the hotel later, I asked the concierge where I could buy a surgical mask.

Morgan Stanley's Tokyo offices were in a medium-sized building in Ote Center, part of a group of about four hundred gleaming miniskyscrapers, just north of the Imperial Palace. Morgan Stanley was one of the first Wall Street investment banks to invade Tokyo. The key to the firm's success was David Phillips, a native of Japan who had spent thirteen years in the U.S. as a youth and had earned a degree from Cal-Berkeley. For non-Japanese banks, Phillips was a bridge between two distant cul-tures. His name had not always been David Phillips. Several years earlier he had changed it from Satoshi Sugiyama, a change that proved a key career move. In the late 1960s he successfully handled Morgan Guaranty's negotiations with the Japanese

Ministry of Finance to open a Tokyo branch. In 1970 the combination of the thirty-seven-year-old's Japanese connections and American name had convinced Morgan Stanley to hire him to open its Tokyo office.

The firm's Tokyo office was an instant success, and in 1977 Morgan Stanley promoted Phillips to managing director. That was an historic move. Phillips was Morgan Stanley's first minority managing director – and the only minority so appointed for another several years. By 1982 the Tokyo office had grown to a staff of twenty, including nine professionals, and had acquired several blue-chip Japanese clients. Still, Phillips was Morgan Stanley's only managing director of color.

Phillips was paid well, but his salary didn't change some of the pervasive antiminority attitudes in the investment banking business, and he often appeared to be a token minority. Robert Greenhill, an investment banking head at Morgan Stanley, seemed to like surprising people who assumed Phillips was white based on his name. Greenhill was quoted as saying, "I've been with David a few times when we are meeting clients, and you can just see their jaws drop." Phillips, meanwhile, clearly knew how to play the investment banking game by its non-Japanese rules, and it wasn't merely because of his Japanese face and American name. He wore expensive suits, smoked Dunhills, and drank Dewars scotch.

During the next decade, Morgan Stanley hired several hundred people to work in Tokyo, and by the late 1980s the firm had the second largest Tokyo office of any U.S. investment bank. The office gained some notoriety during the same period, and in 1990 Tom Wolfe, author of *Bonfire of the Vanities* and *The Electric Kool-Aid Acid Test,* was spotted in Morgan Stanley's Tokyo office, interviewing several straitlaced Japanese financiers, apparently as research for his next novel.

By the time I arrived, the Tokyo office closely resembled the New York office. Phillips had suffered a stroke in 1987 and retired four years later, but his influence was still pervasive. The trading floor was a smaller, more cramped version of the floor in New York. Computer screens were constantly blinking, people were always shouting, papers were scattered everywhere. There were a few notable cultural differences. The secretaries were polite, and many were either older than twenty-five or not blond. Many of the salesmen and traders had done well in college, and some even had graduate degrees. There was plenty of swearing but very little in English. In place of mildewed cheese steak, I spotted a day-old slice of salt-water eel.

It was obvious from the moment I arrived that everyone in the Tokyo office had spring fever. The morning derivatives meeting was filled with juicy trade ideas, and clients were answering our deal inquiries with their own, even more lurid, suggestions. Japanese companies were desperate for profits and would do just about anything, however risky, for a taste. The salesmen were intense and focused. No one even bothered to discuss the subway attack.

I knew the past few springs had been especially profitable for the Tokyo office. Tokyo was growing in importance throughout Morgan Stanley, and DPG employees in New York were struggling to keep some role in Japanese deals. The New York managers had tried to take credit for portions of deals sold in Tokyo, and several New York people worked late nights to accommodate the Far East schedule, but despite these efforts New York was losing power to Tokyo's muscle. I suspected that part of the reason New York had sent me was to spy on Tokyo and, if I could, infiltrate their ranks.

I wasn't familiar with the specifics of many derivatives the Tokyo office sold. From what I had read in their weekly derivatives transaction reports, I knew Tokyo made a lot of money and was the headquarters for some of the shadiest derivatives deals. Often the Japanese trades made no economic sense. Few people at Morgan Stanley, even in DPG, truly understood what was happening in Tokyo. In my short time there, I could only scratch the surface.

It didn't take me long to discover that the social life of American investment bankers in Tokyo is just as bizarre as the derivatives transactions they sell. At night one square block in an area called Roppongi is constantly filled with American expatriates. No one seems to go anywhere else. In a city filled with twenty million people, the few hundred American bankers stick together.

Occasionally the locals take an American out for a good time at one of the notoriously expensive hostess bars, but a couple of nights in Roppongi was enough for me. I was working long hours, trying to learn about the Japanese deals everyone was pitching. By the time I returned to the Imperial Hotel, I was ready for sleep.

Americans in Tokyo expend enormous energy exploiting the bizarre sexual culture, which is cleanly bifurcated between really soft core and really hard core. Just having sex with a prostitute is of no interest to anyone and costs only about three dollars. But getting a hostess to serve you a beer and talk to you costs about three hundred dollars. And whipping a teenage girl with a sharply studded leather belt costs about thirty thousand dollars.

I met people who had done all three. Only the native Japanese salesmen could visit the bargain-basement prostitutes, although they did it often enough for everyone. The Japanese are deathly afraid of AIDS, and they exclude non-Japanese from the local "soap lands," where a good "soaping" (you know what that means) was quite reasonably priced. The more expensive hostess bars were available to Americans. The hostesses there typically were non-Japanese and did not offer soaping. One salesman said he had tired of spending his entire salary on hostesses and saved a fortune by paying two of them to quit their jobs and simply follow him around the one square block in Roppongi.

The most surprising side of Tokyo was the whip-and-chain dark side. Hard-core Japanese brothels made New York's Eighth Avenue look like Candyland. One Tokyo salesman told me about a Korean client who visited Tokyo just so he could go to an underground club where he would beat up a teenage Japanese girl.

The cost, millions of yen for about twenty minutes, was more than made up for in transaction fees.

I obviously wasn't in Kansas anymore, and I stayed close to my hotel room. Even that cost a fortune, beginning with my first authentic sushi experience in Tokyo. I went to Sushi Nakata, a famous sushi bar in the basement of the Imperial Hotel. The chefs all seemed very happy to see me, an American obviously out of his element with pockets of unlimited depth. I ordered and ate six little pieces of raw fish, two of which I didn't recognize. My bill was almost $100. At that rate, I either was going to lose a quarter of my body weight or I was going to bankrupt the firm, $15 sushi piece by $15 sushi piece. The next morning I stopped by the posh Eureka restaurant for a quick breakfast. It is well named. Order a dry english muffin and a cup of coffee, and – *Eureka!* – you owe $25.

After a few days I told one of the secretaries I already was broke and needed more money. She laughed and said that happened to everyone who visited Tokyo. She produced a copy of the Morgan Stanley Tokyo Office Expense Report. The report has a large box at the top of the page, with a line next to the box begging PLEASE PAY ME. I filled out the report, signed it, and several ten thousand yen bills appeared. They wouldn't last long.

If you have visited Tokyo recently, you understand what I was going through, adjusting to the city's high costs. That night I found a moderately priced restaurant with a $50 dinner entree. That wasn't bad. Gradually, I became accustomed to the prices. My room service orders included $8 french fries, a $7 scoop of vanilla ice cream, an $8 glass of grapefruit juice, a $10 cup of coffee, a $6 banana, and several $6 Cokes. After a few days, my $100 dinner entree at Prunier, one of the nicer restaurants in the hotel, seemed like a bargain. I didn't even blink on April 1, when the waiter handed me a 4,500 yen ($45) bill for a hamburger. I knew it was no April Fool's joke.

However, I quickly tired of working on the various bizarre transactions in Tokyo. They made no economic sense to the investors, and they no longer made any sense to me. Japanese companies were using derivatives either to skirt regulations or to create false profits. These trades were starting to make me feel dirty. I knew even a tinge of morality was a sure sign that I no longer was cut out to sell derivatives. Had I had lost my edge? I tried to ignore my sense of right and wrong, but it was no use. I could never work permanently in Tokyo. I decided to stop working and just enjoy my time there.

I took a trip to Hakone, a popular tourist destination. I visited Mount Fuji. I toured the various parks and markets and museums in Tokyo and even saw the cherry blossom festival at Ueno Park, by the city's zoo.

I met with a few Japanese accounts, but no one bought anything. Several clients rejected the trades I was offering because they weren't nearly risky enough.

I thought about offering them a bet on Kansas in the upcoming Kansas-Virginia basketball game, but that didn't seem risky enough, either. What *was* risky was finding a spot to watch the game in Tokyo. The NCAA college basketball tournament had begun, and I was very concerned about seeing the games. I had bet several thousand dollars on Kansas, and I was concerned about the team's three-point shooting.

I had no idea how bleak the prospects of watching a live basketball game in Tokyo were. If you are in any small town in the Midwest and you want to watch an NCAA basketball tournament game, you have about ten thousand choices. If you are in Tokyo, you have only one. There is an American sports bar in Tokyo that occasionally shows basketball games, but even they don't have a live television feed. Instead, Americans who miss basketball wait to receive videotapes of games airmailed from the U.S. After several unsuccessful calls, I begged the concierge at the Imperial Hotel to find me a place to watch the Kansas-Virginia game. He was stumped.

I became depressed and homesick. Even though it was the weekend, I went to the Tokyo office, where at least I could watch

261

the game's score printed on one of the Bloomberg screens. The office was deserted and silent. Every five minutes or so, the screen printed a single line of Japanese characters followed by the score of the Kansas-Virginia game. I sat there sullenly after the final printout indicated that my team's three-point shooting had failed, and I had lost my bet. I no longer liked Tokyo.

Now that I had decided I couldn't work there, it was difficult to go through the motions of doing business. I watched with amazement as one salesman was designing a high-tech options trade that rivaled the AMIT. It could generate a quick capital gain, with 99.99 percent certainty. I halfheartedly pitched the FP Trust idea to several clients who were interested in obtaining AAA ratings for low grade bonds. However, when they discovered the AAA rating would have a subscript R, they rejected it. An R rating might tip off the local authorities.

Near the end of my stay in Tokyo, an earthquake hit. I was in my hotel room when I felt the tremor and heard the clothes hangers in the closet begin to clang. It was my first earthquake, and I was terrified. Was it an omen? My only comfort was my belief that the original hotel, having survived one of the worst earthquakes in history, was rock solid and therefore the newer version of the hotel should be safe, too. But the earthquake sealed it. I wanted to go home.

I later learned, much to my dismay, that the original hotel hadn't been solid at all. It wasn't only the Japanese banking system that was filled with deception and fraud. Even the Imperial Hotel and Frank Lloyd Wright had duped me.

I knew that Frank Lloyd Wright had spent almost four years in Tokyo, from 1918 to 1922, designing and supervising construction of the hotel that he touted as earthquake-proof. The hotel had been built on a foundation of floating pads, which Wright claimed acted as shock absorbers, soaking up seismic motion without transmitting it to the rest of the building. What I did not know was that much research had proved that these stories were myths and that Wright was either wrong or lying. As the foremost

Frank Lloyd Wright researcher in Japan, Nihon University Professor Masami Tanigawa, put it, "A young American architect, who didn't have much work, took advantage of the quake to publicize his success in designing a quake-proof building. That is the truth of the matter."

Although Wright's Imperial had become one of Tokyo's best known landmarks, it had major design problems. It also had severe structural problems. Just after the 1923 earthquake, Japan's Naimusho, the Japanese Home Affairs Ministry, conducted an on-site inspection of damage to buildings in central Tokyo and concluded that many buildings around the Imperial Hotel had survived the quake with much less serious damage than the hotel itself. I always assumed the original hotel had been a skyscraper and was surprised to learn that it had squatted like a three-story stone frog, bristling with decorative volcanic rock and terra cotta tiles but not much structural stability, even for its three stories.

In 1990 Ichiro Inumaru, the hotel's president and general manager, reportedly recalled that after the big earthquake, the entire main building of the hotel started to sink into the ground. The center of the structure was heavier, and it sank more than the rest of the building. Inumaru said the hotel staff periodically had to cut away the bottoms of the doors because of the hotel's sinking center.

Following a struggle to save the original building, a portion of the lobby and facade were preserved in what most architecture critics considered a tasteless theme park in rural western Japan. The village, called Meiji Mura, is set among rolling hills and lakes and is dotted with remnants of Japan's Meiji era: schools, civil buildings, a prison, and even one of Japan's first steam engines. Some architects referred to Meiji Village as a graveyard. Others call it a fabrication or hoax. It certainly contains many of the great fakes of Japanese history, including the old Imperial Hotel. Perhaps one day the AMIT will reside there, as yet another surprising but sad truth about Japan's past.

When I returned to the U.S., I was completely disillusioned. Three years earlier, before my first interview at Bankers Trust in 1992, I knew nothing about derivatives or structured notes or RAVs or ripping people's faces off. Some of my friends even thought I was a nice guy. By April 1995 I had become, in my judgment, the most cynical person on Earth. I now believed everything was a fraud, and I had a well-founded basis for my beliefs. Derivatives were a fraud, investment banking was a fraud, the Mexican and Japanese financial systems were frauds, even Frank Lloyd Wright and the Imperial Hotel were frauds. It was depressing.

The value system I had acquired in recent years included shooting at clients and blowing people up, all in the name of money. There was a reason why my colleagues would have switched to virtually any other job for equivalent pay. Everyone I knew who had been an investment banker for a few years, including me, was an asshole. The fact that we were the richest assholes in the world didn't change the fact that we were assholes. I had known this deep down since I first began working on Wall Street. Now, for some reason, it bothered me.

I was at a pivotal time in my career. It's difficult for some people to understand, but after a few years on Wall Street you can't quit. You can be fired or move to a new investment banking job or die. But you can't quit. You make too much money to quit. Think about it: If you made $500,000 a year, and the only negative consequence to your job was that you became an asshole, would you quit your job? What if you made $1 million a year? Or $10 million? Many of my colleagues had asked themselves this question, and the answer, for most, was that for a million dollars a year, you don't care what you become. Later, after three or four years of making millions, once you've become an asshole, the question of whether to quit is academic. At that point there's no downside; you may as well continue to work on Wall Street until you retire, one rich asshole.

I don't mean to get on a moral high horse here. There is nothing impressive, from an ethical perspective, about my quitting a high-paying investment banking job. If anything it was idiotic. What I mean to convey is the reason why I decided to quit so quickly. For most people in the financial services industry, their job is morally ambiguous. That's the only way to survive. I had believed mine was, too. Moral ambiguity is just fine, especially while your salary is increasing. However, when I began to think, unambiguously, that what I was doing with my life was fundamentally wrong, I simply couldn't do it anymore. I had no choice but to stop.

Back in New York, I told Marshal Salant I needed to talk to him. The conversation went roughly like this:

"Marshal, I quit."

"What? Where are you going? How much is the offer? What will you be doing?"

"I'm not going anywhere. I'm leaving the investment banking business. I'm leaving New York. I'm not selling derivatives anymore. I don't know what I'm going to do. I'll probably practice law."

At first Salant was baffled. He couldn't understand what I was saying, and he eyed me as if I had gone complete crazy. But after a few minutes I think he understood my reasoning. Or at least he pretended to. He said I should take my time and try to make the transition as smooth as I could.

A quick review of my outstanding projects with Salant revealed just how bizarre my dealings at Morgan Stanley had become. The transactions I was supposed to be working on included: several AMITs, a half-dozen different Tokyo deals designed to skirt regulations, CEDNs, Eagle Pier, additional Pre4 and FP Trust trades, several tax-motivated RAVs, a few Mexican derivatives, and a financing structure for the rehabilitation of some Brazilian F-5 fighter planes. I stared at this list. What in the world had happened to me?

The Queen was shocked that I would leave all this behind. She definitely could not understand my reasoning. However, I was not the only one of the Queen's employees to quit. Within a very short time, almost every person working for her would leave her palace. One went to graduate school, one went to London, one went to another division at Morgan Stanley, one went to Goldman, Sachs, two moved to Washington D.C. (including me). Within a few months her RAVs empire had crumbled. She had become a lame-duck queen.

Bidyut Sen interrogated me about leaving DPG. The very few people who had previously left the group had been lured by huge salaries at other banks. Sen refused to believe that I didn't have another job lined up. However, he sensed that I didn't like the business anymore, and I thought he probably was happy to see me go. Earlier, he and I had discussed with one other salesman how certain people are in the investment banking business just for the money, and others are in it for the game. Sen had suggested that John Mack, Morgan Stanley's president, probably would do the job for free because he loved the game so much. He knew I didn't carry the same passion.

Scarecrow said he was sorry that I was leaving, and I think he meant it. He reiterated his belief, contrary to Sen's suggestion, that there was only one reason to be in the investment banking business: money. He, too, had a law degree and said he sometimes wished he had become a country lawyer instead of a money-grubber. He also blamed himself for my leaving. He joked about how I had been as corrupted by the business as he had been. He talked about his role as my mentor, which I found to be a bizarre historical reconstruction. I told him my leaving had little to do with him, which was only a partial lie. He responded that he planned to leave DPG anyway, for greener pastures at Morgan Stanley, and would not be able to continue corrupting me, regardless. I apologized for not visiting the Samurai Sword Museum in Tokyo, and he promised to invite me to the next F.I.A.S.C.O. – a promise he predictably did not honor.

The next F.I.A.S.C.O. was held at a different shooting course, and from what I heard, it just wasn't the same as Sandanona. There were fewer participants, and blowing up those little clays had lost its sense of urgency. Perhaps if the derivatives business resurges in the upcoming years, F.I.A.S.C.O. will once again fuel the aggression of hungry derivatives salesmen. Until it does, it will serve as a fitting reminder of how a few dozen people in DPG saw the "blood in the water" and made $1 billion in two short years.

Epilogue

This book is the story of my journey through the gluttony and dysfunctionality of 1990s Wall Street. But it also is a story about the roots of the 2008 market crisis. Today, when I am asked if anyone saw this crisis coming, I think back to the people I worked with in the derivatives groups at Morgan Stanley and First Boston, and my answer is, "Yes". We invented the products that ultimately blew up the banks. We created the instruments at the center of the subprime mortgage meltdown. We fostered a culture of epic greed, which nearly destroyed the financial system.

Yes, we saw it coming. How could we not?

In this epilogue, I will connect the dots from the mid-1990s through the end of 2008. I will describe how investors and regulators ignored repeated warnings about the hidden dangers of derivatives. I will show how derivatives were at the heart of the collapse.

Without derivatives, leveraged bets on subprime mortgage loans could not have spread so far or so fast. Without derivatives, the complex risks that destroyed Bear Stearns, Lehman Brothers, and Merrill Lynch, and decimated dozens of banks and insurance companies, including AIG, could not have been hidden from view. Without derivatives, a handful of financial wizards could not have gunned down major mutual funds and pension funds, and then pulled the trigger on their own institutions. Derivatives were the key; they enabled Wall Street to maintain its destructive run until it was too late.

The final months of 2008 marked the end of an unprecedented

saga of excess. The mania, panic, and crash had many causes. But if you are looking for a single word to use in laying blame for the recent financial catastrophe, there is only one choice: derivatives.

After quitting Morgan Stanley, I moved to Washington, DC, where I practiced law for two years. Lawyering was considerably different from selling derivatives. I can honestly say that I would not have switched to shoveling manure, as my colleagues might have done for lesser jobs, unless a substantial raise was involved.

During the summer of 1996, Scarecrow tracked me down. He said he had a new job with Morgan Stanley's asset management group. It had been difficult for him to get the job, and he had been forced to compete against numerous candidates outside the firm. The key question in his interviews had been, "What are the most important qualities a salesman can have?" The interviewer told Scarecrow the firm had recently conducted a survey about such qualities and asked him to pick his favorite among: product knowledge, intelligence, relationship ability, and integrity. Scarecrow said he had answered, "Without a doubt, integrity. This is a trust business, and we are selling our trust." That answer had clinched the job.

Later that summer, one of my ex-DPG colleagues was married, and the wedding reception served as a derivatives reunion. We traded stories about our various fiascos and the investors who had lost billions and billions of dollars on derivatives. Everyone looked on the two-year period as a once-in-a-lifetime experience, never to be relived, always to be savored. Most seemed to have mellowed. The Queen was there, but wasn't yelling at anyone. Late in the evening she began apologizing to the former members of her RAVs team for her periodic tantrums. We forgave her. Everyone kissed and reconciled. The scene was almost a last derivatives supper, except that not one of us would be punished, jailed, fined, or even sued.

I don't know how or when Morgan Stanley got a pre-publication copy of this book. But someone at the firm discovered it and, by early October 1997, my old bosses were scrutinizing every word.

Meanwhile, I was settling into a quiet routine, teaching a few dozen law students at the University of San Diego, sharpening my golf game, and preparing for several decades of comfortable, easy living tucked away in a sunny, seventy-degree where-is-he-now file.

I had expected the following reactions to my book: from Morgan Stanley, a curt "no comment;" from my former colleagues, cries of betrayal; from derivatives outsiders, mild nausea and, perhaps, a little greater care in investing. I didn't have a stellar track record on expectations, though. I had been expecting the markets to crash for nearly a decade. I had been expecting the University of Kansas basketball team to win a national championship every year since the last time they won in 1988.

As for my book, my expectations were wrong, yet again.

Within a few weeks, Morgan Stanley started a press war. My former colleagues cried betrayal – not about my exposing their business as a fraud – but about my omitting the juiciest stories (as one early caller put it, I had "barely scratched the surface"). And derivatives outsiders howled they were sick, sick, sick – not about the excesses of the derivatives markets – but about not joining up sooner. During a particularly depressing period, several Irish business school students e-mailed me for job hunting advice, and one derivatives wannabe wrote that *F.I.A.S.C.O.* was "actually the best book I have ever read." I felt I had created a monster.

These people might never have heard of the book if it weren't for a single propitious decision by Morgan Stanley's management. It was this decision that ignited the press war, the battle Hal Lux, Senior Editor of *Institutional Investor*, would later call Morgan Stanley's "public relations nightmare."

The nightmare began when the firm released the following statement, dated Monday, October 6, 1997:

The book is clearly a combination of inaccuracies and sensationalism. Our business is based on consistent and professional service to our clients and customers. We do not engage in conduct that would violate the trust that they place in us. We stand on our record.

I don't know whose idea it was to issue this statement. It certainly came as a surprise to me. I was living in San Diego with my wife of three months, and was adjusting nicely to the gentle purr of academia. My days were quiet and contemplative. Receiving more than one call in a day was jarring.

During the next two days my phone rang several hundred times.

Peter Truell, a financial reporter at the *New York Times*, was among the first to call. Top financial journalists like Truell have thankless jobs. They understand markets better than most bankers, are better educated than most bankers, are more entertaining, erudite, and so forth, yet journalists' salaries are a pittance compared to the fat bonuses of Wall Street salesmen. Nevertheless, on a rare occasion, the journalist gets a priceless perquisite: the chance to saddle up his or her moral high horse and skewer a white-shoe firm such as Morgan Stanley. Truell seemed to savor the opportunity.

He didn't pull his punches, either. His article cited a less-than-spirited defense by Jean Marie McFadden, a spokeswoman at Morgan Stanley, that "I'm not saying it's a nunnery, but this is not the culture of the firm," and noted a lukewarm comment by Monroe R. Sonnenborn, chief lawyer at Morgan Stanley, that firm president John Mack had never said – as I claimed he did – "There's blood in the water. Let's go kill someone." (Another source later claimed Mack had indeed said those words, but had been misinterpreted.) "Monty" Sonnenborn also asserted the economic defense that Morgan Stanley would lose clients if it fleeced them in the way the book described. That defense seemed odd, and I've often wondered since why Morgan Stanley doesn't lose more clients.

Other reporters soon joined the fray. Patrick McGeehan and Anita Raghavan of the *Wall Street Journal* described Morgan Stanley's efforts to "stamp out a brush fire" sparked by the book. Kimberly Seals McDonald, in vintage *New York Post* style, focused on the blow jobs and strippers and sexual escapades, in a full-page piece entitled "Indecent Exposure." Amanda Grove of CNBC broadcast an interview, complete with footage of me writing "MARKET FAILURE" in large letters on the board while teaching my Latin American Financial Markets class.

Within a few days, word spread to trading floors in New York, London, and Tokyo, and the book sold out. Second and third printings were ordered. On October 8, 1997, *F.I.A.S.C.O.* was the third-best selling book on amazon.com, the internet bookstore, in part because books were sitting in a warehouse somewhere in North Carolina, and the only way to get a copy fast was to order it online. October 8 was well before the planned publication date, and my publisher and I were still rubbing our eyes.

So much for the gentle purr of academia.

I took advantage of the media attention to warn anyone who would listen about the hidden dangers in financial markets. I gave speeches to industry groups and regulators. I wrote op-eds for major newspapers. People liked hearing about the face ripping and skeet shooting, but they weren't as interested in the details about AAA-rated wolves in sheep's clothing or the hidden risks in mortgage derivatives. No one wanted to hear about the possibility of a system-wide collapse.

When the U.S. stock market fell 7 percent on Monday, October 27, 1997, I began preaching that the end was near. Market crashes always seem to happen in October, and it had been almost exactly ten years since the 1987 market crash, dubbed "Black Monday." A 7 percent drop alone wasn't much, but because of derivatives it sent shock waves through the markets.

One of the first victims was Victor Niederhoffer, a celebrated and often barefooted squash champion, financial maestro, and hedge fund manager extraordinaire. I thought his fall was a harbinger of doom. I wanted to be sure everyone knew and understood his story, so they wouldn't repeat it on a grander scale.

I met Niederhoffer shortly after the October decline, at the St Regis Hotel in New York. We were there for the second annual

Derivatives Hall of Fame, sponsored by *Derivatives Strategy* magazine, one of about a million new industry publications about derivatives, but the only one with a comic strip.

The conference included most of the biggest names in the derivatives business, including Robert Merton and Myron Scholes, two finance professors who had just won the economics Nobel prize for their research on options. I had been invited to lead a discussion about dealer abuses in the market. Apparently, I was the only abuser willing to talk.

I was thrilled to meet Merton and Scholes, who were making their fortunes at a then-obscure multi-billion-dollar hedge fund called Long-Term Capital Management. But I was most interested in talking to Niederhoffer, who was the lunch speaker. I wanted to hear about the dangerous put option selling strategy that had destroyed his fund.

Just a few months earlier, Niederhoffer had been on top of the world. His excellent autobiography, *The Education of a Speculator*, was selling well, and he was managing more than $100 million of investments, including much of his own considerable wealth. He was both popular and respected, and had an incredible track record: returns of 30 percent per year for fifteen years, with a 1996 return of 35 percent.

Unfortunately, Niederhoffer also had made a big derivatives bet on Thailand. Remember the mouthwatering Thai baht structured notes I had watched First Boston's salesmen hawk when I was a derivatives naif? Those notes, and similar investments linked to the Asian "tiger" currencies, were issued by highly-rated corporations and government sponsored enterprises, such as General Electric Credit Corporation and the Federal Home Loan Banks. The notes looked safe, and paid a deliciously high coupon if the baht stayed strong. That was the bet Niederhoffer had made.

On July 2, 1997, Thailand announced it no longer would peg the baht to a basket of foreign currencies. The baht plunged more than 17 percent against the U.S. dollar, just as the Mexican peso had collapsed on December 20, 1994. The effects were cataclysmic.

The rest of east Asia quickly devalued their currencies, too, and followed Thailand into the dumpster. Asian banks had been feasting, like the fat Mexican banks of the early 1990s, making leveraged bets on their own markets and currencies using swaps, options, forwards, and more complex derivatives. Now, they faced annihilation. Within months, the foreign currency value of investments in east Asia dropped by 50 percent or more.

Derivatives ensured that the ripple effects of the baht devaluation reached well beyond the Asian markets. If a butterfly flapping its wings in Thailand could affect weather in the U.S., imagine what a currency devaluation might do. Investors throughout the world were reeling.

Most of the derivatives causing the pain were traded "over-the-counter" rather than on any exchange. That meant, for example, that Asian banks doing swaps had a counterparty, typically a U.S. or European bank, who expected repayment, just as I would expect repayment if you and I had made a private bet. The Asian banks and companies hadn't lost money on any centralized exchange; they had lost money to other companies, primarily Western banks. The bottom line was that if the Asian banks went bust, their counterparties might lose the entire amounts the Asian banks owed.

The over-the-counter nature of these derivatives trades created enormous potential for loss. For example, U.S. banks had more than $20 billion of exposure to Korea. One Korean investment firm, SK Securities Company, had bet with J. P. Morgan that the Thai baht would rise relative to the Japanese yen, and when the baht collapsed, SK owed J. P. Morgan about $350 million. Other banks – including Citicorp, Chase Manhattan, and Bankers Trust – each disclosed more than a billion dollars of exposure to Asia. This exposure to a counterparty's inability or unwillingness to repay was called "credit risk." Credit risk is a banal non-issue irrelevant to a counterparty until a so-called credit event actually occurs; then, credit risk becomes the central issue mattering all too much. Credit risk was why major banks with Asian counterparties were so worried about the currency declines, even if they hadn't made bad currency bets. And credit risk was one reason why I thought Niederhoffer's predicament was an omen.

When the Thai butterfly flapped its wings, the currency crash triggered losses for Niederhoffer of about $50 million, almost half of his fund. Derivatives traders who lose $50 million, or more, seem to follow a pattern. I used to fall into that pattern playing blackjack in Las Vegas. Perhaps you've had a similar experience. You play a hand of blackjack for $25, thinking it wouldn't kill you to lose that much money. You lose the hand. Then you play another hand, thinking it wouldn't be a big deal to lose $50. Besides, maybe you'll win the hand and get back to even. You lose that hand, too. Then, you lose another hand, and another hand, and another. Pretty soon, you're down $500, an amount of money you really would prefer not to lose. What do you do? Do you quit? Of course not. You do the opposite. You increase your wagers, and start betting to get even. That's the pattern. You look up to the eye-in-the-sky, and a little voice in your head trembles, "If only I could win that money back, I would stop gambling. Forever."

To imagine Niederhoffer's plight, add five zeros to that $500. Now what does the voice sound like? It might sound awfully depressing if the $50 million was your money. But what if the money was, in the words of Justice Louis Brandeis, "other people's money"? Suddenly betting to get even doesn't seem foolish at all. Wouldn't you double-down, at least once, for $50 million of someone else's money? Why not? If you win, you're even and no one will ever care about your temporary loss. And if you lose, do you really think it matters much if you lose another $50 million? After the first $50 million, you've pretty much guaranteed that special someone else won't be inviting you to their holiday party.

So Niederhoffer, like others before him – Nick Leeson of Barings, Joseph Jett of Kidder, Peabody, Yasuo Hamanaka of Sumitomo, Toshihide Iguchi of Daiwa – began betting to get even, taking on additional risk in the hope that he could make back enough money to overcome his losses on the baht. Academics would refer to Niederhoffer at this point as a rogue trader.

By September, he had recovered a bit of the Thai loss, but was still down about 35 percent for the year. Going into October, he began doubling down by selling put options on the Standard & Poor's 500 index futures contract, which tracked large stocks.

Remember that a put option is the right to sell some underlying financial instrument at a specified time and price. In the trader's parlance, or Corvette lingo, if you bought a put option, you might pay $1,000 today for the right to sell a Corvette for $40,000 some time during the next month. You would make money if the price of Corvettes dropped. If the price of a Corvette dropped to $30,000, you would make $10,000 – the $40,000 you could have sold a Corvette for, using the put option, minus the $30,000 you could have bought a Corvette for in the market (less the $1,000 premium you had paid).

Whereas the buyer of a put option wants the price to go down, the seller of a put option wants the price to stay the same or go up – but definitely, please, don't go down. The more the price goes down, the more the seller of the put option has to pay the buyer. In our example, if the price of Corvettes dropped to $30,000, and we had sold put options on 100 Corvettes, we would have lost $900,000 ($1 million less the $100,000 premium we had received). The strategy of selling put options does not carry the one benefit Morgan Stanley touted for some of the riskier products it sold: "downside limited to size of initial investment." In this case, you could lose more than everything. A put seller's downside is limited only by the size of his or her imagination (and the fact that prices usually don't drop below zero).

Niederhoffer was looking OK through the weekend of October 25–6. October had not been an especially eventful month, the publication of my book notwithstanding. Niederhoffer was waiting, hoping the options would expire worthless so he could keep the premium and get back closer to even. Remember, he wanted the market to stay the same or go up – but definitely, please, don't go down.

For Niederhoffer, the 7 percent stock market decline on Monday was a death blow. By noon, he was broke. By Wednesday, his funds had been liquidated. The $100 million-plus of his investors' money was gone. One of his biggest investors was in my new hometown, the $3.3-billion San Diego public employee pension fund. Well done, San Diego!

At the conference, Niederhoffer gave a dazzling speech, weaving his philosophical and financial expertise into an absorbing narrative. Merton and Scholes, and the other derivatives hall-of-famers, delicately side-stepped Niederhoffer's recent collapse. After lunch, I approached him, and we talked about his put options imbroglio. He told me some of the details of his losses, and I wished him the best in defending any lawsuits. He signed my copy of his book, which I had brought to the conference, writing somewhat cryptically: "To Frank Partnoy, How Close Fate Has Carried Me to Your Drift. Best, Victor Niederhoffer." He already had read *F.I.A.S.C.O.*

For me, Niederhoffer's story illustrated how derivatives could bring down the financial system. If enough people made enough losing side bets, and then kept doubling down, they could cause major institutions to collapse. Selling options was especially dangerous. Because the downside was potentially unlimited, employees who sold options could put an entire institution at risk. If the losing trades were in the over-the-counter market, not on an exchange, the collapse of one institution would expose others to credit risk. One defaulting bank could become a falling domino that would topple many others.

Indeed, the market declines that destroyed Niederhoffer brought down dozens of institutions that had bet secretly on currencies. However, the Asian crisis was not widespread enough to cause a system-wide collapse. The markets ultimately shrugged off the losses and by spring 1998 the derivatives markets were whirring again.

Regulators, especially Alan Greenspan, the Federal Reserve chairman, were elated that the derivatives markets seemed so resilient in the face of crisis. They agreed with bankers and their lobbyists that no rules were needed; the free markets worked fine on their own. When Brooksley Born, head of the Commodity Futures Trading Commission, suggested that the government should at least study whether some regulation of derivatives might make sense, her colleagues, including Greenspan and Treasury Secretary Robert Rubin, admonished her to keep quiet. Arthur Levitt, the longest-serving chair in the history of the Securities and Exchange Commission, dutifully followed Greenspan's lead.

I thought Greenspan's laissez-faire zealotry clouded his judgment, and I said so publicly (not that he cared, or even heard). He saw no reason for any legal rules to govern the markets. Greenspan even boasted that there was no need for rules prohibiting fraud, because the markets inevitably would discover it. According to Greenspan, market competition alone, without any regulation, was sufficient, because no one would do business with someone who had a reputation for engaging in fraud. To me, Greenspan sounded a lot like Morgan Stanley's public relations department.

During fall 1998, Greenspan and other regulators learned that Long-Term Capital Management, or LTCM, the hedge fund that boasted the intellectual firepower of Merton and Scholes, was suddenly near bankruptcy. LTCM's mathematical models had seriously understated the firm's risks, as well as the degree of correlation among seemingly unrelated assets. LTCM had stacked $100 billion of debt and more than a trillion dollars of derivatives on top of a relatively thin sliver of a few billion dollars of equity from investors.

Like Niederhoffer, LTCM had sold massive amounts of options. It ultimately lost $1.3 billion from that strategy. It lost most of its remaining capital on "convergence" trades – bets that diverging prices of various financial assets would return to their historical relationships. LTCM's derivatives positions were so large that even a relatively small market-wide decline was enough to wipe out its capital. Yet LTCM's models had suggested such a decline was virtually impossible, and would occur perhaps once during the lifetime of several billion universes.

Regulators claimed they were shocked – shocked! – by these losses. Greenspan called the financial crisis surrounding LTCM the worst he had ever experienced. Rubin remarked that "the world is experiencing its worst financial crisis in half a century." Merton and Scholes, the options gurus, were disgraced, and considerably poorer. I thought it was inevitable that, in response to LTCM, regulators finally would implement some rules.

Again, my expectations were dashed. The Federal Reserve engineered a private bailout of LTCM, but Greenspan resisted derivatives regulation. The derivatives lobby, led by Senator Phil Gramm and his wife Wendy, who initially had deregulated swaps in 1993 and had been a director of Enron since then, waited out the storm of criticism. Then, in late 2000, as the country rubbernecked at the Bush *v.* Gore election results, they and Greenspan persuaded President Clinton to perform his last official act, signing the Commodity Futures Modernization Act of 2000. Greenspan, Rubin, and Levitt all supported this sweeping deregulation of derivatives. It was one of the greatest mistakes in the history of financial markets.

It didn't take long for another derivatives firm to hit the fan. When Enron collapsed into bankruptcy in 2001, I once again thought that, surely, this must be the end. The United States Senate invited me to testify as an expert at its first formal hearings on Enron, and I seethed about how the company had become an unregulated derivatives trading firm. I thought I was making some progress when Senator Fred Thompson reacted to questions I had raised about footnote 16 of Enron's annual report, which contained cryptic disclosures of some of the company's most opaque and horrific derivatives deals.

Thompson interrupted my rant to remark that he was familiar

with footnote 16. But when I became uncontrollably excited about our apparent parallel understanding of the Enron fiasco, he interrupted me again and said, in his classic TV drawl, that he was only joking. Since, this was such a dramatic moment for me, and since most people don't believe this story when I tell them, here is the full unedited official transcript:

MR PARTNOY: I would draw your attention to footnote 16 of Enron's 2000 Annual Report.

SEN. THOMPSON: I'm very familiar with it.

MR PARTNOY: If you can tell me what's going on –

SEN. THOMPSON: Just kidding.

When the dust settled after several more hearings, Congress decided to respond to the collapse of Enron, not, as a reasonable citizen might have expected, with rules that actually related to the collapse of Enron, but instead with a law called the Sarbanes–Oxley Act of 2002. SOX, as the law became known, was sweeping and highly controversial. It imposed costly governance reforms on public companies, and had some positive impact. But it did nothing about derivatives.

In response to Enron, I wrote more articles and another book, *Infectious Greed*, in which I traced the thread running through dozens of financial scandals, and set forth a six-point regulatory blueprint for preventing future disaster. I continued to warn anyone who would listen that the derivatives markets were spinning out of control, and could cause the collapse of the financial markets. But every year, my expectations were dashed. The derivatives business surged, profits skyrocketed, volumes increased tenfold, and regulators loosened any remaining rules.

The last chapter of *Infectious Greed* focused on credit derivatives, including collateralized debt obligations and new instruments called credit default swaps. It warned about the problems associated with the use of these derivatives to take on and hide risks, and focused on how people were abusing and mistakenly relying on inaccurate and unreasonable credit ratings. The new deals I described, as of 2003, were the progeny of FP Trust and risky AAA-rated mortgage-backed instruments described in this book. James Grant, the brilliant editor of *Grant's Interest Rate Observer*, bought copies for everyone who attended his 2003 spring investment conference. I gave a talk there entitled "Credit Derivatives: Be Afraid, Be Very Afraid." I testified as an expert again, this time on credit derivatives and credit ratings before the Senate and House, at the invitation of both political parties. This time, no one was kidding.

Even as the chorus of derivatives critics grew, regulators did nothing. James Grant wrote in detail about the dysfunctionality of credit-rating driven derivatives. Warren Buffett denounced derivatives as "financial weapons of mass destruction," and George Soros exclaimed that derivatives would "destroy society." But Congress remained silent. Buffett and his second-in-command, Charlie Munger, put this book on their list of recommended reading, and Munger said *F.I.A.S.C.O.* "will turn your stomach." I suppose anyone in Congress who read the book must have had an iron constitution.

To add injury to my insult, throughout this period Kansas basketball repeatedly dashed my hopes as well. First, the team choked in the second round of the national tournament three years in a row. Then coach Roy Williams left for North Carolina after a heartbreaking loss in the 2003 national championship game. Finally, the new coach, Bill Self, lost in the first round of the NCAA tournament for two straight years, first to Bucknell and then to Belmont, two schools I didn't even know had basketball programs. Bucknell and Belmont? Long-Term Capital Management and Enron? Fred Thompson and footnote 16? It was nearly too much for me to take.

Not long after I left Morgan Stanley in 1995, David X. Li, a thirty-something math whiz from rural China, joined second-tier Canadian Imperial Bank of Commerce. Li was thinking about the same problem my derivatives colleagues and I had addressed with the FP Trust, PLUS, and MX deals: how can you repackage low-rated assets to create high-rated ones?

At Morgan Stanley, we had created dozens of collateralized debt obligations, or CDOs, and we had become quite skilled at persuading the rating agencies, and investors, that they should label an investment AAA, even if the underlying assets were risky. FP Trust was the classic example: a risky and high-yielding financial cake made of crap (Philippine National Power bonds) with a thin layer of attractive icing (U.S. Treasuries).

But FP Trust proved to be too brazen, which is why Standard & Poor's ultimately branded it with a subscript "r." Even the unsophisticated analysts at S&P saw through the simple icing layer and figured out that they shouldn't be giving unadulterated AAA ratings to what lay underneath. Wall Street needed a new way to mix crap together to make it look like real cake.

The mixing process was key. One might reasonably assume that crap would be toxic. But what if you could pool different types of crap, and then extract the unhealthy parts? What if the negative characteristics of some fecal material offset the negatives of others, magically canceling out any risks? Like matter and anti-matter. Crap and anti-crap.

Had I stayed at Morgan Stanley, the question of how to create a better mixing process would have captured my attention. Bankers everywhere were looking for ways to remodel the relationships among assets in a portfolio. The key variable everyone focused on was correlation: the extent to which assets might decline simultaneously. Just as crap might become safer if pooled, financial assets might become less risky when put together – especially if you could show persuasively that any expected declines or defaults on those assets would not be highly correlated. One bond might default, but if you held a hundred uncorrelated bonds, not very many would default at the same time.

Several people discovered good mixing models, but David Li found the best one. It had the most colorful history as well. Li reframed the mixing problem as an inquiry into death, something he knew a fair amount about, and not just because his father, a Chinese police official, had moved his family to the countryside to escape the purges of Mao's Cultural Revolution. Li knew that statistical research into what was known as the "broken heart" problem suggested that people died more quickly after their spouses died. In a not-very-touching move, insurance companies had tried to profit from this phenomenon by denying coverage and raising premiums for bereaved spouses.

Li saw a straightforward, though perhaps implausible, analogy to this insurance problem, through the use of a mathematical formula known as a "copula," a kind of skewed bell curve distribution that describes the probability of death. A default by a company or an individual is like a death. Just as the statisticians had modeled how people reacted when their spouses died using copulas, Li used the same math to show how different assets react when one of them "dies," or defaults. As Li told the *Wall Street Journal*, "Suddenly I thought that the problem I was trying to solve was exactly like the problem these guys were trying to solve. Default is like the death of a company, so we should model this the same way we model human life."

At first, that idea sounded ridiculous, especially to the salesmen who would be charged with dumping the resulting CDO investments on clients. Human life? Broken heart? Who was David X. Li anyway? The first reaction of a typical salesmen, after he asked what the fuck the "X" stood for, would have been to note that "copula" sounded like "copulate."

But once the salesmen learned that the commissions for selling new CDOs were a hundred times higher than those for most other investments, they stood at attention. When they heard these CDOs had high yields and AAA ratings, all they could talk to their clients about was the genius of David X. Li and his new copulas.

Li moved up the ladder to J. P. Morgan Chase. He published his copula model in an academic journal. (If you want to read the article, it's called "On Default Correlation: A Copula Function

Approach," and is in the 2000 *Journal of Fixed Income*, Volume 9, pages 43–54. I can't recommend it as riveting bedtime reading, although I like his reference to the "Frank" copula – no blood relation, I assure you.)

According to the math, huge amounts of risk disappears when you pool risky assets together in a CDO. As a result, a large share of the pooled investment can be rated AAA. Word spread about this result like a game of telephone. Mathematicians explained the model to derivatives structurers, who explained the model to rating agency analysts, who explained the model to salespeople, who explained the model to investors. By the end, the message had warped from logarithmic functions and negative infinity symbols, to fat tails and low correlations, to simply "AAA, pass it on."

Wall Street derivatives arrangers trolled for risky assets to pool using the new methodology. Banks created hundreds of billions of dollars of new CDOs backed by low-rated corporate bonds, emerging markets debt, and subprime mortgage loans. They split the CDOs into levels, or tranches, based on the seniority of claims. The tranches were like the floors of a building built on a flood plain. The lowest floors were the riskiest, and would be flooded with losses first. The middle levels were protected by the lower levels. The highest floors seemed very safe. It would take a perfect storm to flood them. Or at least that was what the mathematical models said.

The rating agencies, primarily Standard & Poor's and Moody's, were willing to rate many CDO tranches AAA, even though the underlying assets already carried much lower ratings – from them. In their eyes, the models could magically transform a pool of BBB-rated subprime mortgage loans into a somewhat smaller pool of AAA-rated CDO investments. These AAA ratings were nearly as preposterous as the AAA ratings for FP Trust, but the rating agencies' mathematical models, including a version of Li's copula, better hid the dubious nature of the ratings. The crap had become cake. Investors either believed the ratings or ignored the ratings' unreasonable bases (as well as the fact that the banks paid the rating agencies triple their usual fees for these ratings). The CDO business boomed, and became the most profitable part of Wall Street.

When mortgage lenders such as New Century Financial Corporation and Countrywide Financial saw the insatiable demand for risky loans, they began making too-good-to-be-true loan offers to anyone they could find. Many people have criticized these lenders for unscrupulous practices. Others have criticized borrowers for taking loans they couldn't possibly repay. Much of that criticism is fair, but it ignores the big picture. The driving force behind the explosion of subprime mortgage lending in the U.S. was neither lenders nor borrowers. It was the arrangers of CDOs. They were the ones supplying the cocaine. The lenders and borrowers were just mice pushing the button.

However, the new CDO mixing process had limits. The models could only convert certain kinds of risky assets into new AAA-rated instruments, and there simply weren't enough of those risky assets. As bankers structured more CDOs, they bought up all of the underlying assets that best fit the profile of the mathematical models. Once these assets were in CDOs, they were stuck there and couldn't be repackaged again. It was hard to believe, but the bankers were running low on risky assets. After low-rated bonds and loans had been pooled once, they were gone, and therefore no longer available to be pooled again.

It was truly incredible, but there simply wasn't enough crap on Wall Street.

This is where derivatives entered the picture. The major banks recently had begun to trade credit default swaps. Credit default swaps are like life insurance: one party pays a premium and receives a benefit upon death, except that, as with Li's model, the death is not the death of a human being. Instead, the "death" that triggers payment is the default on some obligation, such as a corporate bond or mortgage loan.

There is no limit to the number of credit default swap side bets parties can make. If General Motors has a billion dollars of bonds outstanding, you can only get a maximum of a billion dollars worth of fixed income exposure to General Motors. But by using credit default swaps, you can increase your exposure to General Motors without limit. If you want a trillion dollars of exposure, you simply enter into a credit default swap based on General Motors, and then multiply by a thousand. It doesn't matter whether the bonds exist or not. This is a side bet, like gambling on a sporting event. There might be a limit to the amount of exposure you can get to a professional sports team by investing directly in the team, but there is no limit to the exposure you can get from betting on its games.

The Wall Street banks saw they could use credit default swaps to create an infinite amount of crap. They quickly engineered new repackaging transactions, using credit default swaps to clone risky subprime mortgage-backed investments that, when pooled, generated more sky-high ratings. These new deals were known as "synthetic" collateralized debt obligations, because they had been synthetized, or created artificially, through derivatives side bets. Instead of basing payoffs on subprime mortgage loans that actually existed in the real world, the banks created an Alice in Wonderland world and based payoffs on the multiple virtual realities that were down the rabbit hole.

If you were a homeowner with a risky subprime mortgage loan, CDO arrangers might put together a hundred side bets on whether you would default. Through credit default swaps, a hundred investors around the world could be exposed to the risk that you might not make your next monthly payments.

Soon, investors were buying complex subprime-backed financial instruments: synthetic collateralized debt obligations, structured investment vehicles, constant proportion debt obligations, and even some things called "CDO-squareds" (don't ask). The demand for these derivatives-backed investments was a tail wagging a very large dog.

Back when I worked at Morgan Stanley, credit default swaps did not even exist. Yet by 2008, the credit default swaps market had grown to $60 trillion. To put that number in perspective, the entire world's gross domestic product was $60 trillion. The value of all of the publicly traded stocks in the world was less than that. During the same time, the size of the derivatives markets overall had increased from $55 trillion of notional amount in the mid-1990s to an incredible $600 trillion. To paraphrase the late Senator Dirksen, $60 trillion here, $600 trillion there, and pretty soon you're talking about serious money.

By 2006, there were as many synthetic CDOs backed by credit default swaps as there were actual CDOs backed by real mortgage loans. By 2007, insurance companies had joined the banks as major players in credit default swaps. AIG led this new pack; it sold half a trillion dollars of credit default swaps, including swaps based on CDOs. Because all of these derivatives were unregulated, no one could figure out who held what. No institutions disclosed details about their credit derivatives. Lehman Brothers was a typical example – it grouped credit default swaps along with other derivatives, so no one could accurately assess its exposure.

The banks bought staggeringly large amounts of "super-senior" tranches of synthetic CDOs. That term referred to the top floors of CDO "buildings" filled with subprime mortgage loans. They were called "super-senior" and were rated AAA, because the mathematical models said they were senior enough to be safe from even a Noah's-era flood. The banks' positions were similar to those in the Corvette example earlier. The banks had sold put options, except that in this case the options were "out-of-the-money," like a put option on a $40,000 Corvette that would not be triggered until the price fell to $30,000.

Essentially, the banks were selling put options based on subprime mortgage loans. They took in insurance premiums in the form of periodic swap payments from their counterparties. In return, they assumed the risks of a major increase in subprime mortgage defaults. But the trades were labeled "super-senior" and rated AAA. That was a marketing ploy. If they had been

287

called put options instead, it would have been more apparent that they had real downside risk.

The rating agencies's models said these "super-senior" tranches were so safe because they had a large cushion protecting them against losses, in the same way the top half of a ten-story building would be protected by the bottom five floors. According to these models, the probability that a mortgage market decline would go through that cushion, to damage the more senior tranches, was essentially zero.

What did the banks' managers and boards of directors think of these risks? Either they were comfortable with having share-holders bear the risk of major losses in the event of a subprime mortgage decline, or they had no idea what the risks were. Or perhaps some of both.

In any event, managers and directors did not warn shareholders about the massive losses they would incur if housing prices declined so that defaults on subprime mortgage loans increased and became more highly correlated. They did not tell shareholders they had done the equivalent of selling put options based on housing prices. Because so many people had taken out risky mortgage loans – with low teaser rates, interest-only adjustable payments, and no money down – a decline in the price of their homes would put the homeowners deep underwater, with little incentive or ability to repay their debts. Many of them would default at the same time, which would flood even the top floors of a subprime-backed synthetic CDO. The banks' senior officials either hid, or did not understand, this risk.

As long as housing prices remained high, or even flat, the banks and their employees would earn large profits from the subprime CDO insurance premiums. But if housing prices collapsed, the banks would be like a million Victor Niederhoffers or a thousand LTCMs. Anyone who looked closely at the details and understood derivatives could see that the impact of a flood of defaults would be truly biblical. That was why, beginning as early as 2006, many sophisticated investors, including several hedge funds, placed big bets against both the subprime mortgage markets and the banks. Those bets would, almost overnight, make them some of the wealthiest people in the world.

For me, the first sign that my expectations might actually be proven right came during the evening of Monday, April 7, 2008. It had been exactly twenty years since Kansas had last won the national basketball title, when I was a student there studying math and economics. You might find my obsession with Kansas sports misplaced, irrelevant, or even unhealthy. You might find it a mere coincidence that my expectations about both a derivatives collapse and an NCAA basketball championship would be fulfilled in dramatic succession. But coincidence or not, 2008 was a time of vindication for anyone who was a derivatives critic and a Jayhawks fan.

I was in San Antonio, Texas, at the final game of the billion-dollar escapade that has become known as "March Madness." Coach Bill Self had quickly rebuilt the Kansas basketball program, and the team had lost just three games all season. The Jayhawks had easily won their first three games in the tournament, and had survived a scare against scrappy Davidson. In the semi-final game, they had pummeled a North Carolina team led by Roy Williams, the ex-Kansas coach. That set up another potential Black Monday for me, a game with Memphis, which was widely regarded as the best team in the country.

With just over two minutes remaining in the game, Kansas trailed by nine points. Many of the 43,000 spectators packed into the Alamodome headed for the exits. Yet I still genuinely expected victory. I won't dwell on the details, in case any Memphis fans are reading this, but when the ball left Mario Chalmers's hand with two seconds remaining, I simply knew Kansas would win. I got an eerie feeling, something I had not experienced in two decades. *I had been right.*

That week, New Century, the second largest subprime lender

289

in the United States, filed for bankruptcy. Soon after that, Countrywide, the leading lender, went into free fall. The savviest hedge funds increased their short positions and the value of subprime mortgage loans plummeted. Bank stocks began to decline.

In June, Moody's and Standard & Poor's finally had to admit they had been terribly wrong. Moody's downgraded the ratings of $5 billion of subprime mortgage-backed securities and put 184 CDO investments on review for downgrade. S&P placed $7.3 billion of deals on negative watch. One by one, banks began announcing massive losses from investments backed by subprime mortgage derivatives.

Bear Stearns collapsed and was purchased by J. P. Morgan. Lehman Brothers filed for bankruptcy. Merrill Lynch sold itself to Bank of America, which also bought Countrywide. The U.S. government had to rescue AIG, the world's leading insurance company, and the handful of banks that were still standing. By the end of the year, most experts were calling the financial crisis the worst since the Great Depression.

Without derivatives, the total losses from the spike in subprime mortgage defaults would have been relatively small, and easily contained. Without derivatives, the increase in defaults would have hurt some, but not that much. The total size of subprime mortgage loans outstanding was well under a trillion dollars. The actual decline in the value of these loans during 2008 was perhaps a few hundred billion dollars at most. That is a lot of money, but it represents less than 1 percent of the actual market declines during 2008.

Instead, derivatives multiplied the losses from subprime mortgage loans, through side bets based on credit default swaps. Still more credit default swaps, based on defaults by banks and insurance companies themselves, magnified losses on the subprime side bets. As investors learned about all of this side betting, they began to lose confidence in the system. When they looked at the banks' financial statements, all they saw were vague and incomplete references to unregulated derivatives. By the time banks voluntarily disclosed some additional information about their complex positions, it was too late. The dominos already had fallen.

This story was Victor Niederhoffer's writ large. Banks effectively sold trillions of dollars of put options based on subprime mortgage loans. They used credit default swaps to make huge leveraged side bets that the holders of those loans would not default. Because derivatives were largely unregulated, most of those sidebets were hidden from view. Without derivatives, the risks associated with subprime mortgages could not have multiplied and propagated in such sweeping ways.

The 2008 crisis might seem complex and inaccessible, but if you've made it through this book it is easy to understand. As with the options sold by Robert Citron of Orange County, or Nick Leeson of Barings, or Niederhoffer, the strategy appeared to generate profits with little downside risk. Until it didn't.

Ironically, the banks that had prided themselves on ripping the faces off their clients ended up bearing the largest losses. Morgan Stanley was right there, announcing billions of dollars of write-offs. The subprime risks that originally had appeared to move away from the banks returned, like a financial boomerang. This time, the biggest victims were not the banks' clients. They were their own shareholders.

As with previous fiascos, many market participants misunderstood the complexity of derivatives. But don't blame this mess on David Li. He understood the limitations of his mathematical copula model and the downside risks of subprime mortgage loans. And he warned everyone, too. Li told the *Wall Street Journal* in 2005 that using his model could be treacherous: "The most dangerous part is when people believe everything coming out of it."

Where were the regulators? By 2008, Alan Greenspan was long gone. He had helped plant the seeds of the crisis and then stepped down. When Congress called Greenspan to testify about his role, he admitted to some of his mistakes, and was publicly disgraced, his once-great reputation soiled forever. Robert Rubin also suffered searing criticism, in part because he denied responsibility and defended his earlier decisions, but especially because he had been a director and senior executive at Citigroup through the crisis, and had pocketed $115 million in pay even as Citigroup crumbled. In contrast, Arthur Levitt, the former SEC chair, admitted his errors and called for reform. No one mentioned Brooksley Born, the woman all of them should have listened to.

Meanwhile, the men on the job struggled in response to the turmoil. Federal Reserve chair Ben Bernanke and Treasury Secretary Hank Paulson lost credibility as they felt their way through various responses in fits and starts. SEC chair Christopher Cox was criticized for early inaction, even after he embraced regulation of credit default swaps. As of this writing, in early 2009, it appears that the Obama administration plans to implement sweeping financial reforms, but details are not available. When they consider new legislation, I hope they think about derivatives.

Ultimately, what lessons should anyone draw from my experience? I believe derivatives are the most recent example of a basic theme in the history of finance: Wall Street bilks Main Street. Since the introduction of money thousands of years ago, financial intermediaries with more information have been taking advantage of lenders and borrowers with less. Banking, and its various offshoots, has been a great business, in part because bankers have an uncanny knack for surviving century after century of scandal. In this way banking resembles politics. Just as political scandals will continue as long as we have politicians, I believe financial scandals will continue as long as we have bankers. And, despite several bank failures, massive pain, and much consolidation, there is no evidence of the banking profession disappearing anytime soon.

It might seem inconceivable, but in a few years the banks will recover and reemerge. Memories of the egregious excesses will fade, as they always do. Bankers will return to recapture their informational and regulatory advantages. The U.S. government's "Troubled Asset Repurchase Program," engineered by Bernanke and Paulson, ensures that banks will survive to fight another day.

And when they do, the cycle will repeat.

The main reason Wall Street will return is that we will want it to. Our financial culture is infused with a gambling mentality. Even in the midst of crisis, we don't seem to think we deserve a better chance. We continue to play the lottery in record numbers, despite the 50 percent cut. We flock to riverboat casinos, despite substantial odds against winning. Las Vegas remains the top tourist destination in the U.S., narrowly edging out Atlantic City. The financial markets are no different. Our culture has become so infused with the gambling instinct that we afford investors only that bill of rights given a slot machine player: the right to pull the handle, the right to pick a different machine, the right to leave the casino, but not the right to a fair game.

Gamblers are not steady hands. They either play too much, or not at all. When they lose faith in the markets, as they did in 2008, they do not lend or invest. Instead, they swear "never again," and sell at the bottom, when they should be buying. Investment choices oscillate between the financial equivalents of stuffing cash in a mattress and betting on the ponies. That is not an efficient way to allocate capital, but that cycle will continue. It always has. Cash can remain stashed away for only so long. Eventually, what economist John Maynard Keynes called the "animal spirits" will return, and the gambling will begin again.

In this book, I have tried to describe how the most sophisticated part of Wall Street works. These are the people, the products, and the activities that have dominated our financial system. Morgan Stanley is a central player, and is one of the survivors. The bank will do everything it can to rebuild its tarnished reputation: intensive lobbying, tear-jerking television ads about our children's future, elaborate investments in corporate social responsibility, and unprecedented charitable and political contributions. Eventually, that strategy will work. Morgan Stanley will remain among the most prestigious banks, and derivatives will return to dominate global finance. In a few years, some young rocket scientist from the firm might be ripping your face off.

F. I. A. S. C. O.

As the derivatives markets have grown, they have become more volatile and dangerous. At the same time, lobbyists for investment banks have persuaded our elected representatives to reduce the amount of derivatives regulation, arguing that derivatives are used primarily for "hedging" and "risk-reduction purposes." These arguments – plus healthy campaign contributions – have worked. The result is that the regulators lack both power and money, and are doomed to remain several steps behind the finance industry. Could a $100,000-a-year Securities and Exchange Commission investigator ever catch a $2,000,000-a-year derivatives salesman?

At the end of the original edition of this book, published in 1997, I wrote the following:

> Given the dearth of regulation and proindustry balance of
> power, you don't need a psychic to predict that there will
> be another Orange County-like fiasco some time soon. The
> current path seems clear. The financial services industry
> will continue to pay tens of millions of dollars to lobbyists
> and congressional campaigns to fend off regulation.
> Derivatives will continue to cause billions of dollars in
> losses by hundreds of derivatives victims, along the way
> destroying reputations, twisting lives, and emptying bank
> books. Young salesmen will, as I did, continue to join the
> derivatives business and become rich beyond their wildest
> dreams. And Wall Street will continue to argue that there is
> no compelling reason to regulate derivatives. So far, this
> argument has persuaded Congress and the investing public
> not to worry too much about derivatives.
> After reading this book, what do you think?

I have just one last thing to add, for anyone who doubted my claim that obscure financial instruments called derivatives could cause the collapse of the global financial system. *I told you so.*

San Diego, January 2009

294